...The Adoption Paradox humanizes the whole experience in a way that hasn't been done in full since Betty Jean Lifton.

~Shannon Quist, author of Rose's Locket and Mirrors Made of Ink

...mandatory reading for those looking for a deep dive into the complex impact of adoption on those in its wake...

~Patricia Knight Meyer, Black Market Baby and Adoption Reform Advocate and Author @myadoptedlife

...Widner pulls no punches, embracing the both-and nature of adoption's paradoxes...

~Beth Syverson, Adoptive Parent Co-Founder of Unraveling Adoption

This Powerful Book Will Change Lives...Widner's research is unquestionably admirable and all-inclusive, and her voice is undeniably the one that needs to be heard... by all professionals...and the public who have bought into the old and tired "all adoption is beautiful" theory.

~Laura L. Engel, Birth Mother and Author of You'll Forget This Ever Happened-secrets, shame, and adoption in the 1960s.

Jean Widner does a wonderful job of exploring the multiple perspectives and complexities of adoption...

~Sharon Stein McNamara Ed.D., L.P.

...I consider The Adoption Paradox one of the most essential and unflinching explorations of adoption's lifelong impact...

~Jennifer Joy Phoenix, LSWAIC, MH

...Her insightful, nuanced, synthesized narrative is ingeniously punctuated by breathtaking first-hand lived experience testimony of constellation members...

~Suzanne Bachner, Author & Advocate,
The Good Adoptee

...The book stands out for its balanced treatment of the topic...

~Monica Hall, Adoptee, Birthmother,
and Author of Practically Still a Virgin

...Insightful, profound and full of nuggets of information. Highly recommended.

~Simon Benn, Thriving Adoptees Podcast, UK

...This book is a must-read as we work together to build a more inclusive and compassionate world.

~April Dinwoodie, Host of the Born in June,
Raised in April: What Adoption CanTeach
the World Podcast and Founder of Adoptment

...Adoption Paradox is an essential starting point for anyone seeking to honestly grasp the emotional complexities and diverse truths of adoption...

~Brian Stanton, Adoptee, Actor and Playwright of
BLANK and Screenwriter of the film @ghostkingdom

...Widner crafts a narrative that not only tells the story of adoption...all while maintaining a candid, unflinching perspective...

~Tony Hynes, Adoptee, Author of
The Son with Two Moms, Ph.D.

The ADOPTION Paradox

Putting Adoption in Perspective

by Jean Kelly Widner

Ink & Quill **Publishing**

Ink & Quill Publishers

2025

Henderson, NV 89002

The Adoption Paradox

Jean Kelly Widner

Line/Content Editor: Janelle Evans
Interior Design: Jo A. Wilkins
Proofer: Cheryl A. Slinker
Cover: Janelle Evans
E-book Format: Richard R. Draude

ISBN: 978-1-957374-00-0 Trade Paper
ISBN: 978-1-957374-12-3 Hardback
ISBN: 978-1-957374-02-4 E-Book

1. Family & Relationships / Adoption & Fostering
2. Social Science / Sociology / Marriage & Family
3. Parenting / Adoption

Ink & Quill Publishers
Henderson, NV 89002
Printed in the United States of America

1 2 3 4 5 6 7 8 9 10

This book is dedicated to my parents
who raised me, George and Marion Kelly.
Thank you, I love you now and always.

Foreword

As an executive leadership coach and licensed marriage and family therapist, one of the questions I like to ask my clients is, *"Where are you thriving?"* So often when we look for growth, we are hyper fixated on the places where we want to grow, our areas of weakness. We forget that life is a complex experience full of dualities and paradoxes. Likewise, when I speak about my adoptee experience, I intentionally give my adoptive parents credit for the things they did well while being critical when discussing the ways in which they and the industry failed me. Adoption is like that. Life is like that. And while we show gratitude and balance from the places where we are thriving, change and growth are facilitated from critical spaces.

I began thinking critically about how industries and institutions affected me as a black woman. Then, as a former educator, I learned to be critical of the education system and who it is designed to serve and who it is designed to exclude. More recently, as an adoptee and teenaged birth mother, I have focused on critically examining the adoption industry. Through these lenses and more I have learned hard truths about the industries that control our lives and learned to advocate for those who are left out of conversations while being the ones who are the most negatively affected by them. I now focus my work on examining the adoption industry through multiple lenses—as a transracial adoptee cut off from my Black Cultural roots and as a pregnant teen who was coerced to relinquish my son through what I termed "birth mother grooming." What I have learned in my critical examination and advocacy work within the adoption industry is that the popular adoption narrative centers adoptive parents, and leaves birth families and adoptees out.

My work focuses on shifting that narrative by centering on the adoptee in adoption and in understanding the birth family experience. This narrowed view can skew the picture to the opposite extreme, focusing on the negative stories and forgetting the paradoxical nature of the experience.

Enter Jean Widner and *The Adoption Paradox: Putting Adoption in Perspective.* Jean and I had crossed paths in the online adoption community for quite some time but had not been formally introduced until we found ourselves serving side-by-side on Adoption Knowledge Affiliates' Board of Directors. It was here that I learned more about Jean and her unwavering commitment to understand the nuances of adoption, support anyone connected to adoption, and educate all people on the "truth when it comes to how children are treated and raised." Jean is a thought leader, scholar, and respected voice within the community. It has been my honor to serve the adoption community with Jean. In her I have found a kindred spirit.

The Adoption Paradox offers a comprehensive look at all sides of adoption from extensive historical data to contemporary lived experiences told to Ms. Widner by adoptees, birth families, and adoptive parents. Navigating the space as both a storyteller and a truth teller, Jean effortlessly blends first-hand experience with historical, legal, and psychological research, adding a robust look into the adoption industry and giving voice to the often silenced. Motivated by the complexity of her own adoption story, Jean brilliantly initiates a conversation in which the reader can critically examine questionable practices of an industry shaped by capitalism and Western biases, paralleled by the experiences of duality that come from life, relationships, pain, love, and sacrifice.

As a scholar, therapist, adoptee, and birth mother, I was honored when asked to write the foreword to *The Adoption Paradox*. This book is part historical account, part critical analysis, and part biographical portrayal of adoption from the lived experiences of the triad of adoptees, birth parents, and adoptive parents. It is a must read for anyone who is connected to adoption and should be mandatory for those who work within the industry. Not only do I absolutely applaud Jean Kelly Widner for her contribution to the adoption community, I also thank her for this instrumental work that allows space for us to see where we are all thriving while we continue to advocate for, or better, demand awareness and change.

Dr. Abigail K. Hasberry
Licensed Marriage & Family Therapist
Author, Speaker, Advocate

Table of Contents

Table of Contents
(Continued)

The ADOPTION Paradox

Part I - Introduction

Chapter 1
My Adoptee Story

The mother who birthed me, and the mother who raised me both have the same middle name, which became my first name. Neither of them knows this.

My birth mother was a victim of her times. Unwed in 1965, she had no choice other than to place me for adoption. Sent away from the upper Midwest to Washington State, she gave birth to me at a home for unwed mothers. It was there she relinquished me, and my adoption was completed when I was two months old.

My adoptive parents were never secretive about my status. They infused me with a loving indoctrination that I was special and wanted, and being adopted was good. I don't remember being "told" I was adopted—I only remember "knowing" I was.

On the surface, we were a typical happy family. Underneath, there were problems.

My adoptive mother was an addict. She was a victim of the times in which she lived as was my natural mother. Trapped by the expectations around her. When people married back then, they started a family. Those were the rules. Never mind she had already begun her dark slide into depression and addiction, the dual burdens which would haunt her psyche and mine throughout our intertwined lives. I was never certain, and I still wonder if she wanted to be a mother.

When I was little, I took ballet and gymnastics classes at the St. Claire Dance Studio. We had a practice room with barres. In one section was a glass-walled lounge with folding chairs where our parents could see us. I would dance around with the other little girls, springing into the air with my best tour jeté, hoping my mother was watching. She never was. She always sat there with her book, reading not seeing. She never took the time to take in the scene, make eye contact, or give me a smile.

At home, it was as if I had two mommies. One was the happy-faced mommy with her mask fully in place. She acted engaged, smiled, and was fun to be around. Mommy number two was raging, crying, or screaming at who-knows-what. Sometimes she wouldn't get out of bed. I never knew from day to day, or even morning to night, which would be waiting for me. She managed herself with prescription drugs and alcohol. But, of course, as a child, I understood none of this.

By fifth grade, I was in soccer, a mixed co-ed team of youngsters, and both of my parents attended the games every Saturday. My father stood at the sidelines, cheering us on with the other parents. My mom sat in a camp chair and read her book. Afterwards, my friends and I would pile into the back seat with my parents up front. We would eagerly recount the game's events, but Mom wouldn't even know what happened—if we had won or lost. My friends noted her odd behavior and asked why she bothered to come. I couldn't answer them. From my view, I couldn't understand why she had gone to the trouble of adopting me.

Her love felt missing. As an adopted child, you worry you are not good enough, and that's why someone did not want you. Love, logic, or will cannot overcome this constant companion. We need our parents aware of this truth so much more than others.

As adoptees, we are told our noble, suffering birth mother loved us so much she gave us up for someone else to raise. Simultaneously, we're told we're chosen, special, and wanted by our parents. So then love gave you away and love also wanted you. But in my case—rejected me. I was a living, breathing paradox of these truths.

Children are far more intuitive to the energies of those around them than adults realize. As a child, I was tethered to the intentions of my adoptive parents. I needed them in ways I could not express.

I've heard it said there are two primary emotions—anger and sadness—that are the strongest. What I aimed at my mother during my teen years was anger, but what lurked underneath was grief.

Grief from feeling so completely unloved and alone inside, despite looking like I was busy and popular in school. I also had resentment. No matter what I did, I never felt safe. Not that I thought someone would physically hurt me, I could not let my pain show anywhere, ever. This did not fit the narrative of our happy, perfect little family. I do not know where I learned those rules, but they were always present.

At fifteen, my mother began her journey to sobriety. Back then, I hated her for her weakness. In truth, she was strong. I learned she had her own mean-spirited, narcissistic, alcoholic mother to heal from.

As an adult, I know my addict mom wasn't rejecting *me.* She loved me very much in her own way. She just didn't feel she had anything to give. I believe this would have been true whether I had been her natural child or her adopted one. A different source, same outcome.

It was challenging to unpack and separate the effects

of growing up adopted from the problems of being raised by someone with addiction. These effects might surface repeatedly throughout the remainder of my years. But I can't shy away from the effort to reintegrate the inherent pieces of myself that were overwritten or replaced, behaviors born from emotional survival.

An adoption always first begins with a loss. Someone relinquishes us. I am grateful for my educated and financially stable parents and being born and raised in the United States with opportunities denied to others. I also feel the losses and wonder at the differences I may never know. This wondering does not mean I am unhappy or not appreciative of my circumstances. It means only that I am human. The paradox continues.

Reconciling these truths is one of the most important journeys we adoptees need to trek. Our society must understand that adoption does not make a perfect family. It creates a human one. As an adoptee talking to others, I have often found a lingering sense of abandonment or rejection. In their words I often hear a longing to know what might have been. After all, what if my mother hadn't had her addiction? Or, how different would my life be had my birth mother been able to keep me?

Even though my family wasn't perfect, everyone did their best, as did my birth mother—and thus I find myself grateful for all of it.

This is not just my story—this is our story. The question, I think, comes down to this. How do we ensure all sides not just survive, but thrive?

As children, we are innocents. We have no power to affect our circumstances. In my deepest-held instincts I believe most adoptees, to one extent or another, carry wounds caused by the separation from the mothers who bear us. They, in turn, reflect this same pain seared into their souls. These instincts lie in the oldest parts of our brains, inserting themselves into our present being, regardless of how happy we are with our adoptive families. The parents who raise us, I believe, also harbor some sense of insecurity even through their unconditional love for their adopted children.

A Few Words Before Continuing

Writing this book and sharing its stories from different viewpoints is an audacious task. It is also a humbling one. As an adopted adult I can speak for myself and those I have met and interviewed, but I cannot and would never dare to speak for us all. I also am not a parent. Yet in this work I attempt to share the stories of many parents and enough of their wisdom to convey their good advice.

All interviews were conducted in person or over Zoom. Each interview was then transcribed and human reviewed and all were given the opportunity to approve their portions as they appear in the book. Some are quoted from their lived experiences and are also trained experts in adoption-related fields of work and are noted as such when appropriate. Two researchers were also hired to assemble the significant study summarized within.

If a newly adoptive parent is reading this book, hopefully a new awareness of adoption's complexities will surface. These same wishes expand outward to members of their extended family, teachers, clergy members, adoption facilitators, and members of the mental health profession. If one already has older adoptive children, then my hope is these pages will contain "ah-ha" moments where something is clarified. For those who may be pondering adoption to start or build their family, the intention is to give them good advice on what they need to know before beginning. All parents do the job better when they know more, ensuring that adoptions only happen when necessary and making the process better for adoptees is essential.

The book will also outline needed changes to the way adoptions are practiced in the US, including calls to action that many of us in the constellation want enacted.

Each section is designed to immerse you into a central point of view. While I am personally not a fan of labeling people into various groups, it's necessary to define the parts each play within the adoption constellation. They are: adoptee/adopted adult, birth/first parent, and adoptive parent. Some wear multiple labels. Not all of these "name tags" are liked by those who contributed to or will read the book, but they are a way to anchor these complicated and nuanced relationships and convey the depth of their stories to others.

I am endlessly touched and awed by the nearly one hundred people impacted by adoption who have shared their journeys. They speak for themselves, and hopefully you will learn from them. For those who need healing, I hope you find that here, too.

Chapter 2
The Paradox of Adoption

I think that's just part of being adopted: finding peace in your story while knowing that you will still move through the impact of adoption for your lifetime. ~ Isaac Etter

A paradox means you have opposite and dual realities. Adoptees are loved, rejected, celebrated, abandoned, made to feel special, and made to feel less than. They are often both grateful and angry. They are different from everyone else, and yet the same. Regardless of the backstory or the upbringing, they know a reality which contradicts itself.

To understand the paradox, it is best to understand some history. Adopted children have been stolen, sold, loved, wanted, abused, made into indentured servants, used as farm hands, and graced with wealth, education, and opportunities their native birth families never could have afforded them.

In the modern era, many adoptees love their families and feel wanted, safe, and cared for. However, they never see their faces and features mirrored back to them. There will always be differences in appearance, mannerisms, interests, and aptitudes between themselves and their raising family. Depending upon the circumstances, they will not know or have access to their genetic medical information and many other vital and identifying facts about themselves.

Many people do not realize that when an adoption takes

place, the original birth certificate (OBC) often becomes a sealed, secreted, and "unofficial document." A new birth certificate is issued showing the names of the adopting parents on a child's birth certificate as though they had them naturally. This *only* happens in adoption.

The practice of sealing original birth records has far-reaching consequences. It denies the children and adults of adoption access to their identity, as well as their medical history and the birthright of their heritage. It also treats birth parents as though they do not, or never did, exist. This is dehumanizing. Society treats them largely with confusion, disdain, or martyrdom for their selflessness, then all is sunshine and celebrations for the new family.

The public narrative around the practice has most often been dominated by adoptive parents. The average person is still informed about adoption only through beautiful stories in the media, or "the pastor down the street who has taken in all of those foster kids," and "they're such a great family."

All sides deserve their say. Adoptees, birth parents, and adoptive parents each have unique points of view. Complicating these connections are the complex emotions behind these very different lived experiences. Adopted adults' feelings vary. For some, their adoption experience was nothing less than fantastic and they see no ethical, emotional, or moral questions for the practice. Others wish to see it abolished. Their views are as vast as the stars. Some resent the idea that they should listen to anyone's opinion who is not also an adoptee. Others want to interact with the constellation of different ideas and experiences because they find healing in those revelations.

Birth parents also have a wide variety of influences coming from the generation in which they relinquished and their individual circumstances. Some find acceptance that their decision was correct for them at that time. Others emerge years later to realize they were coerced or treated unethically by bad actors. Some become activists for change while others bear the yoke of their shame forever. They, too, have widely different opinions on how adoption ought to be conducted, if at all. Like adoptees, they wish to be heard for themselves and with their own voices.

Validating and hearing this often unheard-from constellation is essential. They tell stories from their inspirational, angry, triumphant, troubled, and grateful voices—in their words.

Adoptees

Kate~
I feel so incredibly lucky. My parents gave me so many opportunities that I would have never had from my biological mother. I used to think she didn't want me, and that hurt. But later, I learned she hadn't had a very stable or happy childhood. When she knew she was pregnant, and my father wasn't going to be in the picture, she did what she thought was best.

Tina~
I don't want to say my parents are reluctant to discuss adoption, but they feel that once that took place, it pretty much ended the whole chapter. Once I became adopted by them, everything was fine. There was no need to go digging into the past. There was no need to find out health-related things. You know you're going to die anyway, so who cares.

When I told my parents I was reunited and found by my biological sister. My dad said, "Well, it sounds like you had a better life with us. It sounds like your mom was messed up."

Yeah, I would be messed up, too, if I had to give up my baby.

Terri~

Day in and day out, I rode the fifty-two bus in West Philadelphia, and while on the bus, I looked at each woman seated and couldn't help but wonder if I was looking at *her*. I thought every woman that looked like me was her. I couldn't fathom what my dad would look like, but I could almost imagine my mom.

As my stop came, and it was time for me to exit, I felt tremendous sadness because I couldn't help but feel like one of the ladies was her.

Susan~

My mom tried doing all these crazy things to "claim" me, instead of letting me be who I am and celebrating the person I am.

One of the biggest fights my mother and I had happened because she had short curly hair. She wanted me to have short curly hair, so she could claim me to the outside world. I can't tell you how many home perms, trips to the beauty parlor I went through to get short curly hair. I grew to resent it. It became this big thing.

"You're not keeping your hair up," she

would say.

"I hate curly hair. What are you doing to me?"

Abbey~

Even though I never questioned whether I was good enough for my birth parents, I felt like it was always a subconscious thought in my head. I always thought I had to be a certain way. I was always a perfectionist, and yeah, I believe part of that was probably because I was adopted. I've had issues with self-worth and being good enough for my parents.

Adoptees often feel their birth mothers did not want them, discarded, set aside, and unworthy of love. Many blame their birth mothers and are unable to move beyond what they have internalized as a physical rejection of them. Others remain solid in their belief, "adoption is awesome!" They feel loved and wanted, and report no adverse effects being separated from their original family.

Why do some feel that profound abandonment while others do not? What forces create this? Biology, environment, or something else?

Birth Parents

This book addresses birth parents rather than simply birth mothers because there are men who experience this too. Before a family is built, one is broken and dissolved. There is coercion and pressure brought to bear on birth mothers in particular, and a staggering load of personal judgment heaped upon them.

Whenever and however an unplanned pregnancy occurs, there are consequences. Prior to the late 1970s, an unmarried woman was rarely allowed to remain a single mother—the culture would not readily allow it. Closed adoptions dominated the process and there was much shame and secrecy surrounding any relinquishment of a baby.

In the modern era, women do and can raise children without a husband or partner. Some unmarried women will adopt a child independently. The culture has progressed, but this shaded history around the secrecy of adoption still has living and breathing suffering from its impact.

Currently, birth parents who relinquish a child usually do so because they, together or singly, cannot feasibly support it. Some will give up their baby because of addiction or criminal behavior and are unable to parent at that time. Women who become victims of a sexual attack will sometimes carry the baby to term and place it for adoption because of their religious beliefs.

Open adoptions try to minimize the emotional pain of relinquishment. In these arrangements, the birth parent(s) remain present in the child's life even though the adoptive parents are the unquestionable caregivers and are solely, legally responsible for the child's welfare. These arrangements are often complex for all involved and create their own set of unique emotional and mental health challenges. But some birth and adoptive parents make this work.

Regardless of the circumstances, birth parents always remember the child they gave up. Even if they come not to regret their decision, and some do believe it was ultimately the right choice, they are often traumatized by what happened.

Ellen~
You have to remember, it was 1973. Our world was changing and there was a lot of the old guard who still believed unwed mothers were garbage. I was treated like garbage by the women I worked with, by the nurses at the hospital, and by the doctors. I was left in the hallway screaming in pain. When the nurse came out, she unceremoniously spread my knees, looked in, and said, "You're not ready. We'll come back when you are." I remember screaming, and she said, "This is what you get for being an unwed tramp. I'm going back in there with this proper married woman to take care of her." That was burned into my brain. So, when that baby girl was taken from my arms, I don't remember anything. I just remember being numb for months.

Ann~
It was like closing the book, but the memories were still there. You don't forget the birthdays and the "this year he would be in kindergarten, and then first grade," but I felt like I had to go on with life. I always knew I did the right thing because I gave somebody else life that couldn't have life. So, I didn't sit back and beat myself up, but the thoughts of those birthdays or wondering what he got for Christmas. Those thoughts always came up.

Mel~
That night after dinner at my parents' home,

we often sat in the TV room. I said, "I've got something to tell you." They let me tell them the story of Candace and that she was pregnant. They were just the kind of parents you'd want because they simply said, "What can we do?" We had only dated a few months and had broken up several months before I learned she was pregnant. But she and her mother had decided they wanted to have the baby and give it up for adoption.

A lawyer was hired, and they took over. After that agreement had been reached, I was told not to reach out to her. I don't know if that was the attorneys talking or Candy saying she didn't want to hear from me. I wouldn't even know if it was a boy or a girl.

Debi~

They contacted Catholic Charities and had me put away in a home. Being the summer of 1967, my mother lied and told her side of the family that I was in Italy with my father's mother.

No one ever knew. It was my secret. I got sent away, came back in August, and went back to school. Nobody knew little Debi had a baby. From that day forth, every single year, my mother and I would get together on his birthday, so we could cry together.

Adoptive Parents

Very few couples choose to adopt without there being some sort of loss in their background. Couples who cannot conceive are often in deep emotional pain. Most have tried multiple times to get pregnant or keep a pregnancy and may have experienced multiple losses and what feels like endless heartache. Many have not fully, or even begun, to grieve.

Queer couples have faced open discrimination for centuries, which continues today. This has often been reflected in state laws on their ability to adopt or foster children, even though gay marriage has been legal in the US since 2015.

People wishing to adopt have many avenues available. Some contact state agencies or other non-profit organizations to help them. Others use the services of a lawyer or private adoption agencies. Some try to find birth mothers on their own via social media. There are even Apps to connect birth and prospective adopting parents.

National adoption statistics for 2022 report approximately one million willing couples are actively seeking to adopt a baby. This contrasts with only eighteen thousand domestically born babies who will be relinquished in any given year within the US. This level of disparity between the available supply of infants and the number of wanting parents has never existed since adoption records have been kept. The child welfare and infant adoption industry is now a multi-billion-dollar enterprise.

> **Gayle~**
> I called everyone. The state was more interested in you fostering and then getting your home study for the adoption process. I wasn't interested in adopting a seven-year-old, as we already had two children naturally, but a pregnancy was too much for me physically, and we wanted a third child.

We got a call from Jewish Social Services. Their attorney who deals with adoption has this baby that's coming quickly, and she needs someone to adopt who doesn't care about race.

It was January. The baby was due February 14th. The birth mom had a woman who was going to adopt the baby, but she never did the home study and approval process. If you wait, then it's even more expensive. You're talking \$30-\$40,000.00 easy because they have to rush all the paperwork. Now here's the mother with a baby, and she has nowhere for the baby to go.

We met at an Olive Garden in town and talked to her for about four hours. She asked us, "Are you equipped and able to raise a chocolate child?" Yes, she actually used that word.

They induced her on February 12th. She called from a local hospital. We walked into the room, and she said, "Here's your chocolate boy!" I said, "Thank you!" That's why he's been chocolate boy ever since because his birth mom called him that.

My breast milk came in. I nursed him. From the minute I held him, I loved him. He completed our family.

I would say this to anyone thinking about adopting a baby or a child. Love it like it's your own, because it is. You have to go into adoption knowing it's yours until you die. No matter what they do, no matter their medical issues, no matter what. He is mine until I die.

I never questioned it or would rethink it, ever.

Beth~
At the time, to go to other countries and other states for adoption was so huge in Utah . I was becoming biased against adoption agencies and some of the things my husband and I had experienced. Is there no feeling behind this? You're just buying and selling children?

I hate to use the words human trafficking, but it almost felt that way. It was just like, "Oh, we just need to get these kids into a home, and we'll make our money." There are fees for this and fees for that. When really, those fees didn't need to exist. I understand it's a business, but it seems outrageously expensive.

Lee~
She's her own person. That part is really exciting. There are two reasons why we're on the planet, to love and be loved. Put that love to the ultimate test, it's not about us. It's about them. It's not even about my journey. It's about me creating a soft pillow for her to rest her head.

The Challenges of the Times

How this society treats unplanned-for children has consequences. As the US dismantles nationwide access to abortion, a gigantic social experiment is happening, and all are watching to see how these changes will unfold. Rescuing at-risk children will be needed indefinitely. Sadly, there will always be parents who cannot, or should not, raise children.

All regulations and laws on adoption need to be evaluated with the greatest care. *Lives are at stake*. This country needs to ask itself some hard questions. Are the safety nets, social services, and modern adoption practices we currently have capable of creating the society we most want, need, and deserve?

Chapter 3
The History of American Adoption

"Adoptee rights are everyone's rights, and they deserve to be protected." ~ DaShanne Stokes

The foundations of adoption were largely about wealth and labor. It is only in recent times it became about the welfare of the child or the longing to be a parent. There are a great many factors which create the legal practice of a child born to one family and ending up, legally or not, part of another.

Adoption sits at a nexus of wealth, social class, race, the subjugation of women to men, sexuality, sex education, and birth control and its availability. Adoption practices have been used to justify apprenticeship, indentured servitude, and to circumvent child labor laws. Children are, and have been, trafficked both domestically and internationally. Through it all, many throughout time have attempted to use adoption with the noble goal of creating loving families and reducing child homelessness, abuse, neglect, and infanticide.

The welfare of adopted children throughout history deserves to be examined in detail to understand how the rights of children and, most especially adoptees, have changed drastically over time. Some historical biases about their status as human beings with innate rights have always been minimized and are to this day.

Adoption's Origins

Adoption originated in Ancient Rome, driven by the need for male heirs to inherit wealth and prevent the state from claiming a wealthy family's assets. Adopting "spare sons" from others became common and was unrelated to child welfare. Adoptees were frequently adults.[1] Only men could adopt, and even widows were barred from adopting heirs. Adoption declined during the Middle Ages as emerging nations such as England, France and Germany prioritized bloodlines.[2] The practice became illegal, and orphanages opened en masse beginning in 1419 with Florence's Hospital of the Innocents.[3]

However, orphanages were overwhelmed and the practice of "foster servitude," became common. Children were placed with families or tradesmen to work in exchange for support. In both rural and urban settings, children contributed labor to family enterprises, helping to sustain themselves. This system provided orphans with modest stability and some skills for their future, although this was hardly a loving or family-oriented practice.[4]

In the 1800s, the Industrial Revolution transformed children's roles from labor providers to dependents. Cities became crowded and men more commonly worked outside the home at a job, rather than as farmers or running their own enterprises. This relegated women to domestic roles, while children focused on schooling and minor chores.[5] In growing cities, poor working conditions and pollution created harsh environments, leaving many impoverished children to fend for themselves. By the 1850s, homeless children, called "foundlings," roamed streets, begging or selling goods. Resources for these children were limited to asylums, orphanages, and almshouses, highlighting the plight of urban poverty during this era.

The Orphan Trains

Driven by a genuine desire to provide a different life and opportunity for such children gave birth to the idea in America that they be sent away from the squalor of the slums and embraced by a loving Christian family on a Mid-Western farm.

The Orphan Trains became the solution, also known as the "Placing Out" program. Charles Loring Brace created the Children's Aid Society and became the program's chief administrator. Between the years 1854 to 1929, it is estimated between 150,000 - 200,000 children were re-homed via this method into the farmlands of the Midwest.

Homeless children, either found on the streets or languishing in orphanages, were put onto trains. As they traveled, the youngest babies or infants were usually taken first. By the time they reached the Midwest, the older youths were nearly all who remained.

In fact, the common term of "putting a child up for adoption" comes from this practice. As the children were often "put up" on the station platform when they arrived and inspected. Then they were fostered or adopted into their new home.

Many of the farmers were looking for labor rather than an emotional bond between parent and child. An example of this is a letter written below:

> "In 1918, the Mayor of Bogalusa, Louisiana, wrote the Children's Aid Society of New York to request some white babies…a car load…by a car load, meaning about thirty to fifty. We do not care to know anything about their antecedents or parentage. All we want to know is that they are healthy. We would

> be interested in about one half Protestant and one half Catholic children, both boys and girls."[6]

Reviews of the Orphan Trains are mixed. Some believe it enabled abandoned children the opportunity for better lives and was a shining example of good Christian generosity from families who took them in. Critics point out it became a labor and employment program for the farmers. Many of these children were not welcomed into a loving family but were in effect, indentured servants.[7]

The Great Depression and Early Adoption Laws

The Great Depression of 1929 caused massive upheaval in every aspect of American life. The average family with one bread-winning husband faced drastically cut wages if they were able to keep their jobs or find work.

For the first time in American history, the birth rate dropped below replacement levels, because parents feared they could not support another child.

Married men and women split up to take work as they could to survive, and children were left to forage for work and shelter. By 1940 1.5 million women were living separately from their husbands, and more than 200,000 children also lived apart from their families, wandering from place to place.[8]

Simultaneously changes were emerging within the rules governing the practice of adoption.

Foundations of Adoption Law in the United States

The laws establishing the practice of adoption in the US were and still are, entirely regulated by each state. They each developed their own practices but also borrowed legislation from each other. Some state's policies became templates for others. The first state to enact a law which prioritized children's needs over adult motivations was Massachusetts in 1851 with its Adoption of Children Act.[9] There are few reliable records documenting adoptions in the US before 1910. By then there were well over one thousand orphanages domestically, housing over 100,000 children. An effort was made to move these children into private homes via the emerging foster care system, the placing out program, and private adoption. However, it was not until 1950 when the US had more orphaned or abandoned children living in private homes versus institutions.

The next significant evolution in policy was the Minnesota Adoption Law of 1917. It provided for the legal adoption of a child with a few specific stipulations: The home of the proposed parents would be investigated by the State Board of Control and deemed safe and sufficient to raise a child. The natural parents must consent to the adoption. If the adoptee was fourteen years or older, they must also agree. It stated the child's name may be changed. The new parents were now the legal parents, and all prior rights from the natural family were terminated.[10] The law was the first provision of its kind, and it sealed the records from view other than the state and the adult parties.

Sealing the adoption records was significant. Before the nineteenth century, it was common for an adoption to be open and more of a shared or combined parenting of the children, and they often kept in contact with their natural kin.

Once adoptions became sealed and secret, then a new priority emerged, which was to hide the fact an adoption had occurred. The concept of *matching* became common practice.

Children were selected and matched with the wanting family, sharing similar skin, eye and hair color, and other characteristics. Religious affiliation was also important. An infant with a biological mother who was Catholic was more likely to be placed with a Catholic family, and the same was true of a Protestant. Between 1920 and 1970, matching was popular, and a normal part of the adoption review processes.[11]

"Matching confronted the central problem of modern adoption. It attempted to create kinship without blood in the face of an enduring equivalence between blood and belonging. The results were paradoxical. Matching reinforced the notion that blood was thicker than water, the very ideology that made adoption inferior, while seeking to equalize and dignify it."[12]

Throughout the 1930s, two significant changes began to occur. One was the branding of children as illegitimate on their birth certificates. This was a common practice, and sometimes, children's birth certificates were a different color than those born to married couples. A *bastard child* was branded forever by the sins of their unwed parents and wielded as a cruel social insult. Through the work of social reformer Edna Gladney of Texas, references to illegitimacy on birth certificates were removed starting in 1933. Other states gradually followed this policy change.

The second major shift was created, in part, by the Great Depression. As the New Deal rolled out, so did the first meaningful child labor laws. As a result, in the late 1930s a child being *"adopted"* as an indentured servant solely for the purpose of their labor, became widely unacceptable. The significance of this change cannot be overstated. Without the social equalizer and the pressures created by the Depression, how long would things have remained unchanged?

As laws governing adoption slowly spread, new attempts were made to create consistent practices. Still, in small towns throughout the US, it is hard to know how much information local authorities had about official adoption procedures.

> **Bobbie, born in 1936~**
> Estelle, my birth mother, whom I met later in life, told me the chief of police and a couple of officers went up to wherever she was with me. I was fourteen days old then. She was told she could go to jail for having a baby and not being married. They just took me away. That's how my adoptive parents got me.
>
> They were supposed to meet Estelle at the County Courthouse in Kansas to sign adoption papers. My adoptive mother told me Estelle never showed up. When my adopted mother died in '92, I found my adoption papers, which were never signed. So, I think I was stolen is how that went. There were no signatures on it at all.

In 1951, there were other major evolutions to the Minnesota law. For the first time, formal definitions were created for the parent, child, petitioner, agency, and the petitions' contents. It was also the first time "the welfare of the child" is part of the formal language in any adoption statute.[13] Those legal developments set the stage for what most other states created from this point forward, and this Minnesota version of the law remained unchanged until the 1980s.

The Baby Scoop Era

It is unclear who first coined the term, "the baby scoop" but its roots lie in two different sources. The first was called the "Sixties Scoop" from Patrick Johnston, author of the 1983 report *Native Children and the Child Welfare System*. It documented the mass removal of Aboriginal children from their families into the child welfare system. The second was in the books written by historian Rickie Sollinger, *Wake Up Little Susie* and *Beggars and Choosers*. Regardless of the source, the term and its accuracy about the events unfolding make it accurate. A new phase in adoption history had begun, altering the lives of millions.

In the years between World War II and 1973, adoptions were at an all-time high. Approximately 1.5 million adoptions occurred in the United States alone, the peak being in 1970, with 175,000 in just that year.[14] The US was not alone. The same flood of adoptions also took place throughout Europe and the U.K., as well as Canada and Australia.

After the Second World War, a worldwide "baby boom"began. Young, unmarried people were part of this same trend, but other specific cultural changes were happening.

In America, the G.I. Bill boosted a young middle class into existence en masse for the first time. The suburbs exploded as most married couples now had their own home, and parked in the driveway was a shiny new car—a large one with big front and back seats made for status and comfort. Into those cars piled teenagers on romantic escapades with newfound freedoms. Gone were the days of chaperoned dates and gentlemen callers in drawing rooms. Dating included new privacy provided by the automobile.[15]

However, there was still no meaningful birth control available for most single people, especially teenagers, nor was there organized sex education. According to accounts from teens who came of age in the '50s and '60s, information about sex was widely shared or gathered by reading illicit books or magazines. Most did understand the basic biological plumbing and the potential consequences of pregnancy, but little could be done to minimize the risks.

The *Comstock Laws* created in the late 1800s were still on the books in many states and severely limited access to reliable information about the sexual act, or education and birth control. In 1961, it was still *illegal in twenty-four states for a physician to converse with a married woman about contraception.* When it came to having sex, teens of the era were told, "don't do it," and this was expected to be enough.

Decided in 1965, *Griswold v. Connecticut,* legalized the use of contraception nationwide but only applied to married couples. Throughout the '60s, some states with more progressive views did make birth control available to young adults on college campuses and other outlets. But it was only with the Supreme Court's ruling *Eisenstadt v. Baird* in 1972 that contraception could be sold to unmarried people evenly across the US.

The consequence of these restrictions, combined with a new, permissive sexualized culture, was a tsunami of unplanned pregnancies. Teenagers and college-aged young adults became pregnant but were surrounded by a society that was not ready for them. Most burdens and judgments were heaped on the young women and girls as the double standard was the prevailing attitude. The manipulation, bullying, and shaming of those young women caused them to surrender their babies for adoption on an unprecedented scale.

This was great for would-be adoptive parents who could not conceive. If you wanted to adopt a baby, plenty were available. Want a boy? No problem. Been trying to have a girl and cannot—you can pick one up easily!

> **Vickie~**
> There was an attorney who worked with the home for unwed mothers to help place the children who were being given up. It all started with my parents when our next-door neighbors who had five boys decided they were done trying to have a girl. So, they adopted one. My parents had two boys, but my mom said that she wanted a little girl too when they brought Amy home [from next door]. So, they put my parents in touch with the lawyer that helped them, and they ended up with me. It took them only a month to complete the process.

The baby scoop era created families with lots of love, joy, and fulfillment. But it also had consequences. Adopted children were told they were wanted, special, and chosen. That they should be grateful to the mothers who selflessly relinquished them and should feel that same way toward the adoptive parents who "rescued" them from a life assumed to be filled with poverty and the stains of illegitimacy. Adoptions were fast, painless, and easy. But few at the time stopped to consider what that was like for adoptees or those natural mothers.

Native Americans and the Indian Child Welfare Act (ICWA)

The tales of the atrocities of the US government against Native Americans are lengthy and well-known. There are two key aspects to note when one looks at any policy regarding them. First, the government primarily wanted their land. Second, that while negotiating for the land, the treaties created recognized the tribes and their people as their own sovereign nations.

These facts set any discussion on the adoption of Native American children apart from African Americans or any other people of color. The government believed that the savage Indian needed to be culturally subjugated to superior Christian values and adapt to American culture.

The Indian Removal Act of 1830 created the policy in the US to forcibly relocate Native Americans from their tribal lands, sometimes far away from their original homes. Beyond that, it extended to the forcible breakup of individual Native families.

Boarding Schools and Cultural Genocide

In 1881 the government directed the Bureau of Indian Affairs (BIA) that school attendance for Indian children was compulsory, or they would be denied basic treaty rights such as rations or clothing.[16] Thousands of Native children were taken from their homes and placed into the Carlisle Indian Industrial Schools. Fifty of these schools spread rapidly throughout the Midwest and Eastern states. The children were forced to speak only English, practice the Christian faith, and cut their hair and wear only non-tribal clothing. These rules intended to systematically remove their culture and assimilate them into the American one.

Henry Pratt founded the boarding schools and created an infamous motto, "Kill the Indian, save the man".[17]

Abuse was rampant. A 1928 report detailed how children were neglected, suffered from chronic health conditions, and overcrowded dormitories with poor sanitation.

A recent report commissioned by the US Interior showed at least five hundred of those children died in the United States, although that number might be falsely low.[18] In Canada, over one thousand unmarked graves were recently discovered with Native children in similar institutions.

In the years between the late 1800s and 1934, the forced allotment of Indian lands by the US government left Native tribes with only forty-eight million acres, forty percent of which was desert or semi-desert.[19]

The Indian Adoption Project

The 1950s and '60s ushered in a new era as Indian boarding schools became culturally unpopular, although they continued operating into the early 1970s. Instead, the Indian Adoption Project was born. From 1958 to 1967, the federal government partnered with the Child Welfare League of America to remove Native children from their families and place them with white ones with the continued goal of assimilating them into white, Christian culture.

The number of children adopted because of the project is comparatively small, about four hundred overall. However, it is important because it is the first and only federal program designed to promote what was viewed as "transracial" adoption at the time.[20]

It is estimated that ninety percent of these adoptions were into white families, and by 1968 there were several tribes that had *all* of their children placed outside their native homes.

Unwed young tribal mothers faced the same bias and judgment for their situation as their white counterparts. However, far fewer resources were available to them. Social workers and others responsible for the safety of children believed they should be "far from the reservation" where there were more resources.

> "As sad and as terrible as the conditions are that Indian children must face as they grow up, nothing exceeds the cruelty of being unjustly and unnecessarily removed from their families...Indian children are removed from the custody of their parents or Indian foster family for placement in non-Indian homes without sufficient cause and without due process of law."
>
> ~William Byler, Executive Director of the AAIA, 1968

The Indian Child Welfare Act (ICWA)

A cultural genocide of Native Americans, had been carried out by the separation of families from their children, organized by the federal government and the Bureau of Indian Affairs. However, Native peoples and their tribes had formal treaties with the federal government that was supposed to protect their rights. Any adoption taking place should have been treated almost as an international adoption. Social workers and adoption agencies were supposed to negotiate equally and fairly with both entities.

"Social workers* and missionaries took children without any color of law...there really was no necessary connection between a court order and losing your child—the caseworker just came and put the child in her or his car and drove away."[21]

In the years prior to the ICWA at least 25 - 35% of all Indian children were with adoptive families, foster care, or boarding schools. 85% of them were with non-native families, even when suitable and willing relatives were available.

Most states kept no statistics about how many of their children in the foster care system were Native American.

Many tribes throughout the US fought in state courts to try to reunite these families. The American Association of Indian Affairs (AAIA) represented and won *all* of the dozens of cases where they intervened. "No one on the other side had even tried to act within the law. It was just Indian kids."[22]

A series of hearings were held before Congress beginning in 1976. Organizers struggled to create a coherent and official argument through the labyrinth of barely believable tales of lawlessness. "A social worker just walked up to your child and took him…and there was never a dependency hearing, never a finding of parental unfitness? These things made no sense in Congress."[23]

Hundreds of tribes and dozens of states reported that Native families were four times more likely to have their children removed and placed in foster care than their white counterparts.

In 1978 the ICWA passed Congress and remains the only binding national legislation on adoption in the US It gave tribal governments exclusive jurisdiction over children who resided on a reservation. The act was and is considered to be the "gold standard" of the child welfare industry and set evidentiary standards higher than for non-Native families. It required that parents be offered crisis intervention services before a child could be taken. And relatives or tribal members, including those from other recognized tribes, are always given placement preference before other options are considered.[24] Ten states with high Native tribal populations have codified their own versions of the ICWA into their own state law.

In December 2022, the Supreme Court heard oral arguments in *Brackeen v. Haaland,* challenging the constitutionality of the Indian Child Welfare Act (ICWA). In June 2023 the court upheld its provisions. Justice Amy Coney Barrett wrote the majority opinion stating, "Congress's power to legislate with respect to Indians is well established and broad. When Congress enacts a valid statute pursuant to its Article I powers, state law is naturally preempted…end of story."

The Past Influences the Present

The impacts of the closed and secreted practices of the past live on today. Those fueled by shame are particularly painful and must be addressed. Unless one is actively seeking to adopt, most of the public remain largely uninformed of the details, or the long-term consequence of adoption. It is assumed to be a positive experience, but this narrative has most often been written by adoptive parents.

Adoptees and birth parents have been far less vocal. But that is changing. Adoption practices continue to evolve, and individuals and families are expanding new conversations about the process.

---

1. Goody, J. (1969). Adoption in Cross-Cultural Perspective. *Comparative Studies in Society and History, 11*(1), 55-78. doi:10.1017/S0010417500005156

2. What is the history of adoption? Adoption.org. (n.d.). https://adoption.org/what-is-the-history-of-adoption

3. Gurney, T. (n.d.). Hospital of the innocents (ospedale degli innocenti). Hospital of the Innocents

(Ospedale degli Innocenti) by Filippo Brunelleschi. https://www.thehistoryofart.org/filippo-brunelleschi/hospital-of-the-innocents/

4. What is the history of adoption? Adoption.org. (n.d.). https://adoption.org/what-is-the-history-of-adoption

5. Seaholm, Megan. "Woman's Body, Woman's Right: Birth Control in America by Linda Gordon (1976)." (2012).

6. Walling, Wright S. (2007) "Adoption Law in Minnesota: A Historical Perspective," William Mitchell Law Review: Vol. 33: Iss. 3, Article 15, Page 8. Available at: http://open.mitchellhamline.edu/wmlr/vol33/iss3/15

7. Website by Regina Talento, Palmer School of Library and Information Science at Long Island University, C.W. Post Campus: http://dlib.openlib.org/home/rtalento/Program.html#:~:text=The%20placing%20out%20movement%20has,the%20years%201854%20and%201

8. https://www.digitalhistory.uh.edu/active_learning/explorations/children_depression/depression_children_menu.cfm. (n.d.).

9. Kawashima, Yasuhide. "Adoption in early America." J. Fam. L. 20 (1981): 677.

10. https://www.revisor.mn.gov/laws/1917/0/Session+Law/Chapter/222/pdf/

11. Adoption history: Matching. (n.d.). Retrieved November 12, 2022, from https://pages.uoregon.edu/adoption/topics/matching.html

12. Adoption history: Matching. (n.d.). Retrieved November 12, 2022, from https://pages.uoregon.edu/adoption/topics/matching.html

13. Adoption law in Minnesota: A historical perspective. https://open.mitchellhamline.edu/cgi/viewcontent.cgi?httpsredir=1&article=1186&context=wmlr. (n.d.). Retrieved November 26, 2022, from https://open.mitchellhamline.edu/cgi/viewcontent.cgi?httpsredir=1&article=1186&context=wmlr

14. Stolley, Kathy S. "Statistics on Adoption in the United States." The Future of Children, vol. 3, no. 1, 1993, pp. 26–42. JSTOR, https://doi.org/10.2307/1602400. Accessed 27 Nov. 2022.

15. Fessler, A. (2007). The girls who went away the hidden history of women who surrendered children for adoption in the decades before Roe v. Wade. Penguin Press.

16. Briggs, Laura. Somebody's Children: The Politics of Transracial and Transnational Adoption. Duke University Press, 2012

17. Briggs, Laura. Somebody's Children: The Politics of Transracial and Transnational Adoption. Duke University Press, 2012.

18. Asgarian, R. (2022, November 10). Texas case could change adoption rules for Native American children and undercut tribal rights. The Texas Tribune. Retrieved April 19, 2023, from https://www.texastribune.org/2022/11/10/indian-child-adoption-scotus/

19. Briggs, Laura. Somebody's Children: The Politics of Transracial and Transnational Adoption. Duke University Press, 2012.

20. Briggs, Laura. Somebody's Children: The Politics of Transracial and Transnational Adoption. Duke University Press, 2012.

21. Briggs, Laura. Somebody's Children: The Politics of Transracial and Transnational Adoption. Duke University Press, 2012.

22. Briggs, Laura. Somebody's Children: The Politics of Transracial and Transnational Adoption. Duke University Press, 2012.

23. Briggs, Laura. Somebody's Children: The Politics of Transracial and Transnational Adoption. Duke University Press, 2012.

24. Briggs, Laura. Somebody's Children: The Politics of Transracial and Transnational Adoption. Duke University Press, 2012.

•Author's Note: the term 'Social Workers' will be loosely applied here, as there are many levels of social workers, case workers and other decision makers within the child welfare system.

Part II – Adoptees

Chapter 4

Foundations

"Love is not a cure-all for an adoptee, but it's a great place to start." ~Christina Romo

Adoption is the beginning of a lifelong process, not a singular event. After the essentials of sustenance, warmth, and shelter are met, most parents assume love is the only thing a child needs. This oversimplification creates problems in adoption.

When a newborn is handed off to a new family, most people believe this happens for the child's benefit. However, the needs of others motivate the entire process.

The combined groupthink on adoption is so pervasive, most don't want to let go of the positive narrative. However, society does not look through the eyes and mind of a child, especially one who is so *lucky* to have been *rescued* by loving and wanting parents.

The presumptions by others overwhelm many adoptees and cause them to believe they are puppets in some sort of play, created for others' comforts.

How parents frame the conversation around adoption and everyone's role in the family is the first, most important fact of that young adoptee's life.

The Framework

Kids take cues from their parents on how to talk about, and understand any important topic. A unique dynamic among adopted children is that historically, adoption was seen as a shameful and secret thing. The importance of how they see themselves within their family and how adoption is talked about, cannot be overstated. It can set the tone for their entire life. "In fact, no other influence [communicating about adoption] has been shown to be greater for adoptees' understanding of their adoption and their connection to the adoptive family than their adoptive parents (Wrobel et al., 2003)."[1]

Rae~

I grew up like a lot of adoptees in a comfortably middle-class family. They had two biological sons of their own who were much older than me. Growing up, I didn't really have a lot of conversations about being adopted. I always knew, but it was also not something that was table talk. It was kind of taboo in the house, or at least that's the feeling I got growing up.

I remember asking about my biological mother. I always knew there was another person who was responsible for who I was, and I was curious about her. Every time I asked about her, this was a very uncomfortable topic for my adoptive mother.

One day, maybe I was nine or ten, I came into the kitchen and on the table was a picture. It was of a woman and a boy. I stopped and looked at it. There was no note or anything.

My adoptive mother wasn't waiting for me. She was doing her own thing. I said, "Who's this a picture of?"

She said, "Oh, that's your birth mom and your half-brother." I didn't even know I had a half-brother, so this was quite a surprise for me.

I wanted to ask more questions, but it seemed uncomfortable for my adoptive mother. She took the picture, and I never saw it again. I was a teenager, and adolescence was affecting me. I'm becoming my own person. But after that, things as far as my relationship with her got very bad, very quickly.

Vickie~

I'd known for as long as I could remember that I was adopted. It was something my parents made sure of. I don't remember how old I was when they told me. I had two older brothers who were theirs naturally, but they had also wanted a girl.

Apparently, when I was really little, I thought all kids were adopted. My mother, one of her favorite stories, is that I got mad at one of my brothers and said, "I wish we hadn't adopted you!"

They had to explain to me that not all children were adopted. I was three days old when they brought me home from the hospital.

It was a private adoption. All I knew about my biological mother was that she was at a home for unwed mothers, as they were termed in the South back in the late '60s.

My parents reinforced throughout my life that I was chosen and wanted. But as an adoptee, I struggled with it for a long time, especially in my teens, that feeling of rejection.

Jody~

They were an upper-middle-class couple who lost a child. They had three children, and they lost their middle one. So, a couple of years later, they said, "Hey, let's get a replacement kid." That was fun for everyone.

Imagine having a couple of children who were ten and fourteen who had just lost their sibling, being told, "We got you a new kid. We got you a new sister." My brother goes from being the youngest to the middle, after I arrived.

I had a friend in junior high who was older than me. He said, "Oh my God, your parents, your family treats you like a poodle." I didn't really understand what he meant until years later when it dawned on me, yeah, they wanted a poodle. They wanted a dress-up doll, and they got me.

Talking About Adoption

When and how children are told they are adopted matters. Conventional wisdom for parents is that a child should not remember being "told" but to "grow up knowing"—and many do. "The quality and nature of the communication between adoptive parents and children are among the most important factors to consider in the ability of a child to develop a coherent adoptive identity, even when faced with uncertainty (Brodzinsky, 2006)."[2]

Numerous studies confirm the earlier a child is told, the better for them. The more normal it is to talk about adoption, the less uncertain and stigmatizing it becomes. Transparency builds trust for children and helps them understand that curiosity about their heritage is normal—because it is. However, if a younger child, over the age of three or four is informed, and especially by someone other than their parent, the effects can be quite traumatic.

> **Marc~**
> When you don't look like everybody in your family, subconsciously you know there's something up, but nobody ever said anything to me. My parents were both very stoic. Didn't show a lot of emotion.
>
> I found out I was adopted when I was seven. My mom and dad were out of town, and I'm walking up the sidewalk with the neighbor to my grandparents' house. Carol, his older sister, says to me, "Did you know that your parents aren't your parents?"
>
> I said, "What? What'd you say?"
>
> That's the last thing I remember that day. It just shocked me, even though subconsciously I think I knew. She was the one who told me I was adopted.
>
> Afterwards, I went back to my grandparents' house. I don't think I went to school that day. It's really unclear. It was a traumatic thing for me. When my mom and dad got back, they explained the situation.

I don't really remember what they said other than I was adopted. They didn't give me any background on my genetic parents. I think they absolutely knew some, because I was adopted through Lutheran Social Services in Sioux Falls, South Dakota.

After that, I had some physical symptoms. I constantly cleared my throat. I wasn't really the same for a while, to the point where my second-grade teacher was concerned about my welfare. I didn't go see any mental health professionals, but things just took their course. I have a sister who's three years younger than me, and she was adopted also.

She's never relayed to me how it was communicated to her.

Terri~

When I was 4 years old, my parents got me a brother. I didn't ask for him, and when he arrived, I didn't know what to do with him. I remember rolling him on the floor because he was just a cute, chubby round ball.

Then, it's 1973 and I'm 12 years old. My brother and I are waiting for the school bus, and we get into an argument. I took his backpack and threw it down the sewer. Out of nowhere he yells out "You're adopted."

"I'm what?"

Robin, our neighbor, caught the bus with us, and she is standing in amazement with me. "What are you talking about? Adopted?"

When I got home from school, I asked my mom if I was adopted. "Mom, Mark said I was adopted."

She says, "Yes."

"What does that mean?" I asked.

"Well, it means that we picked you out of many other kids we could have chosen. We picked you because we knew you would grow up to look like us."

I'm still clueless as to what that meant. I didn't understand what a heavy heart meant at twelve years old.

So, we went to church the following weekend, and I talked to the youth minister.

He said, "You're ungrateful. How can you come to us and say you were adopted? You're not thankful to God for being chosen and part of this family!"

He yelled at me! I was baffled because I didn't understand how someone from the church could yell at a little kid who just wanted to know their identity. Nevertheless, I've suffered and struggled with that until now. From twelve years old to fifty-nine.

The Ultimate Secret - Late Discovery Adoptees

A lie by omission is still a lie. When adoptive parents don't tell their children the truth about their origins it should surprise no one that this can be devastating when found out later. These situations are more common than most people realize, enough so that they have their own acronym, LDAs or Late Discovery Adoptees.

Adoptive parents who are so unable to speak about their own choices, allow their discomfort to harm their children.

Brad~

Growing up, I really didn't think anything was off. I knew I wasn't good at almost anything my parents were good at. I spent my life trying to fit into this mold, thinking it was what I should be.

I tried sports…sucked at sports, hated sports, but my dad was into sports. The stuff I was good at and had skills toward were art and music. I ignored it because that's not what we did.

Fast-forward forty-some years, and my wife and I did AncestryDNA for fun. Three or four years from the date we took the test, this woman reached out to us explaining she was trying to figure out how she was related to me in Ancestry. I knew there were DNA matches. I never even looked. My wife didn't look.

We thought maybe somebody related to my [adoptive] mom. We sent her off on that track and she finally reached back out one day, and said, "Listen, I've done all this research, and there's no way I can find I'm related to your mom."

But this woman says she had a sister who had a baby boy on my birthday in Dallas, where I was born, and she thought that was me. Even then, we still laughed it off. My wife and I were out on a lunch date that day. The whole time I am thinking, I know who my parents are.

When I got home that night, I pulled my birth certificate out. I'd had it for thirty years, never paid close attention to it. It's the first time I ever really looked at it. I noticed my place of birth. Instead of where it says address, name of hospital, mine just had a dash in it.

I grabbed my wife's birth certificate. She was born in Dallas in 1970 also. When I put our birth certificates side by side, everything started looking wrong. Hers looked like an official, typed-out document. Mine looked like a copy made off a microfiche machine, all black background with white writing. My wife's looked like a normal document with signatures on it. Mine didn't have any signatures, but even then I still thought maybe my parents lost my birth certificate, and this was what a copy of that looked like.

One evening, I was mulling over this in our study, when it came to me that my parents were both picture takers of everything. My dad was in the Navy. I've got pictures of them overseas, pictures of them on an aircraft carrier. Of everything. And it suddenly hit me—I had never seen a picture of my mom pregnant.

This, along with the second realization that my mom had been there for the birth of all three of our kids, but not once could I recall hearing a story about when I was born. I'm sitting there, realizing I've never heard a story of my birth. I've never seen a picture of mom pregnant or gotten the standard guilt trip of, "I was in labor with you for this many hours…" *Never.*

Brad creates a plan to try to speak to his father without his mother present. He's on the phone with his dad asking for an in-person meeting, but his father keeps pressing him as to the topic. Finally Brad just has to blurt out the issue.

> "Y'all never told me that I was adopted." I told him how the woman who had contacted me was related to me on AncestryDNA was pretty sure she was my aunt and knew she had a sister who had a boy born on my exact birth date. I was waiting for the "She's crazy. This lady is full of shit." Anything other than what I got, which was "Huh," and dead silence.
>
> I could just hear this drumming, which turned out to be his fingers drumming on his dashboard. We sat on the phone in a weird, awkward silence. Finally, I just said, "Dad, I'm not trying to be a dick. I don't know what else to do here. I know the answer already just based on how you responded, but until you say it out loud, I'm going to keep wondering and not feel like I know."
>
> He said, "Well, Bradley, you're adopted. We've been trying to figure out how to tell you."
>
> I fully believe they were taking this to their grave. Had Ancestry not spoiled that, I would've never known.
>
> The first thing he said was nice. "We still love you. You're still our kid. Nothing has changed."
>
> *Nothing has changed?* In my head, I'm

thinking, *everything has literally just changed. Nothing is the same anymore.*

Then he said, "Well, I probably need to go home and tell your mom you found out." And that's as much as we ever talked about it.

Everything changed in a blink, and people are telling you nothing was different. Oh, shit, everything was different. It's something I talk to people about all the time. It's hard and confusing because, in a way, people are right when they say it. I went home that night and slept in the same bed with the wife I had been married to for twenty-five years. The same kids were at my house. It was the same house. I had the same job when I woke up. Nothing had changed—but *everything* had changed. Everything was wrong and different. But from the outside looking in, if you didn't know that one piece, he was right. Nothing was different.

Getting It Right

Some families seem to do a better job of raising adoptees who are happier and more well-adjusted than others. There are a few characteristics observed in almost all adopted adults, including when they describe themselves as generally happy, love their parents who raised them, and have a great life:

1. Almost all adoptees interviewed experience some longing to know about their roots, who they came from, and have

innate curiosity about their birth story.

2. All adoptees wish they knew their medical history.
3. Many internalize some level of insecurity about being given up for adoption by their birth mother even when they deeply feel wanted and loved by their new family.
4. Most take on some internal responsibility to *protect their parents* from the way others treat them and don't share some of the stigmatizing experiences they endure from peers, teachers, or other important figures.

That last element is important and deserves careful attention. Adopted adults tell stories of things that happened to them when they were as young as three or four and will not tell their parents about these instances. Which is frustrating for parents as they cannot address what they don't know is happening. But if the experience is so universal, it needs to be planned for in advance, and some guidance should be shared on how to cultivate better communication.

Jen Wikelmann is the founder of Inward Bound and a family therapist, focused on adoption and foster care issues. She emphasizes some of this is just kids in general.

But she also says, "The thing that I think is specific to adoption, is that when we go through the stress of being separated from the birth family we're biologically wired to be with, it sometimes plants a seed of shame. As children we're very egocentric. We "make everything happen"—that's very magical thinking. So, separated infants/children can nonverbally internalize "making it happen," and this can become shame. There are also sometimes complex loyalty issues between adoptive parents and adoptees."

Adopted children can often feel as though others look at them as victims who need to be salvaged or saved because someone did, in fact, set them aside for unknown reasons. This can create a "rescuing" scenario between child and parent which can stifle an adoptee or manifest in unexpected ways.

Tammi~

I enjoyed my childhood. If a parent didn't need me and I was meant to be with another set of parents, fine. These two parents were doing pretty good, and I can't imagine life being any different.

My siblings did say on multiple occasions, if I did something they didn't like, "Oh, well, she's adopted. That's her fault." It wasn't very often, but it was usually my sister because we fought more.

My grandmother, Audrey, was adopted. I think she took a special liking to me and we connected on another level. Every summer, we rotated between myself, my brother, and my sister. I planned so I could be there as much as possible. She would tell me all the time, "One of the best days of my life was the day they told me they were adopting you." She said it was hard for her growing up because being adopted, her family wanted to have nothing to do with her.

It wasn't a lot, but there were times when I felt that abandonment. Could I pinpoint a specific reason why? No. Probably around times when Mom was paying more attention to my siblings, and I felt like I was the outsider. Because we were a family of five. You go to a restaurant, a family of four is great to seat. A family of five is a pain in the butt. There would be times I would think, "Maybe if they hadn't adopted me, they wouldn't have to be waiting for a table."

Terri~
My parents were the best in the world. They put me through school—the whole bit—supported every dream, every vision I ever wanted to do, attended every graduation.

One of the things people don't know about adoptees is rejection and abandonment are always there. No matter how much we squelch it and say it doesn't exist, somewhere in the back of our minds, in the deep recesses of our souls, we're always dealing with rejection and abandonment.

We're going to face these things for the rest of our lives.

Isaac~
My parents always got it right when talking about adoption. It was never a secret—never something we couldn't talk about. And it was never something we were made to feel bad to talk about. I didn't always need to talk but also didn't when maybe I should have.

Resilience

Kids are resilient. It's a statement heard often when talking about how a child can, to all outward appearances, seem to weather many storms. But what is resilience?

A simple definition is the ability to be tough, to withstand great pressures or adapt and overcome difficult or challenging circumstances more readily. It's a big buzz word in psychology. Most people are at least familiar with the concept, even if they have never actively thought it through. Consider a group of children all raised in the same abusive household—some emerge able to get help, thrive and have a good life. Others never escape their internal pain and succumb to a life infused with more abuse or addiction. What creates these different responses?

The mental health community wants to understand if this is innate, or potentially a learned response which can be cultivated or taught.

Jen Winkelmann shares, "I remember attending a conference with Bruce Perry, he's one of the forerunners in research and treatment for children who've experienced trauma. He said, "Separation from the birth mother is the single most traumatic event a human being can survive." He went on to say resilience is not a given—it is made and built over time. Some kids might just innately have a little bit more of the raw materials to work with."

She goes on to say, "But it's a dangerous place to camp, hoping that a kid's resilience will spare us the impact of a traumatic event. We shouldn't bank there and draw on that account. Resilience is earned—it's not automatic." Further, she adds, "We talk about this stuff in the adoption community but what's ironic is this is not adoption specific. This is human stuff."

Many adoptees find tools to mend their emotional pains

within the adoption community, and others find different sources. Regardless, a young person or adult benefits when they find their agency and take control of their own narrative.

Vickie~
For me, I remember a conversation with one of my friends when we were in high school. We were talking and she asked if I wanted to ever meet her, [my birth mother] and I was very adamant and said no. I think I was probably sixteen at the time. I said, "She didn't love me enough to keep me. Why do I want to meet her?" She looked at me and said, "Maybe she loved you enough to give you a chance." That's the point where my whole frame of mind on it just flipped, and I started to see it from a different perspective. I tried to start looking at it from her perspective, because I didn't know how old she was at the time she gave me up.

Fred~
It's hard to heal when you're stuck in the muck. I see a lot of adoptees just stuck. They can't seem to get beyond this explosive anger phase, because many go through it one way or another, whether they found out earlier or later. Something triggers it and some just end up bitter through most of their life and never can get beyond it. Others slowly start to work it out.

I learned tools in recovery from alcoholism, things like how to be accountable for your own decisions, how to be accountable for your moods. You've got to feel the pain. I get that, it's part of the required healing process. But if you don't want to dwell there, then you have to go find some tools to help get you out of it so you can move forward. So life can be something besides the pain, because it needs to be.

Simon~

I had a meltdown in a therapist's chair when she asked me about why I hadn't finished my search for my birth mother. I froze in fear and then went red hot in anger, like a volcano. I thought I'm not going to let this anger, this fear, hold me prisoner. So, I restarted my search.

When I got my adoption file, lo and behold there was this letter. There was also a teddy bear from my birth mom, and my mom and dad hadn't told me. In the file there was this fantastic letter from my birth mother to the social worker talking about her wanting me to have something from her.

I felt at one with her. I felt connected with her through a letter she'd written forty-eight years before I saw it. And she'd died probably ten, fifteen years before I got that in my hands.

There have been lots of other healing moments along the way, but that was the most easily understandable because it was profound—the teddy bear.

What can adopting parents do better to create a happier, more well-adjusted adult? The stories do show a helpful trend. Love, honesty, acceptance, and openness are key. It is not simple, as the research shows, but loving and fully showing up for your kids because they are *your kids* is certainly the first step.

---

1. Colleen Warner Colaner & Haley Kranstuber (2010)
"Forever Kind of Wondering": Communicatively Managing Uncertainty in Adoptive Families, Journal of Family Communication, 10:4, 236-255, DOI: 10.1080/15267431003682435

2. Colleen Warner Colaner & Haley Kranstuber (2010) "Forever Kind of Wondering": Communicatively Managing Uncertainty in Adoptive Families, Journal of Family Communication, 10:4, 236-255, DOI: 10.1080/15267431003682435

Chapter 5
The Psychological Impacts of Adoption

"An abnormal reaction to an abnormal situation is normal behavior." ~Victor Frankl

When one looks at the mental health statistics of adoptees as they grow, several patterns emerge. They are four times more likely than the general population to attempt or commit suicide.[1] Beyond that, a survey completed in 2003 showed adopted teens were, "at higher risk in all of the domains examined, including school achievement and problems, substance use, psychological well-being, physical health, fighting, and lying to parents."[2] Clearly, more is happening than most realize as the statistics reflect what many adoptees describe. Even so-called "good kids" cope with unrecognized pain.

Research and other interviews with mental health professionals show these kids breaking into, in general, two different groups: the kids who are fighting, lying to parents and "getting into trouble," and the "good adoptees." These kids fly below the radar, but, when interviewed, still show their mental anguish. Living by being "good so my parents will keep me" means love is being equated with behavior. Of the two groups, it is obvious which is more likely to receive professional intervention—the "problem" child acting out. But is the psychology of the second example healthy, either?

Be My Advocate

An important observation when talking to adopted people is how much they need their parents to be their advocates. It echoes broadly when one looks at essays, memoirs, and articles written by them. There is a desperate need to reinforce to the world at large that adoption is normal, and their parents are proud to be their parents.

> **Hannah~**
> When we moved from upstate Illinois to central Illinois, I was the most ethnic person in my town. So, if I wouldn't have known I was adopted, people would've told me on the first day of kindergarten. I definitely looked Hispanic.
>
> I would get all the names across the board. I would get the "N" word, I would get every derogatory word for Hispanic. I didn't usually tell my parents because…I'm not sure why that is. I'm not sure if I thought that I had done something wrong or if I was afraid it would hurt their feelings.
>
> When I was a little girl, my dad's brother said something. He was not the nicest guy. It was summer, and I was very tan. He said, "You look like a little…" My mom overheard him, and even being a very small woman, she just read him the riot act. He never said that again.
>
> It's weird that I remember it. I was a little, little kid.

Shellie~
Nobody wants to talk about going to the grocery store with my mom and somebody at the register ringing something up, her paying for it, and then, they ring up my stuff and her paying for it separately. You couldn't tell them, "We're all together" or "That's my daughter." Or when somebody says, "Oh, you're such a pretty child. What did your mother do to get you?" And I respond, "Nothing more than what your mom did to get you." But I'm the one forced to apologize because that wasn't ladylike behavior.

At what point do you step up and say, "That's my daughter. I am proud to have her as my daughter." Because if my behavior is good and my grades are good, "Oh, that's great. That's a reflection because she's a teacher, and she's done so well" or "Y'all were so great to take this child in."

How adopted children are treated by their peers, neighboring parents, and teachers influences their identity. Going back to "the good adoptee" scenario, most will assume these kids are doing great. They are generally well-behaved, active and involved at school, have plenty of friends and seem perfectly happy. But in doing so they blend in so well their needs may be unrecognized and unmet, setting up emotional catastrophes which can play themselves out years later.

Jennifer Joy Phoenix, LSWAIC, MHP, says in working with adopted persons of all ages, "Humans pay a very high interest rate on things avoided. Kids who have externalizing behaviors are brought in when they are young. However, those with internalized trauma don't come in until their lives are profoundly confusing at age fifty."

Her close working partner, Amy Barker, LMHC, owner and founder of Adoption Savvy, shares, "The compliant adoptee is suppressing all their emotions, and creating a false self. At least the kid who is throwing a tantrum is saying, "*This isn't okay. I don't like this.*" I have a big heart for the compliant adoptee. Usually, these are uber successful people but struggle in their close, intimate relationships, because everything is broken at the core. Another piece I hear all the time is anxiety. They are perfectionists, people pleasers. But this hypervigilance is actually high-functioning anxiety.

We do see them younger coming in for treatment, but they're typically self-harming. They're the cutters and the kids with eating disorders. All their pain has gone inward"

Psychological Disorders

There is a fine line between *assuming* a child is likely to develop problems due to adoption and being aware of the possibility. Assumptions have a way of becoming true—as if the expectation of a problem somehow creates the fulfillment of a pre-ordained bias. The other extreme is to be so completely disconnected that a parent is insensitive from the beginning.

Regardless, adopted adults do not want to feel pathologized. Most of the "disorders" that some clearly struggle with are born of coping mechanisms. Adoptees as infants and small children are attempting to belong, to fit in and receive needed care from their new families. This is all unconscious and often pre-verbal behavior. Because their minds and personalities are unknown by their parents and still forming, *how they cope* through these changes is what creates their mental health.

Beyond depression or general feelings of unhappiness, adopted youths and adults can develop other troubles at a higher rate than the general population. Identity Disorders are relatively common, with one study showing nearly one third (30.4%) meeting those criteria. This makes the disorder almost four times more common in adoptees than in the general population.[3]

Rejection sensitivity is also noted in several studies and is shown again and again in interviews with adoptees. There is a constant fear from a child—if they were abandoned once by their first mother, then it could happen again. "If they can go and get a baby, then they can take one back," might seem absurd to an adopting parent, but perfectly reasonable to a child.

Dissociative disorders arise when someone feels disconnected from oneself and the world around them or feels uncertain about who they are. According to a survey of adult adoptees done in 2019, "With the large percentage of adults in this study who reported dissociative experiences, it appears that dissociation may be a coping mechanism which is well established by the time an adult client seeks treatment."[4]

Attachment disorders are also common but do tend to appear more in children who were adopted at older ages or who were, for example, in the foster care system or an institutional setting, and are more common with international adoptees. An attachment disorder is when an infant or child has difficulty forming emotional bonds to their caregivers. It can be present as early as their first birthday.

"In a meta-analysis of ten studies on attachment of adopted children, it was found that adopted children were less secure, scoring higher than non-adoptees on both the anxiety and attachment-avoidance dimensions (van I. Jzendoorn & Juffer, 2006), suggesting a link between attachment and the obvious early separation of child and parent."[5]

One way this manifests is the child will "test" the relationships around them, almost anticipating rejection to be the response he or she will find. In adoptee support groups, a general observation adoptees report is they will either: stay in a relationship which is unhealthy because they cannot bear the feelings of aloneness or abandonment, or the other extreme which is the person will quickly cut people from their lives or never let them emotionally close to them. "If I don't let you close, then you can't hurt me" prevails in those instances. Regardless, it is a coping mechanism which helps the child or adult feel "safe," even though it is dysfunctional.

Studies confirm this finding, showing three quarters of non-adopted people were classified as having a secure attachment style while only forty-two percent of adoptees showed those attributes, and that group also scored significantly higher on attachment anxiety dimensions and attachment-avoidance.[6]

Other psychiatric disorders also form and can show themselves throughout their lives. A Meta-Analytic comparison done in 2016, states, "The risk of adoptees experiencing psychiatric disorders, contact with mental health services, or treatment in a psychiatric hospital was approximately twice as high as that of non-adoptees. Elevated risks were observed for attention-deficit/hyperactivity disorders, anxiety disorders, conduct disorders/oppositional defiant disorders, depression, substance use disorders, and psychosis."[7]

Hannah~

I was a pretty good kid. I played the piano. I was in band, I was in 4-H. I did a lot of stuff and got good grades until about fifteen. Then everything sort of crashed because I stopped eating, which affects a lot of things. I had an eating disorder, and this would've been '84, '85.

I end up in an adolescent care psych unit, close to home. I was there two years in a row, because one year I overdosed. And then the next year, I was still not really eating. I mean, I ate some, of course, and by the way I was also still a cheerleader, still on the track team. My grades kept going down. I was a distance runner in track, so now, when I sit and do the math I realize. My God, I was hardly eating anything—five hundred calories a day.

I'll always remember this. My father asked them at the hospital, the psychiatrist, with a medical degree at a children's adolescent care center, if he thought my eating disorders, my mood swings, all of the things crashing down on me, could have anything to do with me being adopted? The doctor said, "No, absolutely not."

But there was research out there by then, and my parents were very smart people. But if a doctor tells you, "No, that's not it," what are they supposed to believe?

If he would've said, "there's this thing that happens with adoption when you take a baby from her mother, that sometimes the trauma can come back years later. Also, she's sixteen and she doesn't look like you. When you're coming into your own identity, sometimes having some genetic mirroring, helps soften the blow of adolescence. So yes, adoption probably does have something to do with these things."

Instead, they are left not having answers. They think, "Did we do something? What did we do? What could we have done better?"

I'm very fortunate I made it through. But no thanks to the medical community.

Betsie~

I was an RN and I worked in child mental health. While I was dealing with my own adoption issues, I worked in an inpatient unit with mostly teenagers.

I calculated that about twenty percent of our patients were adopted as I was informally keeping a list of how many patients we had and how many were adopted. I would think that any doctor or treatment team would be wondering what's going on here if two percent of the population is adopted and twenty percent of our patients are. Why is that?

This was in the '80s and I tried to bring these statistics up multiple times. They had me doing staff in-service around adoption and working with families. I wrote a manual for them about some of the issues, but it got little traction. Nobody was diving into the statistics. And the degree adoption was swept under the rug...It didn't sit right with me.

In 2024, the National Council for Adoption (NCFA) released a survey on adult adoptee perspectives on a wide variety of topics. The majority of respondents (57%) were born between the 1960s-80s.

One of the questions asked was how many of them had wanted access to some level of post adoption support services. Depending on the source of their adoption, over half of those adopted individuals from either domestic adoptions or foster care felt they could have benefited from some sort of mental health intervention.[8]

The Blank Slate Theory

Known as the Tabula Rasa theory, the idea that all humans are born as a mental and emotional "blank slate" has deep roots in psychology dating back to Aristotle. This theory postulates that all behaviors are learned and when a baby is born, it can become literally anyone or anything regardless of genetics or biology.[9]

These ideas have been cited by some of the world's most renowned psychotherapists, including John Locke in the seventeenth century and Sigmund Freud in the nineteenth century. Their philosophy comprises the basis of modern thought on behaviorism and still influences mental health professionals today. It endures even in the face of many philosophers and psychologists such as renowned Harvard Professor and author Steven Pinker, who have taken direct aim at the theory and pointed out its many flaws.[10]

Sharon~
My adopted mother used to quote this to me. She said, "I don't know what your issues are, but they told us at the Children's Home Society

> you wouldn't remember anything. What does a tiny baby know?"
>
> I kept trying to explain, "Well, I think these feelings I have of depression or sadness... they're related to having been adopted." She couldn't buy any of that. It was the prevailing theory at the time.

A great number of adopting parents were told, particularly in the Baby Scoop era, they were to not worry about any prior events. Their child would come to them as a "blank slate." This conventional wisdom was so commonplace few ever considered otherwise, and this was during a time where more adoptions took place than in any other period. However, even while the debate between "nature versus nurture" will always endure, there is yet another concept which has become at least as pervasive and important.

All prior studies and explorations on the impact of adoption lead to this most pivotal premise called "The Primal Wound."

The Primal Wound

Within the subculture of adoption, few theories are as celebrated and simultaneously controversial as "The Primal Wound". The book with the same name, published by Nancy Verrier in 1993, calls out the idea that separating an infant from its mother is always inherently traumatizing.

Adopted people flocked to the book, many crying out, "finally someone understands how I've always felt." Others have called it dangerous because they say it creates a generalized view that all adoptees are "damaged" and perpetuates negative stereotypes. Adoptive or would-be adoptive parents have called the book and the theory "terrifying" because they feel it sets up a scenario for failure from the beginning.

One huge issue for many adoptees is the debate in and of itself is yet one more way others dictate to them about *how they should feel* about their adopted lives—especially when many wish to see simplistic descriptions of what are far more complex and nuanced experiences.

Is Separation Trauma Real?

Many studies show that all newborns come into the world with deep and knowing bonds biologically and psychologically formed with their mother in utero. Babies in the womb hear and know their mother's voice and those around them. They become accustomed to the smells and cuisine of the mother as it is their sole source of sustenance. It has also been shown that seeping through the amniotic fluid are hormonal messages conveying the mother's emotional state around the pregnancy.

In return, the baby is sending stem cells into the mother's blood stream throughout pregnancy, causing the mother to instinctively react to the minute changes and movements of her unborn child.

Therefore, within the first moments of birth a known, tangible bond exists between this new life and its mother.

As infants, all humans are completely dependent upon those around them. So, when an infant is then passed over to a "new mother" for care and feeding, on a deep level the baby knows it is not with the same mother. Intricately woven into this bond is also the idea the mother will automatically seek her baby and work hard to obtain him or her over any other.

But then, what does the subconscious mind of an infant register when the mother it knows does not appear no matter what it does? This is one of the many questions raised by the theory—what is the unconscious reaction to this perceived abandonment?

This is the root of the primal wound, or separation trauma. The natural mother is made bereft by an adoption, and the infant has also experienced a profound loss—and since an infant cannot clearly express itself, what it feels or thinks, is unknown.

Critics of The Primal Wound

Adoptees are not all in agreement. Some clearly bond with the message while others reject it whole-heartedly. The debate divides the community, creating a rift in philosophy and varied views on adoption. Those who believe the "wound" theory will dismiss those who don't, saying they are in denial. That same bias has the potential to influence and affect the validity of any serious study of the concept.

Some professionals dismiss the premise entirely. Dr. Charles Nelson is a Professor of Pediatrics at Harvard Medical School and a leading expert on how early childhood neglect, abuse, and other negative parental environments affect children. He said in an interview in 2013, "there is no scientific evidence to support the primal wound theory that all adopted people carry a scar from being separated from biological parents."[11]

He states countless people who've been adopted especially in the first two years, but even beyond, are doing great, and "a theory that says just because they were separated from their birth mother leaves a permanent wound is just false on the face of it."[12]

Another critic of her work is Dr. Michael Grand, author of the book *The Adoption Constellation*. He criticizes not the premise itself so much as the solution she proposes. He says, "[The Primal Wound] captures for some adoptees the experience of pain and grief and loss that so many others have denied them. In that sense, it's a very important and moving book. I was moved as I read it."[13]

His critique is the notion of attachment upon which the idea is based means the child who is adopted experiences the loss of the first parent, and then carries it forward to the new parent. Verrier's assessment that the pain of separation can then potentially (or always) be solved by reunion. But reunion is not always helpful for either party. "[14]

How significant the primal wound trauma may be and the extent of its impact, and how universal this may be, is what fires up such a vast debate—even by people who have read and appreciate Verrier's work.

Supporting Research

Significant research has been done on maternal and infant separation on mammals in both mice and monkeys.

Many studies have been done on rodents, showing early life stressors including maternal separation "affect both acute and long-term development of neuroendocrine, cognitive, and behavioral systems"[15] In rats, separating the pups from their mothers, even when receiving other feeding and care from other rat "mothers," behavior changes are observed similar to anxiety or depression. Prolonged separation appears to increase these results when compared to the control group, (not separated pups). Even as adults, the maternally separated rats displayed abnormal behaviors, particularly in lowered food consumption and an increased startle response, indicating anxiety.[16]

Other models with rhesus monkeys show when separated from their mothers within the first six months of life, these subjects "demonstrate increased distress and passive behaviors" compared to their peers who were maternally raised. The monkeys also have increased cortisol (stress hormone) and display "diminished ability to handle stressful events and exhibit numerous exaggerated behaviors" compared to those raised by their mothers.[17]

Another study on rodents does show differences in these responses based upon the gender of the animal. In general, maternal separation appeared to affect the female rats more than the male rats when exposed to the same types of traumatic stress. Both male and female rats, however, were more likely to develop post-traumatic stress disorder (PTSD) as adults if they experienced early life stressors.[17]

One article produced in Australia regarding newborns to two years of age, says trauma of all sorts can have a "serious effect on babies and toddlers," and that, "many people wrongly believe babies do not notice or remember traumatic events. In fact, anything which affects older children and adults in a family can also affect a baby, but they may not be able to show their reactions."[18]

The article also notes regardless of the cause of the separation, the infant will not only register the loss of their parent, but the infant is also coping with their situation. The stressors induced by having to manage them within a baby whose mind and nervous system is not set up to understand what is happening, is in and of itself, potentially damaging. Furthermore, this trauma can make its ability to bond with its caregivers more challenging.[19] Combining this information with the statistics on the rates of suicide among adoptees, and other mental health concerns paints a troubling picture.

The Way Forward

Assume for a minute Verrier's work is correct. Also assume this can impact the infant's ability to bond with its new adopting parents.

What now? Plenty of children struggle to bond with distant or emotionally unhealthy biological parents, act out in school, and feel unheard, unloved, and unseen by their families. Sadly, many people desperately lack emotional connections with those around them.

However, those "looking in" at adoption often fail to understand this population for whom is denied a blood, familial, or close connection—they are the only group told how "grateful" they should feel for their situation. Imagine being told someone should feel lucky for their loss, their trauma, or even their abuse? It is this frustration at not being validated for their feelings, which has so many adopted people later in life rising up with the need to shout, rather than continue to whisper their pain.

Maybe the way to look at the primal wound is less literal. For those who keenly relate to it, what if the power is in asking adoptees to "lean in" to the psychological pain they feel rather than hide from it? If large numbers of adopted adults have rallied around the book and its ideas, then they should not be dismissed. Many adoptees state that when they were young there was no language which matched their experience.

Psychologists and parents who completely dismiss the primal wound, do so at the peril and well-being of their children. Dr. Marcy Axness, PhD writes, "There are those who consider the primal wound to be a platform for adult adoptees to do yet more blaming and complaining, rather than 'getting on with their lives'... But only having walked into that emptiness inside me, and felt it—finally, deeply—

and grieved it. This, in my hard-won experience, is what effective healing is about: not 'fixing' it, but facing it."[20]

When talking to Sharon Stein McNamara, Ed.D., L.P., adoptee and adoption competent therapist, she shares, "You've got these kids, the relinquishment trauma is primary. I do the grief work of this really, really, horrible thing that happened when you were a baby, and you have feelings about it. Let's touch those feelings and let you cry. You need a compassionate therapist who is capable of hearing that level of pain."

Regardless of the primal wound discussion, themes emerge around healing which are consistent. There are also common strategies parents can follow: love, openness, respect, forming a positive narrative with the child and most importantly *letting them tell the adults in their lives how they feel*, instead of the other way around.

Amy Barker, adoptee, birth mother, and adoption & trauma therapist says, "Can the trauma of infant separation be healed? I wouldn't do this work if I didn't believe that was possible." Her practice, Adoption Savvy, specializing in almost all facets of adoption competent therapies, says, "To me, it's like if your arm was severed in a terrible accident, could you still live a fulfilling life? Yes. You wouldn't live the same life if you had both of your limbs. You would have to adapt. It's going to look different, but you can have a happy, functioning life. We can get there, but it is hard work."

Some may cringe at this analogy, but anyone who has experienced some life-altering event will say they are forever changed by it. They carry it with them and must learn to thrive either because of, or despite it.

No one should have the language of the primal wound thrust upon them, most especially as children who may have trouble reconciling its depth.

Children deserve to speak their minds and express their feelings in productive ways which do not revolve around a narrative, or what their parents or society expects of them. This includes their feelings about being or looking different, or not fitting in, and curiosity about a first family or another mother.

Adoptees all process their experience differently. Moreover, this will likely change throughout their lives as they pass key milestones causing them to re-evaluate their feelings about being adopted.

What they are fighting for, more loudly and clearly than ever, is the right to define their own experience. Dismissing *any* individual's point of view for not fitting a narrative, whether an old one or a new one, is harmful to the larger cause—to be heard, valued, and understood.

1. Keyes MA, Malone SM, Sharma A, Iacono WG, McGue M. Risk of suicide attempt in adopted and nonadopted offspring. Pediatrics. 2013 Oct;132(4):639-46. doi: 10.1542/peds.2012-3251. Epub 2013 Sep 9. PMID: 24019414; PMCID: PMC3784288

2. Miller, B.C., Fan, X., Christensen, M., Grotevant, H.D. and Van Dulmen, M. (2000), Comparisons of Adopted and Nonadopted Adolescents in a Large, Nationally Representative Sample. Child Development, 71: 1458-1473. https://doi.org/10.1111/1467-8624.00239

3. McLamb, Lee J., "A Survey of Dissociation, Identity Distress, and Rejection Sensitivity in Adult Adoptees" (2019). Honors Undergraduate Theses. 606.

4. McLamb, Lee J., "A Survey of Dissociation, Identity Distress, and Rejection Sensitivity in Adult Adoptees" (2019). Honors Undergraduate Theses. 606.

5. Robertson, E. G. (n.d.). REMNANTS OF ADOPTION: REJECTION SENSITIVITY, ATTACHMENT AND ADULT INTIMACY ISSUES.

6. Robertson, E. G. (n.d.). REMNANTS OF ADOPTION: REJECTION SENSITIVITY, ATTACHMENT AND ADULT INTIMACY ISSUES.

7. Anika E. Behle & Martin Pinquart (2016) Psychiatric Disorders and Treatment in Adoptees: A Meta-Analytic Comparison with Non-Adoptees, Adoption Quarterly, 19:4, 284-306, DOI: 10.1080/10926755.2016.1201708

8.Hanlon, R., Davi, N., Quade, M., & Lindner, A. (2024). Profiles in adoption: Adult adoptee experiences. National Council For Adoption.

9. Fritscher, L. (2022, November 26). Why the psychology theory of Tabula Rasa you can unlearn bad behavior. Verywell Mind. https://www.verywellmind.com/blank-slate-definition-2671563

10. Pinker, S. (2002). The Blank Slate: The Modern Denial of Human Nature. Penguin Books.

11. Davenport, D. (2021, April 26). Does the primal wound really exist?. Creating a Family. https://creatingafamily.org/adoption-category/does-primal-wound-really-exist/

12. Davenport, D. (2021, April 26). Does the primal wound really exist?. Creating a Family. https://creatingafamily.org/adoption-category/does-primal-wound-really-exist/

13. YouTube. (2020, November 5). Primal wound new theory with Michael Grand author of adoption constellation | Jeanette Yoffe. YouTube. https://www.youtube.com/watch?v=oZgsbk17UQw&t=80s

14. YouTube. (2020, November 5). Primal wound new theory with Michael Grand author of adoption constellation | Jeanette Yoffe. YouTube. https://www.youtube.com/watch?v=oZgsbk17UQw&t=80s

15. Neurobiological consequences of childhood trauma - the Journal of ... (n.d.). https://www.psychiatrist.com/wp-content/uploads/2021/02/15380_neurobiological-consequences-childhood-trauma.pdf

16. Neurobiological consequences of childhood trauma - the Journal of ... (n.d.). https://www.psychiatrist.com/wp-content/uploads/2021/02/15380_neurobiological-consequences-childhood-trauma.pdf

17. Neurobiological consequences of childhood trauma - the Journal of ... (n.d.). https://www.psychiatrist.com/wp-content/uploads/2021/02/15380_neurobiological-consequences-childhood-trauma.pdf

18. Knox, D., Stout-Oswald, S. A., Tan, M., George, S. A., & Liberzon, I. (2021, November 12). Maternal separation induces sex-specific differences in sensitivity to traumatic stress. Frontiers. https://www.frontiersin.org/articles/10.3389/fnbeh.2021.766505/full

18. Department of Health & Human Services. (2010, January 27). Trauma and children - newborns to two years. Better Health Channel. https://www.betterhealth.vic.gov.au/health/healthyliving/trauma-and-children-newborns-to-two-years

19. Department of Health & Human Services. (2010, January 27). Trauma and children - newborns to two years. Better Health Channel. https://www.betterhealth.vic.gov.au/health/healthyliving/trauma-and-children-newborns-to-two-years

20. In appreciation of the primal wound - creating a family. (n.d.-a).https://creatingafamily.org/wp-content/uploads/in%20appreciation%20of%20the%20primal%20wound.pdf

Chapter 6
The FOG

"Adoption loss is the only trauma in the world where the victims are expected by the whole of society to be grateful." ~ *Reverend Keith C. Griffith, MBE*

Within the adoption community, "The FOG"* is both a metaphor and an acronym—Fear, Obligation, and Guilt. It also describes the emotional transformation some adopted people experience later in life. They "come out of the fog."

Many adults have a positive framework around adoption that stays with them their entire lives. They had good experiences as children, and this shapes their overall view.

Later in life, others shift to a different opinion. Maybe they were mistreated or felt disassociated from the family who raised them. Even with a happy childhood, some emerge with a more critical eye, especially about access to personal information. Often hidden or repressed for decades, new feelings can emerge as adults hit key milestones. They change how they see their family or how they were treated. For some this happens when they become parents. They see what they lost lying in their arms.

> **Tina~**
> With the birth of my first child, the first biologically related member of my family, I wondered how my bio mom could've walked out of the hospital without me. It messed me up for a while.

Some come to feel used by a system that did not honestly or ethically benefit them, that insisted they were unable to remain with their first mother, other people always making choices for adoptees.

Most adoptive parents will share what they know about why a child was placed into their care. But sometimes that information will be incomplete, or even incorrect. What is so important to understand is that these feelings can and do emerge even when that adult loves the parents who raised them. Feeling the "fog" lift, and one's emotional attachment to their adoptive parents is not a mutually exclusive circumstance.

Even good, decent, and loving parents do not receive guidance on the specific needs of their adopted children. Thus, they can fail to understand what is happening in front of them. Although, to the adoptee it is obvious.

This disconnect is agonizing. It causes an unhealthy dynamic between the parent and a "rescued" child who was salvaged from the assumed poverty of life with a single mother. It creates an inherent fear of losing what they have, the obligation to be grateful, and to feel guilty if they do not. All these emotions and expectations are put onto the tiny shoulders of children who are assumed to be perfectly fine in this win-win-win scenario.

> **Li~**
> I just know what I've heard growing up and what I've heard as I've grown older. "Oh my God, you're so lucky."
>
> No matter how much your parents love you, no matter how much they say you are their child, we will do anything for you. And no matter how true that is, you will still always to some extent feel like you have to pay

them back. You have to give a part of your life to them.

And if you don't succeed in certain ways, you're somehow tarnishing this wonderful gift you were given and how dare you not meet ridiculous expectations.

You could have been begging for food in a developing country and now you have all these things and you still screwed it up. What's wrong with you?

It just comes with an immense amount of pressure and society doesn't understand. People say these things to be comforting and to give people perspective, but what you're really doing is putting pressure, weight, and a lot of guilt on us.

Coming Out of the FOG

Many adoptees prefer the statement "I am adopted" versus "I was adopted." The first is an identity in a life-long process. The second is an event. For a great many, being adopted is a part of who they are and something that will evolve with them as they grow.

Emerging from the "fog" can happen suddenly, or over a gradual number of years or even decades. Support groups, online forums, and social media have exploded in the past ten to fifteen years, creating new and powerful adoptee interactions. Their views vary widely, and the community is often in conflict with itself. Some believe adoptions should no longer be allowed. Others are perfectly happy and don't interact with many of these vocal support groups or advocates.

Adoptees who have come out of the fog will often find

it harder to relate to friends and other family members who have not. These are profound shifts in their identity as adopted people.

Dirk~
What does coming out of the fog mean? It means when you realize the truth of what adoption is. I grew up thinking adoption was fantastic. I got great parents. I have a good family. I could have been raised by drug addicts or who knows? For me it was gradual. It really hit when COVID did, and my wife saw Angela Tucker on Red Table Talk on Facebook.

She gave her story. She's black, raised with a white family, and she's talking about those issues. And my wife told me about it. So, I watched it, and I was blown away. "Wow, there's another one of me." Because that's the one thing I always felt, "There's no one else like me." I'm a one-off. I'm this dark kid in this white family, in this white town. I didn't think anybody else could ever relate to that. It was step one in coming out of the fog.

Things started falling into place as far as the whole rejection thing, and why I did X, Y, and Z. Thinking, "Well, that's just how I'm wired." No, I did those things because I'm adopted. Slowly it all came out.

I've got two other friends who are adopted—guys my age—and they're both still in the fog. It's frustrating, because I've talked to one of them a little bit and he's starting to thaw. He's starting to have questions about it.

The other guy's in total denial, he's still in the, "No, adoption's fantastic," thing.

But it's quite a metamorphosis. I've always had anxiety issues. But it used to drive me mad because I kept saying, "You have nothing to be anxious about." Now I know what it was. Again, I can't point to my adoptive parents, and I can't point to my birth parents either. It's maddening in that way. There's nowhere to cast blame. Yes, I had it great, but I'm also pissed."

Since coming out of the fog, I realize how lonely that place was. Because whenever anything bad happened, I never, ever, never told my parents. I always wanted to protect them.

Hannah~

In 2018, I met an author who was a birth mother, and she was writing about her story. It was the first time I ever thought about adoption where it was really, whoa, I need to go find my story. I don't know how to describe it, except my head kind of exploded. She said, "They told me, you'll forget this ever happened, but I didn't, and I found my son." Literally, that was the day I decided to start searching for my birth mother. Of course, there was more to it.

When I got my original birth certificate, I found out I had been born at a maternity home. My story actually was very similar to what this woman, Laura Engel, talked about in her maternity home.

The first book I read was "The Girls Who

Went Away," which was all the birth mothers talking and it just...blew my mind.

My adoptive mother didn't know I was born in a maternity home, but she knew my eldest brother had been. I have two adoptive brothers as well. And she always said, "I don't think they were very nice to women in those places. I don't think they treated women very well. You don't understand how it was back then." And I was like, yeah, yeah, whatever.

But as it turns out, she was correct. That was also my story, my birth mother's story. Ironically, when I met this author, I was writing about women and women's choices, and lack of choices.

I was writing historical fiction based on my adoptive great-grandmother who died trying to hasten her cycle back in 1925 with a poison. I'm writing about choice and everything that went with that. But it didn't occur to me that in the late '60s, not only did women not have that choice, they also didn't really have the choice to keep their children.

But it was always so weird to me when I stepped away from it a couple of years later. I thought, holy cow, I walked in there writing about women's choices, thinking that I knew all about women's rights, but I didn't. My mother was sixteen when she had me.

Adoptees have a multitude of life experiences and no "one" point of view is "right" for all. Some will liken the moment they come out of the fog akin to the famous scene in the movie *The Matrix* – take the blue pill or the red pill.

One changes a life forever, while the other keeps them in their original state of being. Coming out of the fog can be painful and jarring.

Coming Into Adoptee Consciousness

Another model to reference these experiences is called "adoptee consciousness,"[1] created by JaeRan Kim, Ph.D, herself an international adoptee, and Associate Professor at the University of Washington, can be best described by the model below:

Image credit: Branco, S.F., Kim, J., Newton, G., Cooper-Lewter, S.K., and O'Loughlin, P. (2022). Out of the fog and into consciousness: A model of adoptee awareness. *International Body Psychotherapy Journal* 22(1), 53-66.

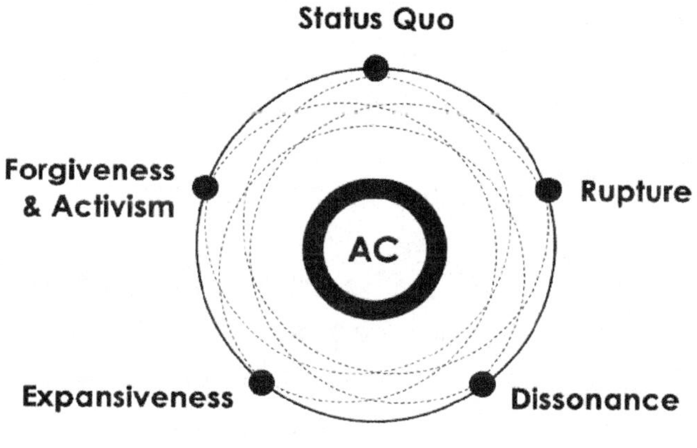

In this model of thinking about the concept of adoption awareness, there are several phases or touchstones which a person can move in and out of over the course of their lives and experiences:

- **Status Quo** – the adoptee sees life as they always

have and the dominant narrative fulfills their existing needs.

- **Rupture** – this is the moment when that person encounters facts or information contrary to their prior way of thinking. This can be sudden and alarming or more gradual and can repeat in different ways over their lives.
- **Dissonance** – tension and contradiction dominate as the adoptee may feel torn between these two narratives. This is painful and some adoptees will revert to their prior status quo way of being.
- **Expansiveness** – embracing the complexities and the duality of how one can feel about adoption and its effects allows everyone involved to understand the paradoxical nature of adoption and its full impacts.
- **Forgiveness and Activism** – adoptees being able to forgive those who may have failed them by not knowing, and understand there are systems at work larger than their individual families. This can also inspire them to become agents for change.[2]

Healing and Recovery

Many adopted adults find healing through support groups. Some write and find solace and clarity through that process. There are now fiction and non-fiction movies, television shows, and documentaries that share adoption stories from a variety of views. Netflix has several such films, and adoption was one prominent storyline in the popular network show, "This Is Us."

Secrets die when light is shined upon them. More than a few adopted adults, as well as birth or adoptive parents have become adoption-informed therapists. They share that many in psychology and family therapy programs in colleges and universities still have much to learn about adoption trauma.

Dr. David Brodzinsky, Ph.D. Psychologist says, "For a variety of reasons, mental health professionals typically do not receive the training required to fill adoption-related counseling needs and, too often, they do not fully understand why such training is necessary or mistakenly believe the knowledge they already have is sufficient." These professionals take on this additional training that most have found invaluable in dealing with the needs of children and families in the adoptive and foster care system.[3]

But even with these obstacles, the National Adoption Competency National Training Initiative created a curriculum to certify that a therapist is a "Adoption Competent Therapist." Now, a professional must meet organized requirements for this training to receive this designation.

> **Sharon Stein McNamara~**
> The more we can untangle this bag of complex stuff the better. There's secrecy, there's lies, there's karma. Because it's secret, it's not allowed to be brought out in the open and worked on and understood. So, the real piece of pain that is so traumatic I think, for adoptees, is the secrecy.
>
> Why can't we just be transparent and open? It's just going to add to the person's dimensions of who they are. Why would you want to be blind about what your child brings?

Today, brave souls take on new work in adoption. Parents team up with their adult children to teach, help others, and share stories. There are podcasts, books, seminars, online courses, support groups and resources. These all combine to help parents better understand the needs of their kids. This work is healing, both for themselves and in the effort to make adoption better for everyone.

---

1. Branco, S.F., Kim, J., Newton, G., Cooper-Lewter, S.K., and O'Loughlin, P. (2022). Out of the fog and into consciousness: A model of adoptee awareness. *International Body Psychotherapy Journal* 22(1), 53-66. "Dr. JaeRan Kim also acknowledges the following contributors to the posted graphic image: including Susan Branco, Grace Newton, Paula O'Loughlin, and Stephanie Kripa Cooper-Lewter."

2. Branco, S.F., Kim, J., Newton, G., Cooper-Lewter, S.K., and O'Loughlin, P. (2022). Out of the fog and into consciousness: A model of adoptee awareness. *International Body Psychotherapy Journal* 22(1), 53-66.

3. Home - nti. NTI - National Training Initiative. (n.d.). https://adoptionsupport.org/nti/

* Author's Note: the origins of the term "the fog" come from several sources. One is from the book by Betty Jean Lifton, Lost and Found who first wrote about "waking up from the great sleep". The second by Susan Forward & Donna Frazier in their book Emotional Blackmail who describe a FOG and use the term as an acronym.

Chapter 7
Multicultural Families and Adoptee Perspectives

I think we live in a better world when everybody can realize there's a level of pain here, and that if you want it to be beautiful, you have to move through it together. ~Isaac Etter

Families that integrate different cultures or races into their mix become microcosms of race relations in America. This can happen through marriage and then subsequent children or divorces. Then new relationships, marriages, and additional children spread across extended families. It also happens in adoption, be that domestic, international, or via the foster care system. Their experiences are diverse. In general, Caucasian parents adopted a child of a different ethnic heritage, although there are some exceptions. This chapter focuses more on the common situation and will highlight the lived experiences of seventeen transracially adopted persons interviewed for the book.

Their stories vary widely, yet there are similarities as they grew from childhood into adults who struggled with finding their identity. More so than other adoptees, they try to intuit the ways they "fit" into the world around them and contain unique perspectives.

Race and Ethnicity

Before going further, some definitions might be helpful. Race and ethnicity are often used interchangeably, but they are different. Race is typically used to define a category of people who share similar physical traits, such as skin or hair color. Ethnicity relates to one's cultural and geographic heritage. Commonalities in language, dress, modes of religious worship, and other characteristics connect these groups of people beyond their physicality. One general way to describe it is, "Race is something you inherit while ethnicity is something you learn over time."[1]

Adoptees do not always agree with each other about the terminology they want others to use, both within this specific segment and in general. The most common term used is "transracially adopted." However, the prefix "trans" in the multicultural family is somewhat of a misnomer, as it means to "change", but this is not what happens. Every member of the family stays who they are. A multicultural family is another way to identify these families, and this is how this chapter will be identified, but not everyone will agree with this terminology either.

A child born in the US is by default already part of this culture. Conversely, an overseas adoption brings a child from a different country with its own language, history, and cultural traditions who are then expected to assimilate. The complexities contained within their journeys reflect some of the larger struggles within America.

The first experiences of these adoptees' lives cement both their place in their families and how the world perceives their adoptions into a family where the members look visually different from one another.

> **Tina~**
> My father was black. My biological mother was white. My adoptive family is all white, so it wasn't like they could pretend I had been born from them.

Then we adopted my brother when I was about five and he's also transracially adopted. That kind of cemented things for me. You can go get a baby and it doesn't have to look like you. I was born in 1971.

Jacob~

I grew up in our small town my whole life. No negativity ever. I was born in 2002. People obviously noticed because I would hold my mother's hand walking by. I'm black and she's white and yet everyone says, "Hey, how you doing?" No negative reactions. Since I grew up here, everyone has known me from a very young age, and we were always out. So, everyone already knew. They all loved us, really.

Sometimes at school people wouldn't put together the last names. They would say, "Oh, that's Jacob S." And I would say, "Yeah, that's my sister," but I never encountered racism or anything like that. Even if—maybe I did one or two times—my brother and my sister always stood up for me. They always had my back.

Dirk~

It was in 1960. I don't know who lied, my birth mom or the adoption agency, or both, but they said I was Hispanic. So, I was adopted under the premise that I was Hispanic. I found out through Ancestry that my dad was black and my mom was white. So that was a pretty wild realization in 2014.

Layers of Complexity

Under the most ideal circumstances parenting is hard. Then, add in adoption and it gets more challenging and complicated. Now, if that same family has adopted a child from a different nationality, race, or culture, more layers of complexity have piled on. Some parents have adopted alongside their own biological children. Some will adopt multiple times.

Multicultural families' lives can often be explored through two different aspects. The way in which they interact internally, and the way the outside world reacts to their family. First comes the impact from adoption and how a family was created or expanded. Adopted children experience everything described in the prior chapters. How their parents first frame their story to them is primary. If they have siblings, they are also part of this essential foundation.

These children are still dealing with the separation from their birth mothers and the psychological impacts as they process being adopted. They will also frequently hide things that happen to them in the outside world from their parents. It's an internal landscape full of potential landmines these youngsters are already navigating.

If adoptive parents lack confidence in how to have candid, hard, discussions about race in American culture, that youngster will find themselves without adult guidance—maybe when they need it the most.

It becomes a lot to manage, and the child may feel alone. They need to be listened to and supported by strong parents who are willing to help them respond to situations as they arise. Remember, both the parents and their child may lack the benefit of their lived experiences guiding the way. This group of adopted kids need advocacy from their parents at a much more fundamental level and with increased awareness.

Tina~
It was very awkward. I had some bad situations when I was younger because my parents, I think, really didn't understand how the world would view our situation. They had on rose colored glasses. Oh, we've adopted this baby, and things are great. Her life's going to be great, and she's not going to experience any of these things because we never experienced these things growing up. We never dealt with discrimination or racial slurs. Being white they didn't have any of that. So, they didn't prepare me.

I remember the first time I was called the "N" word. I had no idea what it meant. I was only five, but I knew it was something bad because of the way people reacted. I had a friend with me, and my friend yelled at the kid that called me that. I just remember being frozen and stunned. I didn't know what to say. It's only been in the last ten years I've even been able to tell my parents about it.

Things got a little bit better when my brother joined the family and he shared some of the same experiences. Then they were able to see, oh, I guess things are different for brown people. Because, for us, we were always in white spaces. Even when you try to feel like you're not standing out—you're standing out. You are.

Marika~

It was a constant question. "Who...what are you? Are these your parents? How is that your sister? You look so different...so exotic!"

I didn't know what I was because I didn't have information on my birth father. My birth mother was white, so the colored part of me was...? I didn't know.

My parents were trustworthy people, but I didn't share a lot with them. I had this anxiety to hide the bad things that would happen. Like a stranger talking to me and holding me too close in the alleyway, which you should go and tell your parents because that's uncomfortable and weird. I wouldn't do it. There were so many things I just felt I couldn't share because I worried I would be looked at as a problem. Then I found my adoption file.

It had a sheet of paper, handwritten, with things about both of my birth parents. Her name was Stephanie. She liked tennis, basketball, and music. His name was Brian, and he liked basketball. And it said he was Armenian. I thought, "Oh my God, I'm Armenian?" That's not on the list of all the million people who had guessed my ethnicity. It's kind of like a game show.

There would be people who were black, and they would say, "I think you're black."

"No, I'm Armenian."

"No, I'm pretty sure you're black."

But I got in trouble because I went into the file. [My parents] said I was sneaking. They told me, "That's our file." And I'm thinking, *is it your file*? But I'm young and I felt very nervous when I got caught. But I was curious. How could they not know I wanted this information? They said, "You have to wait till you're eighteen."

Dirk~

When I was five, my parents got pregnant and ended up having two girls, one in '65 and one in '67. My parents are white, so we had an interesting looking family.

My parents were great, but we never talked about adoption. We never talked about me being different. Every now and then, they would say, "Well, just tell people you're Spanish." That didn't always work.

I do remember one time, I was probably about four, I saw my reflection in the car bumper. I wasn't very tall, but back in the day all the bumpers were those chrome metallic things. I could see my reflection and I moved my arm, and I was like, "My God, that's me." I couldn't believe how dark I was, and it freaked me out. I remember running in the house and telling my mom. I know she comforted me, and I walked away feeling okay about it, but it's weird.

Several of the above scenarios display what is known as "genetic bewilderment." A term first coined in the 1950s when researchers were attempting to understand the poor adjustment of some adoptees into their new families.[2]

These concerns can begin very young, and the best way to overcome them is through a strong connection between children and their parents. This sets the stage for how these families operate with each other. There is the genetic/adoption piece, then the race/cultural element on top of that. Some members of the family may be more open to hearing and responding to these complex needs than others. One example is contained in this story here.

Li~

I'm never going to be Hispanic enough for the Hispanic side and I'm never going to be white enough for the white side. I'm always going to exist in this weird in between that a lot of adopted kids I've known fall into. It's hard because as humans we naturally want to fit in. But if you're that person you kind of accept it, this piece of you that's always going to feel a little lonely. I brought it to my mom, and she laughed at it. Not for a malicious reason.

She just thought the whole thing was so ridiculous. Absolutely preposterous. My attempt to try and explain to her what it feels like being caught in this weird limbo was next to impossible. Because she'd never experienced or faced anything like that. When I was adopted, none of that was ever considered for interracial adoptions. Which, at that time, shut me down. Because if you're just going to laugh at my pain, why am I telling you anything?

I started therapy when I was twelve. At fourteen, my therapist said, "We're going to start unpacking the adoption." I started asking questions. My dad's always been a champion of me knowing that side of me. He started showing me all this stuff. He started

> explaining things. My mom was more of, well, you know, that's not really who you are. She didn't understand what she was doing was muting a massive part of my life. It hurt and it was really not okay.

Li's mother loved her daughter but was missing what her essential needs were. Fortunately, her father was there to help and was more open to finding ways to guide her. Below is an example of a family that seems to get it right. Learning from this story below could be worthwhile for many.

> **Zach~**
> I was the first child for my parents. From there they went on to have nine younger children, and five of them were also adoptees. So, we're a large family, mixed with a lot of adoption. Both my parents are white and I'm black. And one of my brothers is also black and half biologically related [to me]. I have a heightened sense of gratitude for the fact we got to grow up as brothers. So that is a neat thing where otherwise my family are of the same race. When conflict came up, like a question or inquiry from a peer, they would always talk about it. They weren't, "Kids are just being kids." I think they knew there are some things where, yes, kids are kids and not everything necessarily needed a heavy, major discussion. But when it came to adoption, they didn't sweep things under the rug. They'd ask how it made us feel? My parents kept reassuring us that we could always come to them.

Simple openness and honesty was the recipe that allowed me to grow up feeling I was okay with being adopted.

A situation that stands out happened while I was in middle school, maybe twelve. We had taken a road trip to somewhere in Ohio. At the time my parents had started getting into working out and were really into it. For those of us that were the older kids, they were trying to get us into physical fitness and different sports than the ones we may have done in school.

There was a beautiful, huge gym near our hotel where we were staying. So, we were going to work out the next morning after we got there. I was not thrilled to be doing that as a middle schooler, but my parents called the gym the night before to ask what their protocol was surrounding identification for the kids, and because they also had a daycare center they wanted to use.

They said, "Oh, you just have to sign everyone into where they're going to be."

We walk over in the morning. We stood in line watching other families doing exactly what was laid out to my parents. We get to the counter and the person on the other side says something like I need to see proof of who these children are. I immediately knew what was going on. They just couldn't fathom it because we didn't all look identical. How could we be these people's children? How can we be siblings? Who are they?

They told the person they had called the

> night before specifically about this, so we knew what the protocol was for this establishment. And we also watched other families following what was outlined, and it was unfair to be assuming we weren't their children.
>
> After a back and forth for a bit, eventually a manager was called out. They did let us go through and we begrudgingly worked out. My younger siblings went to the childcare center, and all was well, and we were fine afterward. But it was definitely a situation we talked about on our walk back and into the hotel. How unfortunate it is that these things do and will happen. Not all people are going to understand that some families can look different. But they also asked how we all felt and was there anything any of us wanted to say or ask about?
>
> That follow-through afterward—in addition to the claiming—I will always remember. My parents did not back down and really advocated for us as their kids.

A survey recently conducted by the NCFA (National Council for Adoption) shares a great deal of information about adoptees' views in general and includes multicultural input. In reviewing the survey results, it's important to state the NCFA is a fundamentally pro-adoption organization whose mission is to serve the adoption community and the agencies and professionals who facilitate adoptions in the US.

Conducted in 2023, over 1,247 eligible respondents were surveyed from foster care, private, domestic, and international adoptions. Of those surveyed, 447 were from international adoptions and a total of 475 participants said they were of a different race than their adoptive parents.[3] Here are two key questions within the survey below, and their responses:

Race and Adoption

The following two questions were only asked to those who answered they are a different race/ethnicity than their adoptive parent(s).

Survey Question: Do you believe your adoptive parent(s) did a sufficient job at discussing issues of race/ethnicity with you?

Adoptive Parents Job Discussing Issues of Race/Ethnicity	Foster Care N = 33	Private Domestic N = 57	Intercountry N = 385
Sufficient	48.5%	19.3%	53.8%
Insufficient	51.5%	80.7%	46.2%

Table 30. Adoptees' views on parents sufficiently discussing race

Survey Question: Do you believe future adoptive parents should be allowed to adopt a child who is a different race/ethnicity than they are?

Adoptive Parents Should Be Allowed to Adopt Child of Different Race/Ethnicity	Foster Care N = 33	Private Domestic N = 57	Intercountry N = 385
Agree	78.8%	48.2%	89.5%
Disagree	21.2%	51.8%	10.5%

Table 31. Adoptees' Views on Adopting a Child of a Different Race

According to these respondents, those adopted from foster care or internationally felt their parents did a better job of framing and communicating about race than did those from private domestic adoptions. This also appears to affect their views about transracial adoptions overall.[4]

Later in the survey respondents were asked a series of open-ended questions and given free-form expression. Themes emerged around the need for adoptees to feel they "belong" with their families, and the need for the parents to be "child-centric". When speaking specifically to those transracially adopted individuals, the survey shares:

> Adoptees discussed the importance of addressing the complexities of adopting a child

> of a different race or culture. Many stated issues of race were inadequately addressed, referencing family mindsets of colorblindness. One adoptee recalled, "They just acted like I was their biological child. I am Native American. I wish they would have done anything more than the nothing they did to raise me with some of my tribal traditions… They did not see the value in helping me understand who I was."[5]

This feedback is set against the backdrop that most adopted adults know their parents were doing their best. Also, according to the survey results, the majority said overall they were satisfied with their lives.[6] So parents are trying, and still sometimes missing what their child needs. It is an opportunity for more informed education and preparation for these parents before adopting, which also means improvements are possible.

Bias and Racism

Biases and prejudices can come from within a transracial family, from outside sources, or both. They are painful experiences for these adoptees regardless of their source or how prepared they might be to respond.

> **Li~**
> I was born in January of 1989 in Guatemala. By the time I was in high school, the whole border wall, the illegal immigration thing, the dreamer stuff, was really starting to come to the forefront. I remember they were staging walkouts in the schools in Las Vegas and, if

> you were Hispanic, you were supposed to walk out.
>
> Well, up to that point, I never really got along with the Hispanic crowd. They would always make fun of my accent. You know, "Why don't you speak Spanish?"
>
> I remember telling someone my parents and I were going away out of the country for a vacation, and I got the question, "Are your parents drug dealers?" Another friend swooped in and said, "No, they're white."
>
> I never really hung around that group. But I started experiencing racism from both sides, the Hispanic *and* the Caucasian side of the world.
>
> "Go back to your country." "Why don't you speak English?" "Are you an illegal?" Things like that.
>
> But from the other side, it was, "Oh, you're so white, you act white." "You have an accent that's weird. You shouldn't ever speak Spanish, you're so choppy in it." "You're either with them or you're with us."

Sometimes adoptees deal with multiple challenges. Anthony Hynes was a former foster youth who was adopted by his two mothers when he was three in the mid 1990s. He is also now a Training Specialist at the Center for Adoption Support and Education (CASE). He specializes in advocating for families with diverse upbringings and works to better prepare them for both pre and post placement.[7] Here is a small piece of his story.

Anthony~

I suffered as a lot of interracial adoptees do with feelings of racial inauthenticity. There are two stories I tell about Janet [my one adoptive mom]. and I've recently added a third. One, I remember when I was about twelve. Mary, my other adoptive mother, had recently died. I was at a place called Mark's Kitchen, which was a local restaurant we went to all the time. It also doubled as a convenience store. They had little gum packets at the front. I was at the cashier and there were five, six people behind me.

I paid for the thing I'd picked out. Then she said, "Are you going to pay for that other thing?"

I said, "what do you mean, the other thing?"

She said, "The thing you put in your pocket."

I said that I hadn't put anything in my pocket.

She said, "Yes, you did. I saw you put something in your pocket. You need to pay for that."

I unfurled my pockets and showed there was nothing there. Even that wasn't enough.

"I saw you."

I remember that there was an elderly black woman standing behind me who said, "I saw him. He didn't put anything in his pockets." Other people also behind me were looking at her in an accusatory way. And this is a pretty liberal area where everybody wants to think they're not racist.

The cashier felt embarrassed and eventually let it go. I don't remember her apologizing. Maybe she did.

I went home and told Janet. She went to Mark's kitchen and spoke to the owner, Mark, about it.

She said, "This is not acceptable."

Mark said, "I know." And that person was fired. Within the week they were gone.

I've heard that a lot of white adoptive parents say, "Oh, you're imagining things." Or, "Did you put something in your pocket? Maybe you did, maybe you forgot."

She didn't do any of that. She said, "Nope, this happened." Going down there, talking immediately to the person making this happen, showing young Tony that he doesn't have to take this and he can stand up for himself when these things happen too. That was helpful.

I want a lot of parents to see they can serve as a shield. Their kids don't have control over a lot of things, but parents do have control over who their kids are interacting with.

The second story I tell is about allyship. When I was adopted, my mom Janet, her sister, apparently said something racist about them adopting me. To this day, she said she doesn't remember what the phrasing was, but she feels it was racist. And she hasn't spoken to her own sister in thirty years.

I also share a third story now. And that's one of us interacting during the Freddie Gray riots in Baltimore. I went to school at University of Maryland, Baltimore County which is ten minutes from Baltimore City. So I felt very connected to what was going on.

We were watching the news coverage on TV, and Janet turned to me, and said, "Why do they always destroy their neighborhoods?" I knew what she meant when she said "they." I told her, well, first of all, they don't own these neighborhoods 'cause they aren't their neighborhoods. Two, they're frustrated about all the different things that have happened in the last three centuries. We've seen it throughout history.

I was surprised she said it because she's a very smart woman. She gets so many books on race and racism, books by black authors and memoirs, and civil rights figures.

But it was a reminder to me that just because she's gotten things right in certain ways, doesn't mean she doesn't hold racial bias or say prejudiced things.

Support, Services and Training

Adoptees and their parents can benefit greatly by early intervention and training. CASE mentioned above is only one of many such facilitators. (Other sources are included in the Appendix). Youths of all ages and backgrounds can benefit from some friendly, adoption-competent counseling, and so can their parents, regardless of racial or other complexities.

If all parties can open the doors to honest communication, that can help. Some adopted adults find healing with their parents later in life. Others may have to step away, and some do become completely estranged from the family that raised them. But adoptees want and need a safe harbor from the beginning.

Isaac Etter, a black, transracially adopted man along with his Caucasian mother are now co-facilitating adoptive parent training with his organization, Identity.

Isaac~

My relationship with them has been on a steady incline for the past couple of years, which has been really good to see. I didn't connect with them in a deep way for so long. We just didn't have that much to go off.

A couple years ago, me and my mom got close when my dad was going through a rough time.

My parents went on this journey of trying to understand race, what was the problem, what was going on. They ended up reading a lot of books they saw I was reading. When I came home, it was like coming home to a new place. They really had decided to get it and understand me and love me, instead of just rejecting it and making me feel bad for caring about race.

We started to work more and more on my company, Identity, and I started to speak more. My family also was a part of that. I was getting better at training families. The more I worked with them, the more I learned. So, it wasn't just taking what I learned from my family anymore, it was what I was learning from agencies, from families, from other adoptees. The work got a little bit deeper, and that translated into our home. Then my parents would read or see my stuff and they would have their own reflections.

Do we want children of color going into homes that don't want them? Probably not. But it's the ethics behind it all that gets really confusing, because adoption's becoming more "mail order bride" than family building.

We are the continuation of both our birth parents and our adoptive parents. So, we hold this really confusing, and I think at times conflicting, history. Because we can't help but be in the ancestor line of our birth parents, whether we know them or not. Whether we've ever known them or not, they're inside us to a degree. But then we also carry all this weight of our adoptive parents too. So, their mistakes, their unresolved trauma now has somehow also intermixed with ours. It's just so much to carry as an adoptee.

---

1. https://www.diversityresources.com/learn-the-difference-between-race-and-ethnicity/

2. Barn, R.; Mansuri, N. "I Always Wanted to Look at Another Human and Say I Can See That Human in Me": Understanding Genealogical Bewilderment in the Context of Racialised Intercountry Adoptees. Genealogy 2019, 3, 71. https://doi.org/10.3390/genealogy3040071

3. Hanlon, R., Davi, N., Quade, M., & Lindner, A. (2024). Profiles in adoption: Adult adoptee experiences. National Council For Adoption.

4. Hanlon, R., Davi, N., Quade, M., & Lindner, A. (2024). Profiles in adoption: Adult adoptee experiences. National Council For Adoption.

5. Hanlon, R., Davi, N., Quade, M., & Lindner, A. (2024). Profiles in adoption: Adult adoptee experiences. National Council For Adoption.

6. Hanlon, R., Davi, N., Quade, M., & Lindner, A. (2024). Profiles in adoption: Adult adoptee experiences. National Council For Adoption.

7. https://adoptionsupport.org

Chapter 8
International Adoptions

"One day you will tell your story of how you overcame what you went through, and it will be someone else's survival guide." ~Brene Brown

The United States is the founder of international adoptions, and its first source was South Korea. When WWII ended, the country found itself caught between the Soviets and the West. The subsequent Korean War broke out in 1950, and in 1953 an armistice was signed leaving the country fractured into two parts. The North under the control of the communists in China and the Soviet Union; and the South which moved to align itself as a western ally and establish a capitalist, democratic style of governance.

In the wake of the war was extreme poverty and a substantial lack of resources. Nearly eight hundred orphanages in South Korea were established by 1954.[1]

The Southern Korean people and its leaders felt an obligation to the United States, for rescuing them from the prior thirty-six years of Japanese occupation as well as their current liberation from the communists. Harry and Bertha Holt, an Oregon farming couple, traveled to Korea with an altruistic desire to help, and already had a strong history of missionary work behind them. They gained the ear of Korea's leadership and proposed the solution of adoption to reduce the number of starving children South

Korea was struggling to provide for.

The Holt's were devout Christians and established a network of local allies to begin adopting Korean children into the US. The Holt's themselves adopted eight children. Almost immediately in the US, the rush was on. Their local network of equally devoted Christians were highly motivated to adopt these children in need. In 1961, Korea passed the Special Adoption Assistance Act bringing major changes to how children were cared for and prioritized adopting them out to other countries.[2]

In America, the Holt's had connections to nonprofits such as the Child Welfare League of America and the US Children's Bureau. In 1955 they submitted a proposal to congress called The Adoption by Proxy provision. This allowed for families to adopt and bring a child from a foreign country without needing to travel abroad. While some child welfare agencies denounced the plan, the program was implemented.[3]

Some parents are moved to adopt because of their Christian values. Others have the altruistic desire to help those struggling in other nations, and yet still other parents just want a baby regardless of the source. Sometimes prospective parents find that wait times can be shorter with international versus domestic adoptions.

> **Noel~**
> I was seven years old when my parents started the process of adopting me. It took them two years because they started in 1975. I came to the US in '77. They didn't tell me ahead of time what was going to happen. They said, you're going to this other house, I think they call it a foster house.
>
> I remember eating lunch or dinner. The

head foster parent came over to me and said, "Your dad's here to pick you up." *What dad?* It was a shock to me. And they said you're going to America. I didn't think it was real because I wasn't prepared.

I remember, Wonder Woman was [playing on the TV] and it was my favorite show. I never got to finish the rest of it.

I just went along with this strange guy. We went shopping somewhere. My dad was in the military, and we got an escort to go back to the hotel. We were there for a few days and then we got on a plane.

I remember there were other kids getting adopted by these families, but those families didn't know how to get over to Korea. My dad ended up bringing, I think, eight or nine kids over. We brought them to each location we landed. That's where the parents were. We dropped them off as we were coming to the US. We went to New Jersey.

Carrie~

I was adopted at the end of February 1984. What they know about my time in Korea is very limited. They gave me a birthday in September, but the paper trail started in November. The story says that I was found by a woman at 5:30 in the morning outside her house in Korea. They have these gates around their houses, and she heard me crying or she came down and saw me. She supposedly called the police, and they referred me to the adoption agency.

> This was in Busan which is on the Southeast coast. Within a couple of days, I was taken up to Seoul. That's where I was placed. First at a baby's home and then with a foster mother. I was with her for the rest of the time. That's all I know. The Korean name they gave me was probably given by the adoption agency. My birth date—I don't know where that came from. One of the documents says there was a piece of paper that had the birth date on it, but there's no evidence.
>
> My adopted parents lived in Maryland, and they started the process. It happened so fast. I looked at their paperwork and it was that same fall I was born. So, it happened within five, six months. All the paperwork, applications, the home study, all of it.
>
> In Korea, they have an escort. The foster mother gives me to this other woman who then takes me along with many other babies at the same time over to America. I landed in Virginia, with a bunch of other babies.
>
> My mom always says that I was very, very alert. I was looking around at everything, and her interpretation was always that I was very smart. And my interpretation is I was shocked and freaking out.

In total, South Korea is the source of the largest number of international adoptees. There are an estimated 200,000 - 250,000 adoptees from Korea into the US, Europe, and Australia, and is the largest diaspora of adoptees living outside of their home country. It also became the model for how other countries would create and continue the practice.

The Holt International Adoption Agency remains active and is the largest agency with this focus in the US.

The Surge and the Decline

The peak year for international adoptions into the US was in 2005 with 22,991 adoptions and as of 2021 the number has plummeted to 1,785.[4] Between 1990 and 2004, approximately 150,000 children were adopted into the US. [5]

A multitude of factors contributed. The "one child" policy in China was dominant, and the infant care institutions in that country were flooded with babies, primarily girls. Korea's government continued their program but also at this time was the fall of the Iron Curtain. Institutions in the former Soviet Union along with many other occupied countries were overwhelming local resources. Central and South America, along with adoptions in various African countries became more common. The world, it seemed, was flush with babies needing homes, and American families were thrilled to provide.

> **Mikayla~**
> I was born in 1999 in Kharkov, Ukraine. I spent three months with my birth mother, and then was placed in an orphanage, and then transferred to a specialized orphanage, although it gets kind of hairy. During that time, kids couldn't be adopted out to foreigners if the child was under five, unless the child had medical issues.
>
> So, I was placed into the specialized orphanage and a lot of my paperwork says that

I had a lot of health issues, but once I was taken to the States, those issues didn't exist. They were just put on my papers so I could get adopted out.

My parents went through the process after they had a couple of miscarriages. My dad brought it up to my mom and she really wanted a little girl because I have two older brothers. They were just finishing high school when I was adopted. I think a lot stemmed out of the continuous trauma of losing a baby and going through that. They found out about adoption through the church, and they got connected with an agency.

They gave them a list of countries to choose from and they picked a random one that turned out to be Ukraine. They handed them a book of babies with pictures, and they selected one but [the agency] talked my parents out of adopting that baby. They did that another time and got talked out of it. They ended up giving my picture next and the agency finally allowed them to go through with the process.

My parents flew out to Ukraine in 2001, I believe. They spent two weeks over there and met me three times. I have it on tapes and stuff. I look so confused. They would take me out to the hallway, and they would meet with me, and they would try to call me.

I am one and a half, closer to two years old then. I was [given] the birth name, Margarita and that was changed to Mikayla. I cannot begin to explain the confusion in my face that my parent's captured on video as they were holding me in the orphanage calling me Mikayla. It's another loss that I believe families adopting internationally need to recognize.

A Unique Kind of Trauma

Listening to the stories told by international adoptees as adults often challenge the assumptions held by their non-adopted peers in the US.

The bias that America is the greatest nation on earth is often present in these adopting parents. It is true that a great many in this population live in material abundance. Millions enter the US both legally and illegally to participate in the opportunities for freedom, education, and prosperity denied elsewhere. Legal immigrants to the US go to great effort to become citizens, establish residency, and gain lawful employment.

Throughout history, children have been conscripted into the military in guerrilla warfare in Africa as well as Central and South America. Children may languish in orphanages and age out in their later teen years. Some children have been uncared for, malnourished and died due to starvation, war, and natural disasters. Youngsters are forced into slavery and illegal child labor and mistreated with astonishing cruelty.

The presumption is that any child is lucky to be plucked, or "chosen" from their plight in an orphanage and taken to the United States. But these children do not generally have any perspectives of what they are "missing." However, it is important to understand several common factors in the above stories, and thousands of other internationally adopted individuals.

1. They are most often not orphans—in gen-

eral one or both of their parents are alive. These children have been placed into care for a variety of reasons. Their families could not afford to provide for them. Their unwed mother was shamed into relinquishment, or they may have been institutionalized for other reasons. They may have special needs, or were placed temporarily, and their parents intend to return once their living situation stabilized.

2. These children are often completely unprepared for what is happening to them, even when old enough to understand. Their caregivers do not always explain these events in advance.

3. Many of these adopting parents are not well informed or educated about how their child may perceive what is happening. Their expectations may not match this new reality. They also often do not know the accurate details of how these children were treated and what physical, medical, or mental health challenges they may face.

4. There is often even less information being given to the relinquishing parent(s). Several books— "The Child Catchers", by Kathryn Joyce and "Somebody's Children", by Laura Briggs document at length the corruption, coercion, and deceit that has happened internationally, as well as the cultural misunderstandings contained within international adoption.

One story shared below is what was learned when this

adoptee from Korea found her birth mother. She was three when adopted into the US. Her mother had a relationship with a man who had another family she did not know about. He was Korean but living in Japan and traveled back and forth frequently. He financially subsidized the mother, (his mistress) for several years. But eventually pulled that support and went back to his family (with nine other children) full time. Here is the story told by Corissa from her birth mother at their first meeting.

Corissa~
She pulled out this stack of photos and then my heart completely melted. I had always lamented over not having childhood photos, no photos of myself as a baby. I needed to learn about this life I had before I came to the States.

It was me as a baby up to the last photo of us together. I'm dressed so well. I am in these cute little outfits and little hats, so it was a strange disconnect between what I thought was my life, and then this. [During this time my mother is pleading with my father to keep supporting us.]

But a woman had befriended my mother and told her, you know she will have a much better life if you adopt her out. There are American families looking for [a baby like her].

This woman who befriended my mom told her, "You're going to have a really hard life. And she's going to have a much better life over there. You'll be able to reunite with her when she's sixteen. They're going to raise her, but you're still going to be connected."

She would bring American snacks. There's

> a photo of me she had in her stack of me with a can of Pringles.
>
> She convinced my mother this was the right thing to do and the best thing for me. After my mother brought me to the orphanage, she was having doubts. She went to the army base where this woman was living near. She'd been told [this woman] was somehow tied to the base.
>
> They all said, "Oh, she's not here, you never should have trusted that woman."
>
> And she was, "What? What!" She had brought me, or someone brought me on her behalf, to the orphanage with my mom's understanding my parents were in the country, that they were taking me right from that moment on.
>
> Then I told her that, no, I was at the orphanage for a month and a half. It was one of the times she broke down in my lap. She couldn't believe that I was at the orphanage for that long. She thought I was gone. That was one of the moments she really lost it.

Corissa's story demonstrates the coercive and deceitful practices of some adoption agencies and their agents, whose interest was in finding adoptable babies rather than finding homes for children who had been willfully relinquished. Consider what it would feel like for these mothers who may have been duped into handing over their children, regardless of what brought them to that point.

Now, flip that script to wonder what any of these adopted children might be experiencing. Imagine being a small child, but old enough to be aware. Around you are familiar sounds of the words spoken, known smells from the cooking and preparation of food, the common tastes of that nourishment. You are surrounded by a living situation that is familiar and other children and caregivers you are bonded to. You only know what is familiar.

Imagine being pulled away from that. This child is put on a plane or other transport and taken to the other side of the world from everything they know. Who is then expected to assimilate without complaint, and as they age, are assumed to be grateful for the opportunities granted to them.

Many internationally adopted adults outwardly appear to thrive despite these early losses. They focus on their education and become successful in their careers. The complexities of their lived experiences surface for some by the way they are treated due to their ethnic background. Most straddle between two worlds—the one they came from, and the one they are living in now. How they feel about their life experiences differs widely. The biggest take away may be when one encounters an internationally adopted adult is to *ask them* rather than *assume* how they feel.

Adults are almost universally grateful to good parents. These adopted adults however have also struggled with their identity and are often completely bereft of any family history from their homeland, native culture, and heritage. Their documented dates of birth may be complete fiction.

How They Fare

One study from 1990 showed more problems with externalizing behaviors in the 2,148 internationally adopted participants, ages ten to fifteen, when compared to their non-adopted counterparts.[6] Some sources cite nearly the opposite, stating that researchers "found that international adoptees had consistently fewer externalizing behavioral problems than domestic adoptees." The authors speculate that the adoptive parents of international adoptees may be better prepared than those done domestically.[7] Many international adoptees support this point of view, while others strongly contest it.

A more recent article from 2015 in "The Professional Counselor" calls out one oddity in this multi-cultural landscape. Citing that, in general, children adopted overseas show higher rates of attachment, social, and emotional problems than their non-adopted and domestically adopted peers. However, this was not as universal as expected. International adoptees from China apparently are showing themselves to have "better adjustment outcomes" when compared to international adoptees as a whole.[8]

China is statistically the second largest source for international adoptees into the US. Because of the influences in China, 90% of these adoptees are female infants.[9] The reasons for why they tend to fare better are unclear. The article speculates this may be due to the one-child policy held in China from 1979 until 2015. The families placing these children into institutions were generally healthy, and the issues regarding their placement were different. In other countries there may be a higher prevalence of malnutrition, or children abandoned because of disabilities or other familial challenges.[10]

Children who have spent significant time in institutionalized care, most infamously those who have come from the Soviet Union or other former "Eastern Blockade" countries were not treated as well as infants from other circumstances. "Following the breakup of the Soviet Union in 1990 and the growing media attention that subsequently occurred, Western families became aware of the large number of children warehoused in deplorable living conditions."[11] Many families were unaware of the long-term impacts to early childhood development when they adopted them into America.

Stunted growth was common and observed in one study on Romanian adoptees—85% of whom were developmentally behind age-appropriate norms. Other common issues with children from these state-run orphanages are an increased risk from a wide variety of health challenges, such as anemia, hypothyroidism, rickets, lead exposure, and inadequate vaccinations. This same study in 2005 estimated that 94% of these internationally adopted children experienced developmental delays.[12]

The length of time in institutionalized care appears to affect the outcomes for these children. The researchers "demonstrated that children who were institutionalized longer showed less improvement and remained functionally below children with less orphanage exposure."[13] Furthermore, the longer these children stayed in such care, the harder time they had developing secure attachments. Deprived of consistent human contact, these children also experience developmental delays in language, as well as fine motor and social skills.[14] Just like any other group of children who have some harmful or traumatic experiences, they will develop coping mechanisms. These are natural and should be expected. An awareness of different cultural norms should also be noted. What may be considered normal behavior in the US may not be the same within another culture.

Their New Life

Most children want to go along and get along with the people around them. Others are more strong-willed. There are many things these well-intentioned parents get right, and a few things that can be very confusing to their children.

Puma~

I grew up in Michigan in a very ethnically diverse city, which I can't thank my parents enough for. They already knew it was important for somebody from a different country to not be the only person from a different place in their community. That was a conscious decision on my parents' part.

I wasn't consciously dwelling on it while growing up, but it was a subconscious thought all the time. I know I don't look like you guys. I know I don't look like my sister, especially when we stand next to each other, and we introduce ourselves as sisters and then people have the same look, which is curiosity at first. Then we have to be, "Yes, we're adopted, that's why we don't look the same..." before anyone could ask, I felt like we had to say it because I would get a lot of weird assumptions.

People can be ignorant, and they don't start with a question. They start with an assumption question such as, "Oh, are you Chinese?" Then I would tell them a lie. I didn't tell them I was from Kazakhstan because every time I said it no one understood where that was.

And it was really embarrassing because I also didn't understand that much. So, I decided at one point to start saying Russia because it's directly under Russia.

Noel~

The first day, it was the first time I slept on a bed. The orphanage in Korea in 1977, we didn't have beds. Just a blanket and pillow on the floor.

I remember I slept a long time. My grandparents came to visit because they wanted to meet me. They all stood around my bed staring at me, trying to get me to wake up. My mom said I slept sixteen hours or something.

The kids accepted me there in my neighborhood and they all wanted to play with me. I remember my mom coming to me and saying, "Do you want to go play?" I understood that, so I went out and played, not having to know any English. That was a really good experience.

Then my parents put me into a private Catholic school, and she let the principal know my background. They all knew who I was, and they were really nice to me. I really enjoyed that school very much.

That summer we went backpacking in Wallowa Lake up in Oregon for two weeks. To me, coming from an orphanage was not fun. You sleep on the ground. That's what I did before. Americans think that's fun but, for me, it wasn't. I ate food that I wasn't used to. Processed foods. I remember macaroni and cheese and not liking the stuff. It made me throw up.

I didn't know that I had altitude sickness. I was sick the whole time up in the mountains. Certain altitudes make me sick. As an adult, I learned that.

I cried the whole time because it wasn't fun for me. I don't think they understood that. They thought I was being a spoiled brat, and nobody understood I had altitude sickness.

Back home, my mom decided to send me to swim lessons in New Jersey. I cried the whole time because I felt abandoned and was afraid. There was a lot of miscommunications. I think people don't understand when someone comes from another country the language barrier, and the culture shock that happens. I didn't understand a lot of things.

Mikayla~

I wasn't a cuddly child. I was very independent. I remember seeing a tape that I don't think was supposed to be kept because it was taped over a show. But the scene was my mom when she came into my room. I was probably two or three. I'm crying and repeating a word. The word is probably Ukrainian, but I'm not sure.

I think my mom recorded this for my dad to see because he would work out of the country a lot of the time. She came in and said something like, "Mikayla, stop crying." I'm in my crib, in the dark, and she turns the camera to herself. She says, "This is what happens ev-

> ery night. She won't sleep. She doesn't want anything. I don't know what to do."
>
> I think that's indicative of what it was like in those early years for me. A lot of confusion. I felt loved. I just never felt like I fit in. My mom didn't know how to help me. We never really connected on any shared hobbies or anything. So, I would say I felt like I didn't belong.

These adoptees know that for the most part, their parents love them and are trying their best. Contained within their stories are also moments where parents can learn. At times, they need to think about how their child experiences life. The good news is that over the past several decades, resources have improved. Cultural family camps for various groups have formed throughout the US. They gather families with similar adoptee backgrounds to celebrate, learn, and immerse themselves in that heritage. More psychological research is being done on these blended families and continues to emerge. The (APA) American Psychological Association has many articles and resources for parents,[15] and adoptees are entering into the fields of social work and psychology and becoming adoption competent therapists. However, some families will have significant struggles, sometimes to an extreme level.

When Things Go Wrong

If parents are not properly informed and prepared for what they are taking on, the consequences can be severe and irreparably affect a multitude of lives.

Puma was adopted from an orphanage in 1997 from Kostanay, Kazakhstan. Her mother, a Ukrainian immigrant to the US, had an older son from a prior marriage but longed for a girl. When she and her new husband visited the orphanage in Kazakhstan, they fell in love with Puma but also met and dearly liked another little three-year-old girl who had an older nine-year-old sister. The country would not allow the siblings to be separated, so they brought all three little girls back to the US.

Puma~

It was a really big change. I think, in my parents' visions for their future, they thought they were just going to bring home one daughter, but they ended up bringing home three. Jackie was three years old, I was four years old, and Casey was nine years old.

So, Casey was kind of the wrench in my parents' life from then on, unfortunately. Casey really, really struggled.

She was a very mad, angry child. She was separated from her mother by their own child protective services, brought into an orphanage, and then just five months later was given up for adoption to two Americans. She was furious about it. She acted out a lot throughout our childhood, creating a lot of turmoil in the family.

So, my childhood and my upbringing weren't really what my parents had hoped for. It ended up being a very tumultuous one where there were a lot of conflicts. I found myself trying very hard to be a good daughter.

There was a lot of chaos between my parents and my older sister. A lot of stress and pain and hurt. I was always the mediator. I loved my parents and my siblings, but they didn't love each other. I was doing the best I could do, throughout my whole life, to keep everybody content.

It's really unfortunate because Jackie was only three. She didn't understand what was going on.

Casey ended up getting sent away.

My parents thought it would be best to send her to a boarding school because they thought she was an inconsolable child, and these schools were very popular during the 2000s. They were these correctional institutes, where they take troubled children and break their will and try to rebuild them. They're in the Midwest, very remote and secluded. Casey was unfortunately sent to one of those when she was in high school at age sixteen.

I was eleven years old when she got sent away. They explained it to me the best they could to a child. In my head, I said, "Okay, that is what it is." Casey's gone, she's not here right now. She's at school. We moved on with our lives. She's been estranged [from our family] since she was eighteen.

There are tons of issues nobody understands. I'm not talking about it to my friends or anybody in my life or my family. I'm just trying to exist and have a happy life, but my parents were visibly stressed and overwhelmed. Some things that I disagree with my parents' parenting, is them relinquishing an already relinquished child.

> Shortly after my older sister was kicked out of the house, Jackie started acting up and following in the exact footsteps of my sister. Being out late, talking to the wrong people, and getting into dangerous situations. Almost exactly the way Casey had.
>
> I think she was confused and lost as well, and she was in her own rebellious stage. So my whole childhood was just watching my parents wig out and not know how to handle these children. They were out of their depth, and they knew it and they thought the best thing was to send them somewhere where they thought people could handle children like this.
>
> And that's exactly what happened. They sent Jackie away too.

This is the worst-case scenario, and no one is tracking how frequently it occurs. Adoptees already experience a relentless fear they were unwanted. To then give up on a child who has already been dislodged from all that was familiar regardless of why, is hard to comprehend. Parents can feel desperate when they cannot control the behavior of their teenager that is chronically unsafe, or even dangerous to other members of the family. This is why having parents pre-educated with realistic expectations is so important. It's another reason to cultivate relationships with counselors who have experience in adoption trauma. The wrong advice, even if given by a well-intended but not adoption competent trained therapist, can be devastating.

Disrupted adoptions are horrendously painful for the adoptee. Some of these youths are being sent away to boarding schools, wilderness programs, and psychiatric treatment centers. Some are being rehomed or dumped into the foster care system.

These facilities are part of the "Troubled Teen Industry". It's a big business, largely unregulated, and highly lucrative for the operators.[16]

No one is keeping data on adoption disruption, but experts say it is happening with increasing frequency. According to a 2008 Los Angeles Times article, "a decade long-study of 5,750 Illinois children adopted from foster care through the mid-1980s found a rate of 6.5%." It is with international adoptions that experts are seeing an increase now.[17]

Some of these camps actively market themselves to adoptive parents, and even specifically to those who have adopted internationally.

Corruption

International adoptions have a sordid history of corruption dating back decades. A New York Times article from 1981 shared that authorities discovered an international ring worth millions of dollars where children were kidnapped or purchased and sold with forged birth certificates. Victims on the receiving side were in the US and Europe, and the trafficked children came from Columbia, Peru, and Ecuador.[18]

In 1995 Ukrainian authorities busted a similar ring where local doctors were involved in a scheme to sell babies to unsuspecting adoptive American families.[19] But this history of transporting and selling children across international borders goes back further. "Between 1930 and 1975, several thousand Canadian-born children were adopted by families in the United States. Most of these children were very young infants, and most were the children of unwed mothers." These Canadian "Black Market Baby" rings were charging American families between $2,500 to $10,000.[20]

Diana's story as a late discovery adoptee includes the revelation, she was a black-market baby. She recently found out she was most likely adopted and had never been told. In trying to understand what happened, things kept getting increasingly bizarre.

Diana~

I got my birth certificate, there was false information on it. My parents' names were on it, but their ages were completely wrong, the places, previous births—it said none. How could that be? I have an older brother, and he says he didn't know anything. He couldn't remember if mom was pregnant or not. He was still a kid, so he didn't realize it.

I called a man who was the foreman to my father's factory. He said, "I'll have to call you back. I have to speak to my lawyer first."

"What do you mean?" And then he says, "Well, I was with your father that day when we picked you up."

Then he hung up and that was the last I heard from him.

A friend of mine in Las Vegas found a man who was from Canada who told him, "I need to call her." He left a long message saying he was a friend of my father's. He says in his message, "He had made the arrangements for your mother, and I know who she is. And I'll call you when I get back to Montreal.

He had taken my mother across the border,

he said. The plan was to go to New York and have the baby. But things didn't turn out that way and I was born in Montreal.

My birth certificate says I'm born in New York. That's where a felony was committed. It's falsified. He took the baby, me, across the border. First, they went to Plattsburgh, New York, and then on to Lake Placid. That's where my adopted dad, with the foreman, picked me up. My mother, my adopted mom, was not with them.

Through my search, I have discovered four people he placed babies with. I believe he was part of the Montreal black-market baby ring.

I was sold. There were no adoption papers. My brother was legally adopted out of Jewish services in New York, but it turns out they lied because my brother's not Jewish according to his DNA.

The man who arranged it all said my parents were on a waiting list. He made it sound like she was also Jewish, which became very appealing to my parents. There was a Jewish baby coming and they wanted to jump the line, basically. "If we do it this way, we can get you a baby." That's what happened.

Guatemala

This extremely poor country in Central America has a long history of political instability and human trafficking. Recent decades have left the citizens in challenging circumstances. As recently as 2006 nearly half of rural homes do not have electricity or running water. Ruled by a dictatorship with unethical and Communist tendencies, a UN-brokered peace deal in 1996 began to stabilize the nation somewhat. But it also increased its popularity for potential US adoptive families to enter the country.[21]

> "There are stories of kidnappings and coercion, of women tricked into giving up their children, of teenage girls paid to have babies, of nurseries filled with infants ready for sale. And there's plenty of money involved.
>
> Each US couple shells out roughly $25,000 to adopt a child, the birth mother receives about $3,000, and the middlemen—US adoption agencies and Guatemalan lawyers—keep a sizable chunk of the fee. There is fraud on both sides. The lawyers are notorious for sidestepping laws to line their pockets, and several US adoption agencies have swindled couples out of thousands of dollars."[22]

Not all mothers placing their babies for adoptions were doing so voluntarily, or for pay. Some report being drugged, physically restrained, or lied to. [23]

In 2008 all international adoptions in Guatemala were stopped by the government due to allegations of corruption. The scandal echoed throughout the adoption world and American parents scrambled to defend their families or those adoptions still in process as court cases ensued to hold the traffickers accountable.[24] It is estimated by the US State Department that as many as 30,000 children were adopted into the US between the 1990s-2008.[25] At its peak, it was estimated that 1 in every 100 live births ended with the infant being adopted out of the country, primarily to America.[26]

Li~

I was born in January of 1989 in Guatemala.

It just so happened I was the chosen child, and they were telling them, "She's so beautiful, she's healthy, she's this, she's that." And they said, "Okay." Then they told them, "We do have other ones if you would like to see them."

My parents were genuinely horrified at the thought of having baby after baby paraded out for them to make some sort of choice, forget the other four that we just saw. That was a terrible feeling for them.

When I was in college, we found out about the scandals and the arrests. The breaking news was shocking and frightening. Shocking because I don't care what situation the parent is in, you don't steal someone's child from them. Who was okay with this? That's appalling and disgusting.

It was also frightening because immediately we knew, or I knew at the very least I might not be a citizen. I stayed in touch with a group of people from Guatemala and I got a text from them one day telling me about this. She basically said, "Check your citizenship, make sure everything's legit because already one of us has to go back now and get everything redone because she just found out she's not a citizen."

I called my parents, telling them to check all the paperwork. You need to make sure everything is legit. Are we sure I am a citizen?

Are we sure I was legally adopted?

My dad being who he is, went through everything with a fine-tooth comb, double, triple checked, called the lawyers they worked with, called everyone to just make sure I was okay.

Even though he confirmed everything was legitimate and everything was fine, you still carry that uneasiness around with you.

Ukraine

Gaining its independence in 1992 after the USSR dissolved, the country became a popular choice for international adoptions and remains so. The recent war between Russia and Ukraine has expanded an already questionably ethical system. Due to the lack of resources and leadership, the country has struggled for decades. The poverty rate in 2018 places it as one of the poorest countries in net wealth,[27] even prior to recent events. Then, in February 2022, Russia invaded the country and full-scale war broke out.

Russia pounced on Ukrainian children, immediately. So far it is estimated that 19,000 children were removed from Ukraine and transferred to Russia or territory within its control.[28] It appears the country was not doing so purely to take possession of land and human assets, but with the specific intent to adopt them to Russian parents. The country also simplified the adoption process to help more adoptions process quickly.[29]

Others were also looking to "help." Six-term Washington House of Representative Matt Shea has many far-right connections. A probe concluded in 2019 that his activities "amounted to support of domestic terrorism," and he was suspended from the Republican Caucus. He did not run for reelection in 2020 and instead became a minister of his own church, On Fire Ministries.[30]

In February 2022, Shea showed up in a hotel in a small town in eastern Poland three hours from the Ukrainian border. He was with dozens of children he claimed had been evacuated from an orphanage in Mariupol. He said he was working with a Texas organization, Loving Families and Homes for Orphans. After his appearance on a local television show the media started to investigate and found Loving Families was not a registered adoption agency.[31]

Fortunately, this attempt to move the children into the US was prevented, but Shea was not alone.

> "On social media, numerous people have posted requests seeking information on how to adopt, host, or foster a war 'orphan' from Ukraine. Former *Real Housewife* Bethenny Frankel announced on Twitter that she had an apartment building standing ready to house 157 orphans currently taking refuge in Poland. In the UK, a brief political battle broke out between two members of Parliament after one accused the other of slowing the transport of forty-eight purported Ukrainian orphans to Scotland, while the second charged that it was 'wrong to move children without attempting to reunite them with their family first and without the agreement of their home and host governments.'"[32]

The word "orphan" is often misused. Many countries, Ukraine among them, have a long history of institutionalized care for some children. They utilize boarding schools for education and will often use their local "orphanage" to temporarily house their child. Parents may need to move or encounter extreme changes to their living circumstances. Such as a war.

> **Mikayla~**
> How does that make me feel? Thank you for asking because I think I've discussed this with my therapist, I've discussed this with my parents, I've discussed it with my friends, and no one understands that it makes me feel terrible. I don't know how to sum up in words, but it makes me feel like I was smuggled. And there's something to my story that I am missing that I don't know. I don't like that feeling. I don't like the principles on that. I think it's extremely unethical.
>
> They had a baby crisis at the time. So, they just needed to move them through as fast as possible and get around the laws. That's how it happens.

International adoptions into the US continue to drop, but according to the most recent data from 2022, the most common incoming overseas adoptions are from, (in order): Columbia, India, South Korea, Bulgaria and Ukraine. If one visits the Holt International website, they advertise children available where they operate in: Bulgaria, China, Columbia, Haiti, Hong Kong, Korea, Mongolia, South Africa, Taiwan, Thailand, and Vietnam.[33]

An estimated four million children are currently victims of trafficking, the dominant reason being labor in domestic services, factories, or agriculture.[34] Currently, there are five nations who will not allow outgoing international adoptions: Cambodia, China, Ethiopia, Guatemala, Nepal, and Russia.[35] Some of these bans are political, as in the case with Russia, and China, but the majority are due to concerns about a lack of ethics and trafficking.

But even beyond these concerns for adopted individuals, are problems surrounding issues of citizenship which have been neglected for decades.

Citizenship

Not all internationally adopted children between the 1950s to the year 2000 were made citizens. Numbers vary, so the exact amount is unknown. Some sources say the numbers are between 15,000 - 18,000,[36] while others cite as high as 35,000.[37] But first, an explanation is needed of how this happened. Prior to the year 2000, all children adopted from another country into the US, still had to go through the naturalization process. The responsibility for this was on their adoptive parents.

Many of these parents relied on their legal advisors and adoption agency personnel to begin this process for them. Some failed to complete the paperwork, and others were told, incorrectly, that adopting their child was enough.

Most of these children grew up going to school, got a social security card, driver's license and the other common trappings of the modern paper trail. Troubles often only erupted when the adult adoptee tried to get a passport, apply for an SBA loan, or have a need to prove what was assumed—their citizenship.

The fallout for these men and women is a staggering blow. In 2000, President Clinton signed into law the Child Citizen Act, which guaranteed that any adopted child entering the country who met the citizen requirements were automatically made US Citizens. This law took effect in February 2001. However, it left a gap. The law only applied to adoptees already living in America who were under the age of eighteen, and those adopted afterward. Lawmakers intended to revisit the bill to close the loop. But then, September 11 happened.

Little has been accomplished since. Each of these adopted adults have been left to fend for themselves to try to maintain employment and stay in the US, which is their home. A citizenship application can take 18-24 months to complete, and the filing fee alone is $1,170, never mind additional legal fees or other costs, and the hours of time the process takes.[38] *They thought they were citizens.* Most of these people are frustrated beyond measure at their situation.

Shamefully, at least 35-50 legally adopted individuals have been deported back to their country of origin.

Legislation has been introduced to fix the problem but so far none has passed. The Equal Citizenship for Children Act has been introduced into congress that would retroactively address the gap for these folks. A separate bill, the Adoptee Citizenship Act of 2024 has also been discussed which would make the task of filling less arduous. It is past due for congress to address the needs of these adoptees.

A rallying cry from the public is needed to move this legislation forward. Without additional help, these adoptees lobby, watch, and wait.

---

1. Rev. Dr. Janine Myoung Ja, (2022a). Adoption: What you should know. Findaway World. AdoptionHistory.org. ISBN: 9798644111633

2. Chung Y, Ahn H, Lah TJ. Child welfare policy and services in Korea. Int J Soc Welf. 2022; 31: 33–44. https://doi.org/10.1111/ijsw.12478

3. Rev. Dr. Janine Myoung Ja, (2022a). Adoption: What you should know. Findaway World. AdoptionHistory.org. ISBN: 9798644111633

4. https://www.statista.com/statistics/249414/intercountry-adoptions-involving-the-us/

5. Mason, P., & Narad, C. (2005a, February 24). International adoption: A health and developmental prospective. Seminars in Speech and Language. https://www.thiemeconnect.de/products/ejournals/abstract/10.1055/s-2005-864211

6. Verhulst FC, Althaus M, Versluis-den Bieman HJ. Problem behavior in international adoptees: I. An epidemiological study. J Am Acad Child Adolesc Psychiatry. 1990 Jan;29(1):94-103. doi: 10.1097/00004583-199001000-00015. PMID: 2295584.

7. Keyes, M. A., Sharma, A., Elkins, I. J., Iacono, W. G., & McGue, M. (2008). The Mental Health of US adolescents adopted in infancy. Archives of Pediatrics & Adolescent Medicine, 162(5), 419. https://doi.org/10.1001/archpedi.162.5.419

8. https://tpcjournal.nbcc.org/all-foreign-born-adoptees-are-not-the-same-what-counselors-and-parents-need-to-know/

9. https://tpcjournal.nbcc.org/all-foreign-born-adoptees-are-not-the-same-what-counselors-and-parents-need-to-know/

10. https://tpcjournal.nbcc.org/all-foreign-born-adoptees-are-not-the-same-what-counselors-and-parents-need-to-know/

11. Mason, P., & Narad, C. (2005a, February 24). International adoption: A health and developmental prospective. Seminars in Speech and Language. https://www.thiemeconnect.com/products/ejournals/abstract/10.1055/s-2005-864211

12. Mason, P., & Narad, C. (2005a, February 24). International adoption: A health and developmental prospective. Seminars in Speech and Language. https://www.thiemeconnect.com/products/ejournals/abstract/10.1055/s-2005-864211

13. Mason, P., & Narad, C. (2005a, February 24). International adoption: A health and developmental prospective. Seminars in Speech and Language. https://www.thiemeconnect.com/products/ejournals/abstract/10.1055/s-2005-864211

14. Mason, P., & Narad, C. (2005a, February 24). International adoption: A health and developmental prospective. Seminars in Speech and Language. https://www.thiemeconnect.com/products/ejournals/abstract/10.1055

15. https://www.apa.org/monitor/2023/10/supporting-international-adoptions

16. https://www.americanbar.org/groups/litigation/resources/newsletters/childrens-rights/five-facts-about-troubled-teen-industry/

17. https://www.latimes.com/archives/la-xpm-2008-jan-20-na-adopt20-story.html

18. https://www.nytimes.com/1981/08/16/world/ring-in-columbia-kidnaps-children-for-sale-abroad.html

19.https://www.washingtonpost.com/archive/politics/1995/03/22/ukrainians-charged-with-stealing-babies-for-overseas-adoptions/2135aca6-2fe2-4fad-b9bb-5f4a347dc0e1/

20. “phony mothers” and border-crossing adoptions: The Montreal-to-new york black market in babies in the 1950s. (n.d.-a). https://www.researchgate.net/publication/236816169_Phony_Mothers_and_Border-Crossing_Adoptions_The_Montreal-to-New_York_Black_Market_in_Babies_in_the_1950s

21. Garigan, M. (2007). Of note: Guatemala’s adoption industry. SAIS Review of International Affairs, 27(2), 179–181. https://doi.org/10.1353/sais.2007.0029

22. Garigan, M. (2007). Of note: Guatemala’s adoption industry. SAIS Review of International Affairs, 27(2), 179–181. https://doi.org/10.1353/sais.2007.0029

23. https://www.bbc.co.uk/sounds/play/p03ght88

24. https://www.cbsnews.com/news/guatemala-adoption-fraud-may-hit-us/

25. https://www.nbcnews.com/news/latino/painful-truth-guatemalan-adoptees-learn-they-were-fraudulently-given-away-n1095066

26. Joyce, K. (2013). The child catchers: Rescue, trafficking, and the New Gospel of Adoption. PublicAffairs.

27. https://www.kyivpost.com/post/7924

28.https://www.nytimes.com/interactive/2023/12/26/world/europe/ukraine-war-children-russia.html?utm_source=pocket-newtab-en-us

29. https://www.yahoo.com/news/russia-announces-adoption-thousands-children-104931080.html?

30. https://www.salon.com/2022/03/22/ukraines-kids-latest-target-for-the-christian-adoption-industry/

31. https://www.salon.com/2022/03/22/ukraines-kids-latest-target-for-the-christian-adoption-industry/

32. https://www.salon.com/2022/03/22/ukraines-kids-latest-target-for-the-christian-adoption-industry/

33. https://www.holtinternational.org/adoption/

34. https://www.worldschildren.org/child-trafficking-statistics/

35. https://adoption-beyond.org/what-countries-can-americans-not-adopt-from/

36. https://docs.house.gov/meetings/JU/JU01/20200923/111028/HHRG-116-JU01-20200923-SD005.pdf

37. https://www.nbcnews.com/news/asian-america/adoptee-adam-crapser-denied-relief-expected-be-deported-n673426

38. https://www.immigrationhelp.org/news/us-citizenship-processing-time

Chapter 9
Foster Care Alumni

*"Within the foster system,
I received care, but not parenting."*
~Hunter

Content warning: this chapter contains descriptions of physical and sexual abuse against children.

The termination of parental rights due to a determination of neglect or abuse creates severe consequences. It is the gravest and most serious responsibility of any governmental body to break apart a family for any reason. The presence of a county Child Protective Services (CPS) worker knocking on someone's front door is inherently frightening. If a child is separated from their parents, a sequence of events is set in motion that is traumatizing to every member of the family.

Statistics and Demographics

Foster care is intended to be temporary housing for a youngster if a family is in crisis. Conversely, adoption has always been intended to be the replacement of one family for another. The goals are, and always have been, different.

Federal funding for foster care was added to the national budget for the first time in the 1960s and provided for the state's financial burdens in caring for children in the system. By the 1970s there were approximately 500,000 children in the foster care system.[1]

Statistically, the numbers of children in the foster care system in the last twenty years has generally averaged between 400,000 to 450,000. The lowest number in the past twenty years was in 2022 with 369,000 children in foster care.[2] Contrast that with the overall child population (those aged zero to seventeen) in 2012 was about 74 million. Therefore, roughly .5% of the children in the US are in foster care, as an average.[3]

The public money spent on child welfare is substantial. In 2022, over 3 million children were involved in an investigation. Approximately 729,000 of them received some sort of services or assistance, and about 150,000 of them entered the system.[4] In 2024, the federal child welfare budget was $11 billion dollars,[5] which was less than 1% of the $5.6 trillion-dollar national budget.

However, the majority of the funding for foster care still comes from the states, and their budgets vary widely. The most recent number that can currently be quoted was from 2020 where the states spent $31.4 billion dollars on child welfare.[6] Potential impacts from the pandemic are not cited.

There are roughly twice the number of children in need of housing than there are homes for them. Households caring for multiple foster care children have become the norm.

Foster care adoptions are already the largest source for all adoptions in the US and often have the most challenges. The budgetary concerns, and the human costs of these vulnerable children and youths, make the topic of foster care in the context of adoption necessary.

The traumatizing circumstances experienced by these families ripple outward into society, creating consequences beyond their personal stories.

How They Got Here

Nationally, most youngsters placed into care are there because of a report of neglect rather than abuse. The statistics vary depending upon the source. One survey from the Department of Health and Human Services shows as of 2022, 63% of the children referred into the system were placed due to neglect:

Circumstances Associated with Child's Removal	Percent	Number
Neglect	63%	130,289
Drug Abuse (Parent)	36%	73,921
Caretaker Inability To Cope	14%	28,083
Physical Abuse	12%	25,836
Housing	9%	19,406
Child Behavior Problem	7%	15,375
Parent Incarceration	6%	12,142
Alcohol Abuse (Parent)	6%	11,922
Abandonment	5%	9,758
Sexual Abuse	4%	8,329
Drug Abuse (Child)	2%	4,637
Child Disability	2%	3,840
Parent Death	1%	2,513
Relinquishment	1%	1,789
Alcohol Abuse (Child)	0%	707

NOTE: These categories are not mutually exclusive, so percentages will total more than 100% and counts will be more than the total number of entries.

U.S. Department of Health and Human Services, Administration for Children and Families, Administration on Children, Youth and Families, Children's Bureau, https://www.acf.hhs.gov/cb
Preliminary Estimates for FY 2021 as of June 28, 2022 (29), Page 2

However, a different source, Casey Family Programs, which is a nonpartisan child welfare consultant agency, cites that 84% of all referrals to child welfare are due to neglect. They also state that 94% of all reports of child maltreatment do not have a repeat occurrence within six months.[7]

The distinctions between neglect and abuse are important. Neglect is influenced by a lack of resources, unemployment, drug and alcohol abuse, generational poverty, and the increasing costs of housing. If a family is struggling to make ends meet and, for example, is unable to keep basic utility services in place, is that neglect? Or a mother who works at night and leaves her children alone for a few hours because she is unable to find care for them or afford such. Is that neglect? What if the child is not attending school regularly or malnourished? These are the tougher questions that must be answered in real time when a CPS worker responds to a domestic situation they must evaluate. Hunter's story examines these issues.

This young boy was living in the Las Vegas area, and his mother likely worked as a sex worker in a nearby Nevada town where the profession is legal. He was largely left to himself and ended up in the foster care system along with his brother.

Hunter~

My mom would just leave. Now that I'm older I think she was a prostitute. I remember her throwing around the name Pahrump a few times. While she was gone, I would just roam the streets, walking into kids' yards and playing with their toys and stuff.

I didn't have shoes so I would pour water on my feet because the gravel by the road got hot when the sun hit it. So, I'd carry around water bottles and dump them on my feet.

Now that I think about it, I don't know what I ate. I would throw eggs in a plastic thing and microwave them sometimes. I remember eating a lot of bread and stuff. I remember it specifically being a problem, because for a year I couldn't grow. I was small for my age, about fifty pounds at eight or nine or something.

She was never violent with me or anything. She went out, earned her money, however that was, and then came home. But she wasn't hitting the cocaine in front of me. We were living in a trailer next to this junkyard.

My older brother was pretty good at going to school. He was just a lot more well behaved than I am. It was pretty far away to travel to school, that's why I didn't like doing it. Our mom had this giant box of mixed-up shoes, and I was not going to go through them. I just wouldn't go to school. I prefer to be a hood rat and go through people's yards. And if there was a kid playing, I would start playing with him. That's what I did on a day-to-day basis.

One time, during school hours, a cop saw me with no shoes on. They picked me up and I took him back to my little trailer in the junkyard. My mom wasn't there.

That day when she left, we were supposed to go to someone else's house. That didn't happen because I got in trouble. Then they went and got my brother, and they took us to Child Haven. This is why me and my brother aren't close. He blames me for getting taken from her because I didn't go to school, so, technically, it's my fault.

This was the second time that Hunter and his brother had ended up in the system. Eventually, their mother loses custody of both boys.

> The first lady that I stayed with, the foster mom, Miss Meredith. She just put us in a room with nothing. Just a bed and white walls and dressers. She would just lock us in there. We couldn't leave. We were not allowed to go watch TV or anything like that. There were two beds. So, she just kept you in your room with whoever else was there, and you weren't allowed to go out. But there were other kids there too, not just me.

Hunter went on to describe the fact that in both of his initial foster care placements, he was sexually abused by older, more powerful boys who were also in the foster system.

Hunter was certainly being neglected. He was malnourished and undoubtedly missing key developmental milestones from his chronic truancy. His mother's regular absences at home could have, and one could say likely would have, eventually led to other concerns or negative events in his life.

However, he was not being abused. That only happened after he entered the system. When one evaluates the treatment from his first foster care home, it is hard to argue for replacing one kind of neglect for the other.

Unfortunately, things didn't improve for him, as he ended up being in over a dozen different foster care homes before he aged out of the system at eighteen. At least two other sets of foster parents abused him during his tenure. Which then begs the question, was he really better off? Could there not have been a program that might have helped him and his mother and brother stay together in better circumstances? Did this mother deserve to lose custody of her children? Hunter and his brother end up separated, which is a disturbing trend in the foster care system.

Some children have good luck and receive loving care from the onset and are adopted by great parents. Here is a story of two baby twin girls who are likely alive today because their natural mother relinquished them to the system to protect them from a violent father.

Tracey and Stayce~
We did eventually find our biological mother and our older sister. From what we heard, our dad was very abusive. I believe there were a lot of drugs involved between my parents. At some point, my dad made my mom get in the car with all of us and threatened to break the leg of our older sister if my mom did not sign the adoption papers. She did and there was a stipulation that they had to keep us together.

Another thing we were told, apparently, we moved from hotel to hotel. But [our biological parents] would put us to sleep on the couch and leave. I don't know if they were gamblers, out drinking, or what. But we would wake up and there would be no one there and we would just cry for hours because we were alone.

He was Jewish, but somehow, we ended up being adopted through Mormon social services. The story was that he opened the phone book, put his finger down, and that's where it landed. We were in foster care for a while.

Apparently when we arrived, we were in rough shape. Our hair was so knotted they had to cut it. We were so filthy they had to just scrub us. We were not in good condition.

Whenever people would come to see us at the foster care home, we would run behind our foster mom and hide.

When our adoptive parents came and saw us, we actually ran up to them, called them mom and dad. We let them tie our shoes like it was meant to be.

We always knew we were adopted. But for the first year, every single night, one of us would cry. They would get us to sleep. Then the other one would cry. They would get us to sleep. Finally, we realized, "Oh, we're crying and someone's going to come." It took a year before we got past that. It was finally comforting to know that someone was going to be there for us and take care of us.

Our parents were always completely open and honest. We would talk about everything. To this day, we still do. There was no such thing as a secret in our house.

When we got to meet our biological mom, she was just so happy that we were together. That was her biggest thing.

The Impacts of the System

It is hard to go any length of time in the US without hearing a story about a tragedy caused by some failure of the foster care system. A child will be murdered at the hands of their natural parents, or by the foster caregivers. The media runs stories about overloaded case workers. The failures of the CPS system are paraded around for all to see. Criminal trials may or may not happen, and someone will likely be fired or go to jail. Politicians will criticize the policies of their predecessors and call for reforms. Then the world goes on. No one wants to see a child in danger, and public outrage at the unending systemic failings accomplishes nothing.

Just like with every other human endeavor, some case workers, foster, and adoptive families do good work helping these youngsters recover from their traumas. They display patience, fortitude, resilience, and compassion few appear to possess. Others fail miserably or cause more harm. Many will say, and not wrongly so, to fix the system. It should be fixed. *But how?*

How Bad is It?

The kids are not okay. Reports on child abuse nationally are grim, even with the understanding that most children are removed due to a determination of neglect rather than abuse.

An analysis of the 2010 National Child Abuse and Neglect Data System show that 80% of all perpetrators of abuse and/or neglect were the parents, 85% were biological parents, 4% were stepparents and 1% was cited to be adoptive parents. The remaining 10% were extended family or undefined as "other."[8] Note, data regarding rates of abuse of adoptive parents is not consistently or regularly gathered because they are legally "the parents" and no separate distinction is made. The report also says that a slight majority of the abusers were female, 54% versus 45% male.

Here are a few key facts about these youngsters' journeys and the impacts of their being in care:

- Up to 80% of children in foster care have mental health problems, compared to the

general population of 18-22%
- Because of these reported issues, foster youth are prescribed psychotropic medications more often than kids outside of the system, which costs millions of dollars a year in Medicaid expenses.
- Factors contributing to the mental and behavioral health of children and youth in foster care include the history of complex trauma, frequently changing situations, broken family relationships, inconsistent and inadequate access to mental health services and the over-prescription of psychotropic medications.
- Because of the complex traumas faced by children and youth in foster care, alumni experienced posttraumatic stress disorder at a rate nearly five times higher than the general adult population.[9]
- Maintaining relationships with relatives and kin can increase stability, reduce trauma, and help children maintain a sense of family, belonging, and identity.[10]

High numbers of abuse in foster care have been reported for years, and there does appear to be a correlation that the longer a young person is in the system the likelihood of abuse increases.

One study published in 2021 examined 184 homeless former foster youths from a drop-in center in Hollywood, California. Of the 173 who completed the reporting process, it appears nearly 60% of these youngsters were abused during their foster care journeys.[11]

Table 4 Abuse in foster care (n = 173)

	All youth (n = 173) n (%)
Foster care abuse	
Parent physical/sexual abuse	44 (32.12)
Sibling physical/sexual abuse	50 (36.76)
Verbal abuse	84 (60.43)
Group home abuse	
Group home staff physical/sexual	38 (27.74)
Group home residents physical/sexual	42 (30.15)
Verbal abuse	61 (44.85)
Kinship care	
Kinship caregiver physical/sexual abuse	35 (27.78)
Kinship- other family physical/sexual abuse	39 (30.95)
Kinship verbal abuse	54 (43.20)
Any abuse	94 (59.49)

Source: Yoshioka-Maxwell, A. (2022). Experiences of abuse: Homeless former Foster Youth and their experiences of abuse in out-of-home care. Child and Adolescent Social Work Journal, 40(6), 787–796. https://doi.org/10.1007/s10560-021-00810-8

Another study from 2016 separated the difference in reporting between the youths in the system, and the investigations by their caseworkers. The study followed nearly 400 youths who aged out of the system in Illinois and interviewed them two separate times.

Forty-six percent of these youths reported poor treatment from within the system but less than half of those, 21%, are backed up by case workers.[12] Kids *do* lie. However, these youngsters have already been removed from their homes, potentially having been neglected and/or abused. If then this happens to them *again*, and they are not believed, one can only imagine how powerless and invalidated these young people must feel.

The Influences of Poverty

Jerry Miller, the associate commissioner for the US Children's Bureau at DHH states, "The role that poverty plays in child welfare decision-making is a topic that has yet to be meaningfully confronted and addressed. Poverty is a risk factor for neglect, but poverty does not equate to neglect. The presence of poverty alone does not mean a child is unsafe, unloved, or that a parent lacks the capacity to care for his or her child. Poverty can make it more challenging for parents to meet certain of their children's needs. We must be resoundingly clear that a child should never be removed from his or her family due to poverty alone."[13]

It is a factor that is hard to define, as in Hunter's story. Sometimes poverty combined with crushing bad luck causes a child to end up in foster care. A story told here from the Human Rights Watch is another example of the struggles people face that can result in the removal of their children:

> "Amelia Smith, a fifty-two-year-old woman from Oklahoma, was the primary caregiver for her eight-year-old son, her aunt with Down Syndrome, and her forty-year-old husband, who had lupus. The demands of caring for her husband, aunt, and son left her unable to maintain paid employment, so she relied on public benefits for support. The family lived together in a modest mobile home without running water, but bought and stored water in large containers.
>
> Child Protective Services (CPS) came to their home for reasons Amelia still does not understand, but the condition of the home

> was a factor in the investigation. "They said [one reason] was because we had no running water, but I had like 12 gallons in my camper. Water wasn't the problem," Amelia...explained that they were looking for a bigger home to accommodate the family more comfortably, but they had not found a place they could afford.
>
> Instead of providing support and referrals for improving the condition of their home or addressing disruptions in their access to water, CPS removed James, their eight-year-old son, from their care...Amelia's husband passed away without seeing their son James again."[14]

The number of children separated from their families in the past two decades due to prenatal drug or alcohol abuse has doubled. In 2019, some 80,000 children, or one third of all removals are cited for this cause. As many as 80% of all foster care cases are estimated to have ties to drug or alcohol usage or abuse.[15]

Beyond the increasing drug and alcohol addiction rates, there is also the historic racial inequalities inherent within rates of poverty in the US.

Color Blind Ambition

Advocates for foster system reform have long pointed out the disparity of race in the rates of removal in families of color over the removal frequency in white families. From 2021, the statistics of children in foster care break down as follows:

Race/Ethnicity	Percent	Number
American Indian/Alaska Native	2%	9,393
Asian	1%	2,025
Black or African American	22%	86,645
Native Hawaiian/Other Pacific Islander	0%	987
Hispanic (of any race)	22%	85,215
White	43%	168,063
Unknown/Unable to Determine	2%	7,144
Two or More Races	8%	30,701

NOTE: All races exclude children of Hispanic origin. Children of Hispanic ethnicity [16]

According to the US Department of Health & Human Services, children of color disproportionately represent the number of youths in the system. African American youngsters are 14% of the total child populations yet account for 21% of the foster care system.[17]

According to the independent research provided by Casey Family Programs:

> "Black children are *more likely* to:
> - Be reported for maltreatment
> - Have their case investigated and substantiated
> - Be placed in foster care
> - Experience longer stays in foster care
>
> Black children are *less likely* to:
> - Experience placement stability
> - Engage with caseworkers
> - Reunite quickly with their families
> - Have access to resources and services to promote permanency"[18]

In 2011, Nassau County, New York became the first to pilot a program to specifically remove racial bias from the initial foster care decision making process. Jessica Pryce, director of the Florida Institute for Child Welfare at the Florida State University College of Social Work led the study along with a team of researchers.

According to data from New York State in 2010 black children were 14 times more likely than white children to be placed in foster care in Nassau County. Prior to the study, investigators would present cases to a committee made up of supervisors, a manager, and an attorney before a child could be removed and put into foster care.

The blind removal study specifically withheld any information that could indicate the race of the child or their family by presenting only the most basic facts, without mentioning the race, ethnicity, surnames, addresses or the location of the party reporting the potential incident. No information about where the child lived was visible along with whether the family was receiving public benefits or any other socioeconomic information. All that was left was the information about the risk factors to the child for their safety.

The results initially were dramatic. In 2010 the number of black children placed into care was 56.7%, and two years later in 2012, that had dropped to 45.5%, or nearly a 12% decline.

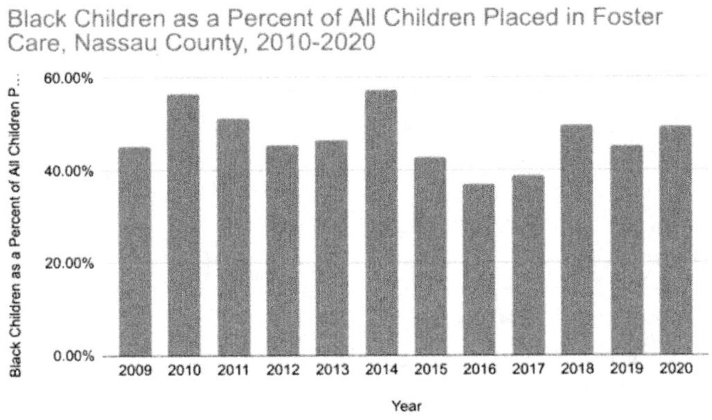

Source: Data provided by New York State Office of Children and Family Services

The long-term data shows that the numbers dropped initially but then peaked again in 2014. Then there is a series of both increases and declines from as low as 35.5% to a high of 61.9%. Experts disagree about how to interpret the data. Critics point out problems with the numbers because, overall, the total number of children referred into foster care in Nassau County dropped dramatically and steadily on an annual basis from 429 in 2009 to just 91 in 2020.[19] Which implies the numbers of foster care youths entering the system are likely influenced by other factors beyond only race.

Pryce has both detractors and supporters within the social work and child welfare community. Regardless, one can make the case that further study is needed, and other agencies across the US such as Los Angeles, Austin, Chicago, and Baltimore, to name a few, are beginning their own studies with their local populations.

The Lack of Consistency

Potentially larger than racial concerns are the lack of consistency within the training and operation of the case and social workers within the CPS system overall. In researching the book, two former social or case workers made themselves available, one of whom will be called Nancy to protect her identity. She ended her employment at a large metropolitan Department of Family Services in her county voluntarily and in good standing after a four-year career.

> **Nancy~**
> When I initially joined the department, I expected to join and work with a certain level of professionalism. I don't know that I always saw or received that, which was jarring from the beginning. I expected people would be

> able to come in and then follow policy and work with families as intended. And where I say professionalism, there was a lot of the human component that would come in where sometimes case workers would make decisions on cases just based on whether they like the family or not, whether they liked the bio parents or not, or the foster parents or not. And that was a struggle because you would butt up against other people, maybe supervisors or managers. You're trying to send a kid home, for example, but they've already got in their mind, they don't like this mom for whatever reason.

The other retired social worker from the Department of Family Services shared that during the early 2000s there was a renewed emphasis from the leadership in her state to focus on reducing removals and improving family preservation. She gladly adapted to these new policies, but said her supervisor refused. "He went on pushing for and removing kids from homes where I didn't see the need. Fortunately, he retired, and I took his place."

These stories get backed up by foster care youths who spend any time in the system where their care will be managed by several case workers, and they will observe differences in personalities that seem to affect their placements and treatment by their foster caregivers.

When talking with Nancy, she made many observations that reinforce the previously cited studies from several different angles.

> **Nancy~**
> If I had suggestions for improvements, it might

be emphasizing that once kids are removed from the custody of their parents and into foster care, it is much harder to send them back home. So, all efforts should be made upfront to keep kids home where possible, if they are safe. But sometimes it was hard. You cross the line of, "Well, are they really unsafe?" Or are you just imposing your own beliefs on what good parenting is? And we would take the kids. People can't think through the consequences of what that means later, terminating parental rights and all that comes with it.

I would say most of the time that initial contact was something to do with lack of resources is what they call it, as a general term. So, not having enough food, showing up to school with poor clothing. The school calls somebody because they're concerned. Not being able to pay your rent. A lot of the time, that's where it starts. Parents not being able to meet the needs of their family. Once they have that initial contact, an investigation begins, which may lead to, "Oh, now there's this we have to look at, or now there's maybe substance abuse or other things going on." But definitely, definitely poverty.

If it was significant child abuse or sexual abuse or a fatality in the family, that went to a special department. I don't know what the statistics were on that. But I wasn't going to affluent homes to knock on the door and check if kids were safe. It's the parents that are on welfare. It's the parents that are already struggling.

There were people I worked with that just said, "Well, that's what policy says and that's it. I'm not going to try to make a case or argue something differently or go out of my way to preserve the family."

That was a challenge for me sometimes. I understood the reasoning behind a lot of the policies—but saw a need to handle this case differently—how can we advocate for that? I had several times where I would go against the grain. But being transparent. The metric I always used was "unsafe." So, if people were trying to use their biases or their opinions, and mark that against policy, it was always, "Is there a safety risk?" Can we back up the fact that they are not in an unsafe situation, then let's push to get them home.

I think the case workers definitely make or break it. Sometimes you get a good one and sometimes you get a bad one. It ends up impacting everybody.

I get to be autonomous and no one's responsible for how I interact with somebody when I go into their home. That means I get to do whatever I want. Again, as long as the kids are safe, that was *my* metric. But that's a lot of variability across a department that has 800 people.

So, everybody's experienced something different. This parent thinks it's supposed to be this way. This foster parent thinks it's supposed to be that way. And that's not conducive to success because there's no standardization.

In attempting to understand what needs to be done to improve the foster care system and the services families receive, patterns do emerge that can help steer lawmakers, caseworkers, and their supervisors to improve these outcomes. They come down to a few key points shared in all the above study and commentary:

- Improve consistency, training, accountability, and focus the foster care workers on safety and family preservation whenever possible
- A greater understanding of how poverty and addiction are impacting people who are capable of parenting and finding ways to better support those families, and investing in their ability to do so
- Focusing directly on the youths in care to ensure their safety both within the system and in their original families

Siblings Separations

Of the ten foster care alumni interviewed for the book, *all* of them who had siblings were separated from their brothers or sisters. There was little or no attempt to keep them together, other than for the twins Tracey and Stacye. However, they had an older sister who eventually ended up two states away in a kinship placement, so they were still taken away from each other. The twins' adoptive parents had known about the older sibling and had their original adoption case worker looking for her, but because there is no sharing of foster care data between states, her status was unknowable.

As siblings move through the system, if they become

adopted, their names will be changed (sometimes both first and last names), the records will likely be sealed, and they will still have trouble locating one another. It becomes no different than any other adoption. But if they remember one another, that can be haunting to them, especially if no one acknowledges their recollections or is helpful to them in their searches.

Shellie~
I kept calling for my brother. I kept telling everybody that I had a brother. Later, I was told he went to live with his father. Of course I couldn't understand. Why didn't my father get me too? Why didn't my father want me? Or why couldn't I go with him?

Jeanette~
I got a strange phone call one day. This woman says, "I have information about your birth family. I would love to speak with you."

I'm thinking, "Who is this?"

She says, "I'll call the next day at 9 o'clock."

I'm waiting by the phone the next day and it rings. I answer it, and it's a man's voice. He says, "This is Patrick. I'm your brother."

I dropped the phone and just completely lost it. "Oh my God, I remember you." Because we had met once before, but that was all.

Desi~
My sister was placed with a family alone because they had been in the hospital I believe for twelve weeks. Upon release, she and my

> brother were placed separately. My sister was placed with a special needs family, because she needed 24-hours round the clock care.
>
> My brother was placed where I was because he was able to heal. So, we were placed together, he and I. Then I think it was three months later we were separated. I was moved to a new home because I was very, very hyper.
>
> I believe it was 2012, I started searching vigorously for my sister. I knew her name and I'm searching, searching, searching. Suddenly, I see her name but with a different last name. Same birthday, same county. She had an unusual first name. This must be her, and ultimately it was. But this was her obituary.

In Desi's family the mother violently abused two of her three children causing them permanent brain damage. Two survivors ended up doing well for themselves. However, one sister was adopted by a family ill-equipped to handle her special needs. She ended up dying in institutionalized care.

One of the hardest truths to reconcile, particularly within the foster care and foster to adopt system, are the random chances that seem to occur, both good and bad.

Adoptee Abuse

When adoptees are abused, it feels especially unfair because of the effort and process adoptive parents undergo supposedly protects them. To then find oneself growing up in a home surrounded by terror and abuse is horrific. This should never happen. But it does, and the child welfare system doesn't track it.

This goes back to the way adoption birth certificates are handled. There are no CPS workers, caseworkers, or agencies that specifically tracks rates of abuse perpetrated by adoptive parents.

Adoptive parents *are* the legal parents. There is no separate distinction to identify them legally within the system. Parents are parents, and the amended birth certificate says they are, and this is separate from foster care, legal guardians, stepparents or other persons who may be cohabiting with a child.

Foster care families are monitored *more* closely than adoptive ones. In most state jurisdictions, once the paperwork on an adoption is complete, no one checks on that family again. A few states do require follow up visits, but they are in the minority.

The home study procedure that screens both foster and adoptive parents is essentially the same. Adoptive and foster parents will talk at length about the paperwork, background checks, interviews, checks of the home and other intrusive examinations they go through. They feel good about passing that and their blessing and qualifications of being cleared to foster or adopt. Natural parents do not have to withstand such scrutiny.

Abuse rates nationally estimate that 16.5% of children are physically abused, and 9.4% experience sexual abuse.[20]

In researching the book, 60 adopted adults were interviewed. Of them, seven were abused by their adoptive families, a rate of 12%, three experienced sexual abuse (5%), and thirteen adopted adults were raised in dysfunctional homes where addiction, domestic violence or mental illness was present, a rate of 22%. While anecdotal, these numbers show there may not be as much security in an adoptive home as assumed.

Adoptions typically involve wealthier families, and a CPS worker is far less likely to come knocking on their door. Even if a report is made, in general, no one is asking if this happens to be a family where adoption is present unless there are obvious multicultural differences. But if asked, there is no formal mechanism for tracking that data.

It is a delicate balance because no one should "other-ize" an adoptive family for any reason. However, surely there can be improvements as it deserves better tracking and awareness.

One final note: If one listens in on adoptee support groups and other gatherings, stories will be shared, particularly by female adoptees, about uncomfortable situations with their adoptive fathers or other male figures in their extended families. Without any blood ties, male cousins, uncles, or grandfathers may feel more permissive about inappropriate sexual contact. Lacking this protection is something adoptive parents should be aware of and occasionally check in with their young person in a thoughtful manner.

A Tale of Two Sisters

One of the most traumatizing and inspiring interviews recorded for the book were the stories told by Jessica and Sara. Born from the same mother about five years apart, their mother was a victim of sexual abuse from *her* father, who then spent her life off track, addicted to drugs, and was both in and out of jail throughout her adulthood. Eventually, she lost custody of all six of her natural children. Unacknowledged and unhealed trauma almost always affects future generations, and this family's story shows how dangerous this becomes.

Jessica~

My mother was a junkie, and I was born in prison. I went to my grandfather, her father, and his girlfriend. She was burning me with curling irons. I wasn't taken from my mother because of drugs. I was taken because of marks on my body and then it came out that my grandfather was molesting me, and that was at three years old.

I was put into the system at that point. My mother was still in prison. My dad was a junkie. I go into the system, and I'm adopted by Jim and Sandra at four years old. I was a beautiful, little platinum-blonde haired girl. They had a lot of money. There were domestic violence cases already open on them. They should not have been able to adopt me.

And seriously, the social worker was friends with my adopted mother. It got swept under the rug. They were multi-millionaires in Glendora, California. We lived in a million-dollar home, and I was adopted at age four. At five, I changed my name. I didn't want to be Sheila anymore. I was born Sheila Marie, and I changed my name to Jessica Lynn.

At age five, my adopted father started touching me and I remember because of my grandfather already touching me, it kind of felt normal. I told my adoptive mom at about age six that my adopted dad was touching me, and she didn't believe me. She put me in a bathtub of vinegar because my genitals were rubbed raw from him and sadly myself

> because the stimulation as a child, I was used to it. She did see marks on me, and she punished me because she thought it was because of my grandfather. She made me apologize to [my adopted father] and he knew what he was doing. I had a beautiful-looking childhood that was just riddled with rape.
>
> My adopted mom, Sandra, was violent. She would hit me, slap me across the face. She put my head into the bricks in the kitchen. Spatulas. Whatever. But I never told her about him, again. There was so much domestic violence going on between them. He would beat her up, and the next morning she'd be in the kitchen making him eggs and toast. It was normal.
>
> I had an adopted brother and an adopted sister. I'm pretty sure he got to her too. She is not okay. I learned to adapt to it and use it. I mean, if it's going to happen anyway...that's where the shame comes in. The self hate. Because I knew if I allowed it, I could get things and not be punished. So, it just continued. It took a long time for me to admit that and just accept it. I really had no choice.

Sara's story starts out similarly, although she is five years younger than her sister Jessica and is the second child of their mother. When Jessica is ten, she does meet her biological mother at some point, and visits with her a few times, even though she is still unstable and using drugs. Both Sara and Jessica have pieced bits of their stories together, even though their memories are often hazy, and the timelines are unclear. But they do know there was some interaction with one another during parts of their childhood.

Sara~

My mother had drug issues, and to my understanding, she was even in and out of prison while pregnant with me. She ended up going into labor. They took her to the hospital, and then she had to go back.

I know I was born addicted to heroin and methamphetamine, and they had to do certain things to save me or keep me alive. I was premature at birth, and under five pounds so they had to make sure I would be okay. I was kind of in and out for the first two years.

That's when I was first in a foster home, Child Haven, and then they assigned me to a family as a foster child, and they eventually adopted me. My parents had just signed up to become foster parents, and I was their first foster kid out of the 25 total years of fostering they did.

They had me for about a year, and then my mom got custody of me again. I went back at about age three, and she did well for a little while, but lost me again by age four.

Because I had already been with the first foster family, the social worker asked them to take me again. Because I would feel familiar and safe rather than rehoming me. So that's how I went back there.

I guess immediately they were looking into adoption and how they could keep me from going back and forth again. I was four now. I had to do some speaking and stuff in

> the courts to CPS. I had reported that [my natural mom] was locking me in closets for hours, saying we were playing hide and seek. It was clear I wasn't being fed properly. When I was two, [before I went back to my mom] I was speaking all these words and starting to say sentences. By the time I came back [to the foster care family] when I was four, I had regressed extremely in my speech and was even mute for a while. I was in speech classes until third grade.
>
> I was also extremely afraid of men. I would cry and scream when my parents would take us to church because I was supposed to shake the missionaries hands upon entering. I'd completely freak out.

Sara gets lucky and is adopted by good parents and a good family. Jessica has the opposite experience. Her adopters are abusive and cruel, almost beyond comprehension. Everyone deserves better than what happened to Jessica.

These young girls grow up in different states, one in California and the other in Nevada. They have little to no communication, and as their biological mother's life unfolds, all her children become lost to her and to each other. Jessica and Sara, now grown women, struggled themselves with alcohol and drug addiction during their younger lives. However, both now are success stories in much different ways. They each have a decade or more, clean and sober. They have worked hard to heal themselves from the early dysfunction of their lives and have bonded in the most unusual and heartwarming ways. They have found two of their siblings, but they are still searching for the other two.

Jessica does eventually report her adoptive father's actions to the authorities and a trial is held. He is not convicted of the charges of abuse against her due to the lack of physical evidence by the time of the trial.

> **Jessica~**
> I really hope that I can let all of this here because I was not heard, and justice was not served. I want you to know—talking about this, you're helping me.

The voices of these marginalized people deserve to be heard and taken seriously. Helping children who need a safe home is always a worthy cause. But our CPS system needs to be more forthright about its failures and become more creative to find better solutions.

---

1. Adoption history: Fostering and Foster Care. (n.d.). https://pages.uoregon.edu/adoption/topics/fostering.htm

2. Trends in Foster Care and adoption: FY 2013 – 2022. The Administration for Children and Families. (n.d.). https://www.acf.hhs.gov/cb/report/trends-foster-care-adoption

3. Child welfare: Purposes, federal programs, and funding. (n.d.-b). https://sgp.fas.org/crs/misc/IF10590.pdf

4. Kpontecorvo@casey.org. (2024, July 16). Foster Care State Data. Casey Family Programs. https://www.casey.org/state-data/

5. Child welfare: Purposes, federal programs, and funding. (n.d.-b). https://sgp.fas.org/crs/misc/IF10590.pdf

6. Child welfare: Purposes, federal programs, and funding. (n.d.-b). https://sgp.fas.org/crs/misc/IF10590.pdf

7. Kpontecorvo@casey.org. (2024, July 16). Foster Care State Data. Casey Family Programs. https://www.casey.org/state-data/

8. Zuckerman, D. (2017, August 2). Child abuse and father figures: Which kind of families are safest to grow up in?. National Center for Health Research. https://www.center4research.org/child-abuse-father-figures-kind-families-safest-grow/

9. Brief mental health and foster care. National Conference of State Legislatures. (n.d.). https://www.ncsl.org/human-services/mental-health-and-foster-care

10. Recommendations-improving-permanency-well-Being.pdf. (n.d.-e). https://www.acf.hhs.gov/sites/default/files/documents/cb/Recommendations-Improving-Permanency-Well-Being.pdf

11. Yoshioka-Maxwell, A. (2022). Experiences of abuse: Homeless former Foster Youth and their experiences of abuse in out-of-home care. *Child and Adolescent Social Work Journal, 40*(6), 787–796. https://doi.org/10.1007/s10560-021-00810-8

12. Havlicek, J., & Courtney, M. E. (2016). Maltreatment histories of aging out foster youth: A comparison of official investigated reports and self-reports of maltreatment prior to and during out-of-home care. Child Abuse & Neglect, 52, 110–122. https://doi.org/10.1016/j.chiabu.2015.12.006

13. Writer, G. (2020, January 22). Time for the child welfare system to stop confusing poverty with neglect. The Imprint. https://imprintnews.org/child-welfare-2/time-for-child-welfare-system-to-stop-confusing-poverty-with-neglect/40222

14. Naveed, H. (2023, June 28). "if I wasn't poor, I wouldn't be unfit." Human Rights Watch. https://www.hrw.org/report/2022/11/17/if-i-wasnt-poor-i-wouldnt-be-unfit/family-separation-crisis-us-child-welfare

15. Naveed, H. (2023, June 28). "if I wasn't poor, I wouldn't be unfit." Human Rights Watch. https://www.hrw.org/report/2022/11/17/if-i-wasnt-poor-i-wouldnt-be-unfit/family-separation-crisis-us-child-welfare

16. Children in foster care on September 30, 2021, AFCARS report - the administration for children and families. (n.d.-b). https://www.acf.hhs.gov/sites/default/files/documents/cb/afcars-report-29.pdf

17. Children in foster care on September 30, 2021, AFCARS report - the administration for children and families. (n.d.-b). https://www.acf.hhs.gov/sites/default/files/documents/cb/afcars-report-29.pdf

18. Sbrown@casey.org. (2024, May 23). Blind removals process. Casey Family Programs. https://www.casey.org/blind-removals-nassau/

19. Childwelfaremonitor. (2021, July 27). The power of wishful thinking: The case of "race-blind removals" in child welfare. Child Welfare Monitor. https://childwelfaremonitor.org/2021/07/27/the-power-of-wishful-thinking-the-case-of-race-blind-removals-in-child-welfare/

20. Day, E., Tach, L., & Mihalec-Adkins, B. (2022). State Child Welfare Policies and the Measurement of Child Maltreatment in the United States. Child Maltreatment, 27(3), 411-422. https://doi.org/10.1177/10775595211006464

Part III – Birth Parents

Chapter 10
The Evolution of Adoption: The Baby Scoop to Open Adoptions

"Not raising one's own child does not make any more sense than not being raised by one's own mother. Both are cognitively impossible to understand." ~Dr. Joe Soll

Of all the people in the triad between adoptees and their two sets of parents, birth mothers and fathers are by far the least studied. Expectant parents that consider placing their child for adoption are a highly diverse and complex group. They do not fit peoples' assumptions.

Many who have relinquished a child find the term 'Birth Parent' offensive. Agencies and social workers created the name back in the Baby Scoop Era. Many now prefer the terms "First Family, First Mother/Father or Natural Mother/Father." This book uses the "Birth Parent" term only to simplify the distinction of roles in the constellation.

At the root of all adoptions is a set of expecting parents. Fathers may not be aware of the pregnancy while others are highly involved. Some mothers immediately know they wish to parent, while others may be uncertain. Regardless, they deserve respect, support, and people invested in their needs.

Everything referenced in this portion of the book is talking about infant adoption only, except when noted.

Birth parents are often assumed to be of defective character or, alternately, glorified for their selfless bravery and love for their child. The truth lies somewhere in the middle. To begin, it is important to start where the highest volume of adoptions occurred, because the practices still shape the modern adoption landscape.

Birth Mothers in the Baby Scoop Era

One can draw a line between the way adoption was practiced prior to the 1970s, and then after. The stories of mothers in the Baby Scoop Era have been covered by several books. The most notable is the groundbreaking work by Ann Fessler, *The Girls Who Went Away*. In it, she combines research along with over two hundred interviews with women who relinquished in those years.

To share that perspective, here are a few stories representing the common practices, pains, and biases that impacted these birth mothers.

In the first story, Yvonne had been accepted to medical school when she found out she was pregnant. Her childhood sweetheart served in Vietnam and returned from the war in 1968, a different person having experienced the trauma of a war veteran.

> **Yvonne~**
>
> We were in love. Once I had finished my medical studies in May of 1973, I realized I was pregnant. At that time, he quite frankly was just in and out of the relationship, and I was not able to force him into being there.
>
> When I discovered I was pregnant, I went to my doctor who ended up being my mentor.
>
> I come from a very dysfunctional, non-communicative family. When I shared with my parents, both my mom and my dad separately, I got a blank face. It was like a blank wall.
>
> "I'm pregnant," I said.

Nothing.

"Did you hear me? I'm pregnant."

I went back to my doctor and said, "I'm not getting any support."

"What are you going to do?" he asked.

"I don't know. I want to keep my child, but I don't have any support." He happened to have a couple or a woman he was treating, he was an OBGYN. I think they'd been married for a few years and were trying to conceive and had not. He mentions this family—that they will give my child a good home. It ended up being a private adoption.

[After the birth] I didn't see my son. I heard him cry. And the situation was that I really thought I had signed the preliminary papers...

I got a call that I needed to pick him up at the maternity ward. So, I went back twelve days later. He had to stay because he had jaundice. I was checking daily how he was doing. When he was ready to leave, I went up and I saw my son for the first and last time.

After I picked him up in the maternity ward and came down in the elevator, I stared at every inch of his face. I was memorizing his face, his nose. I ended up meeting the paralegal in the lobby of the hospital and that was the last time I saw him. There are no words. It was the heartbreak of seeing him and realizing it was the last time, not knowing if I would ever again. That was all sinking in. I bought this yellow plaid blanket to wrap him in and some onesies and diapers. But that walk out of the hospital without him…empty arms are what I call it. Empty arms. Empty arms.

Below, Cathryn's story exemplifies the typical reactions at the time to a young woman from a good religious upbringing faced if she became pregnant while unmarried.

Cathryn~

I was eighteen and almost through my first year of nursing school. We had met at a high school dance a few years earlier. When we had sex finally, I suffered terribly with guilt. This was in 1968. To not be a virgin was a horrible, shameful thing.

I got pregnant and I was horrified. My boyfriend was horrified, our parents were horrified. They asked what we were going to do. He said he couldn't get married. They shouted, "Get out, don't ever come back!" And that was the end of that. I wish, in retrospect, there could have been some reasonable discussion. I didn't know anybody who had a baby out of wedlock and kept the child.

My mother's cousin was a priest, and he gave her the solution, which was to go to Roselia, a home for unwed mothers. My siblings didn't know. I made up stories. I went away.

I was alone. My mother didn't want to see me while I was pregnant, and my shame just kept going on and on. I was Catholic, so I couldn't be punished enough for my own satisfaction.

I was in labor for forty hours, and I was

alone. Nobody came.

The baby was born. I was put under ether for the birth. I woke up, there was no crying, there was just staff around me cleaning up, because, back then, you would go into a delivery room, which was like an operating room.

I said, "What happened?"

They said, "You're all done. You're ready to go back to your room."

I asked why I didn't hear any crying.

They said, "You didn't want to see her, did you?"

"I had a girl? I had a girl?" But I was a Roselia girl, so I said, "No, I guess not." They gave me a shot so my milk wouldn't come in.

I was taken through the service entrance, in the back of the hospital where the delivery trucks were. As I got in the cab, to go back to Roselia, this woman came running out from the hospital with this baby in her arms. She's screaming, "Wait, wait, you have to take your baby. Don't leave yet."

I was told over and over in Roselia, "Don't look at your baby, and for heaven's sake, don't hold your baby. And don't feed your baby, you'll never be able to give her up." That was hammered into my mind.

The nurse said, "You have to take your baby."

I said, "No, I can't do that." She was really aggravated. It was in January—it was cold out.

"Why not?" she said. "What are you talking about?"

I said, "They told me not to. They said to never hold your baby and don't even look at your baby."

"Who said that? That's ridiculous."

"Everybody says it over at Roselia."

"No. Come on now, let's get her out of the cold." So, she put her in my arms, and that's all the time I had. The few minutes that it took to ride in a cab in the backseat, from Mercy Hospital to Roselia, and she had a blanket over her head.

I pulled the cover down, and there she was, she was nine and a half pounds. She was beautiful. That was hard. I said goodbye to her and pictured how our lives would go. We would be on two separate paths, and I would never know her. I had been working for all that time in my head to convince myself that this was not my baby, this was somebody else's. Somebody was going to take her and love her and raise her. I didn't know anything about adoption.

By then I was nineteen and thought I was grown up, but I was a child too.

It was common that these young women were hidden or physically sent away to hide their pregnancy. They were given no choices, and it was rare they had any contact or knowledge of where their baby went after it was born.

After the Scoop

Important changes occurred in American culture in the mid-1970s and '80s. While hardly celebrated, an unmarried woman who had children, or was clearly pregnant, didn't need to be hidden or sent away. Single mothers began to be tolerated, bringing huge cultural changes. The vast majority of homes for unwed mothers closed. For the first time, young women kept their babies in large numbers.

However, closed adoptions continued, and many of the larger non-profit organizations, both religious and secular, transitioned into being large, full-service agencies. Jewish Family Services, Catholic Charities, or Lutheran Family Services became the most common places to facilitate adoption. Larger, more global agencies appeared such as Bethany Christian Services or the Gladney Center for Adoption.

Gradually, policies changed in how agencies, birth, and adoptive parents interacted. For the first time a birth mother or set of expectant parents got a say in who would receive their child. This transition was gigantic because some level of control was now placed into the hands of the natural mother. She could see a bio of wanting parents and some basic information about them.

The agency shows an expectant mother a collection of hopeful parents that the agency has qualified. From that, she can learn something of who they are or read a letter about why they wish to adopt. She learns what city they live in, their education levels, and religious affiliations.

Some level of openness in adoption is born. Expectant mothers and their prospective adoptive parents begin to have limited contact. Phone calls, letters, and even meetings have become more common. This bond is a delicate and precarious thing. It can be used to help share genuine care between these families. Or it can be used to manipulate.

In theory, this limited level of contact can give that

mother a small amount of peace. It is also a tapestry of emotions brimming with desperation, heartache, and desire. One can hope in the best circumstances, that a bond forms between two sets of people that are experiencing something extraordinary over the love of their child.

Ellen~

My parents were migrant workers. I had a very unusual childhood. I didn't grow up in one town. I didn't have any friends. My parents split when I was nine. From that point until I was seventeen, I was passed from one family to another. I finished the last few months of high school on my own—sleeping on couches. I got pregnant, no support system, no family. One of the girl's mothers that I worked with had a friend who was an attorney. I said, "There's no way I can keep this child." I was living hand-to-mouth. Once or twice a month, I would go down to the welfare office and get food. I was not going to bring a child into this world and then subject it to the life I had been living.

She set me up with an attorney who arranged all the paperwork, contacted the adoptive parents, and we executed a contract when I was about five months pregnant. They called me once a week, every week, right up until the time the child was born.

They were wonderful. They were an older couple who did not think they could have children. They had tried and tried and couldn't get pregnant. Very thoughtful, very attentive. It was always a very caring conversation when they called.

Now, did they care about me, or did they care about making sure that I gave them a healthy baby? I didn't know. I have since met this couple and all those thoughts are long gone. They were always concerned about me.

Shellie, Adoptee, Birth Mother~

I wanted to pick his parents because I wanted them to understand the baby I'm giving you, you must love as your own, treat as your own—if you can't do that, you can't have him. The family I chose had two older children at the time, and they already had a mixed child. So, I knew that there wouldn't be as many questions.

[The adopting mother] showed me what it was to be a mother because she would call and check on me. She told me, "It doesn't matter if you choose us or somebody else. Right now, you need a mom. You need to be loved." She did that every day until I gave them my son. They allowed me to name him. They renamed him, but they allowed me to name him so he would have a birth certificate from me, a letter that I wrote him, and a quilt I made him.

His mom was a wonderful woman. She always kept up with me to know where I was because of the deal that I made with her. He was to know about me, but he was not allowed to meet me until he was eighteen. I gave him to a family that could love him.

Beginning in the 1990s, a completely new concept was

introduced into the adoption ecosystem. There would now be fully open adoptions, semi-open adoptions, and closed adoptions.

Open Adoption

- An adoption is considered open when there is a high level of communication in the relationship between a birth mother and the parents who are raising her child.
- The birth mother or father has contact information for the family and can reach out to the adopting parents when she or he likes.
- An open adoption relationship can include phone or video chats, texts, and visits.
- The child grows up knowing their birth parent(s) and the relationship evolves naturally.

Semi-Open Adoption

- A semi-open adoption is one where the birth mother and adopting parents have contact during her pregnancy and they usually meet in person before or right after the birth.
- They exchange calls and/or texts during this time.
- After the adoption, the adoptive parents send updates so the birth parent(s) can be aware of how their child is doing as they grow.

Closed Adoption

- In a closed adoption no information or contact is shared between adoptive parents and birth parents.

This increasing contact between birth parents and others in the adoption system was created, in part, to reduce the appearance of coercion. It was also intended, benevolently, to relieve the emotional pain and grief that a birth mother, in particular, experiences after relinquishing her child.

Many birth mothers report some sense of relief from even a semi-open adoption as they receive photos, letters, and updates. Most of this type of semi-open communication is handled by the agency who facilitates the adoption. The case worker is responsible for taking in all such communications between these two families and passing it on.

Some first mothers do report some sense of peace in picking out birthday cards for their child. Letters, homemade gifts, and presents representing their love and care can be passed on.

But all this communication depends on several factors. First, that the agency and case worker will forward the information. Second, that the birth parents or mother who wishes to remain in contact keeps her address and information current with the agency. Third, that the same effort is maintained by the adopting family as well.

Much can go right or wrong with this process. If a birth mother's life is already unstable, then she may not keep her contact information current with the agency. She may feel unworthy of contact. Also, adopting parents do not always keep their word. They may promise pictures, letters, and updates, but they do not materialize. Or they may move and not stay in touch with the agency or the birth mother. Compounding these issues are the actions of sometimes unethical lawyers, agencies, or caseworkers who fail to keep their promises.

Even with all these uncertainties and risk factors, ninety-five percent of all adoptions are now open to some degree. Some are more successful than others, and the complexities and consequences are never simple.

Chapter 11
Demographics, Myths and Reasons for Relinquishment

Judge not, if you're not ready for judgment. The road of life is rocky, and you may stumble too, so while you talk about me, someone else is judging you. ~ Bob Marley

The paradoxical treatment of birth mothers is even more confusing than what adoptees experience. Adopted children are told that their mothers loved them so much they gave them away, selflessly, to be raised by someone else. Birth mothers receive a much different message. They are often told they cannot possibly raise their child, or they are unworthy. A young, unmarried woman relinquishes her child due, in part or entirely, to these societal pressures. But what if in only a year or two after relinquishment she marries and begins a family. It's a trick of time and circumstance. What changed in terms of her ability to *mother*?

In one moment, she is worthless and unfit, then in the latter, celebrated as a "wonderful mom." However, she is the same person. The line is drawn in the physical world—the house, the job, the financial stability that makes it less stressful to build a family. But these are not matters of the heart, yet the heart and soul are what is shamed.

Many birth mothers will say endlessly that if someone had supported them, just a little, they would have been able to keep their baby. Maybe that support can be physical, such as her partner or family rallying behind her, or emotional or financial help.

But once they have relinquished, they will hear from society and all around them that they were brave and loving and noble for placing their child for adoption. They are also surrounded by the majority of women who say, "Oh, but I could never do that. Give away my newborn baby? Not me." These contradictions cannot coexist, but they are the shoes that all birth parents are forced to wear.

Then they must watch all the world celebrate the adopting parents. There is joy and nothing but rainbows and sunshine for them.

These contradictions and myths deserve to be pulled into the light of day and seen clearly. But who are modern birth parents?

Demographics

The average age of a woman who places a child for adoption is 26 (range 10 - 49). This is according to a survey completed in 2023 by the National Council For Adoption (NCFA). It was completed using both focus groups and a nationwide survey of 1,160 birth mothers and 239 birth fathers in the United States.[1]

Birth mothers are no longer teen-aged girls "in trouble." The age statistic shows they are more mature adults who hold jobs and, while young, are out on their own living responsible lives.

From the NCFA poll respondents, the ethnicity of those birth parents are:

Mothers	**Fathers**
70% White	40% White
12% Black	20% Black
5% Hispanic	18% Native American
5% Asian/Pacific Islander	12% Hispanic
4% Native American	7% Asian/ Pacific Islander
4% Multiracial	3% Multiracial

These expectant parents are also educated. 83% of the

mothers polled had an associate degree or some college, 20% of them having a graduate degree. Fathers also are generally well educated, with 64% of them having some college attendance, 14% of whom also have a graduate degree.[2]

The organization Saving Our Sisters (SOS) supports all members of expectant families and provides information and education to expecting parents considering adoption. From their internal statistics gathered in 2024, when looking at where birth mothers are living at the time before relinquishment, 54% of the women are renting an apartment. 15% are living with family members, 6% are unhoused, 6% are homeowners, and the balance are in some other temporary living situation.

What is more interesting is that nearly *22% of them are married, and 58% of them are already parenting one child.*[3]

All of this combines to paint a picture that does not align with what many people think of when they hear the term "birth parent." They are not "druggies," nor criminals or derelicts. They are functional, blend into society, and most people will not recognize their circumstances. Yet, they are struggling for some support, otherwise they would not consider adoption.

Myths and Lies

Myth: Birth parents want to be hidden.

One of the biggest myths of modern adoption is that birth parents want confidentiality. That has rarely been true. There are instances where because a woman is afraid of an abusive partner, she wishes for an anonymous, closed adoption, but this is infrequent. Overall, less than five percent of adoptions today are closed. Most are open to some degree.[4]

The harsh truth is that keeping birth parents powerless and nameless ghosts is convenient. Even during the Baby

Scoop Era when millions of young women were pushed into relinquishment, they were never promised confidentiality. Keeping these women sidelined was easier for case workers, adoption agencies, parents, and everyone managing the adoption system.

If one visits the Concerned United Birthparents (CUB) website, they declare this clearly for all to see.[5] They advocate for changing laws that deny adopted adults access to their original birth certificates. One important quote from their site states, "We often hear well-meaning people cite "protecting birth/first parent privacy" in opposition to restoring equality to adopted persons. We believe those people are *confusing privacy with secrecy*. Privacy refers to the ability to control information about oneself. Secrecy is the deliberate act of hiding something from others even if they have a legitimate reason to access it. Secrecy is literally what state policy keeps legalized by failing to restore rights to adult adopted persons. It is their birthright to know the truth."

Renee~

There are still so many things wrong with the adoption process of sealing birth certificates. I never knew my son's birth certificate would be sealed. I never knew why they wouldn't let his dad, *who was sitting in the hospital room,* be put on the birth certificate. Mind you, this is 2011.

I said, "He's right there. Everybody knows who he is, why can't he be put on the birth certificate?" In Florida, my son can't get his birth certificate currently. He can't get it whether he is eighteen or eighty. He must go to court.

First, he has to reunite with me. He needs to find me. Then, he has to get my permission. (His letter is already written for him,

> and I keep it in a file.) But then, he's got to go to court, and a judge has to say, "Yes. This is okay for you to have." Which is ridiculous.

If one doubts the sincerity that birth parents wish to have their "privacy" undone, one need look no further for evidence than the numbers who join adoptees lobbying states to open access to their original birth certificates. A recent example is here:

- Connecticut Bill 6105 passed the state House in 2021, in part due to the Catholic Mothers for Truth and Transparency, CUB, and dozens of other support groups. In an article from the CT Mirror, "While we did not feel we had other options, we knowingly signed those papers. Most of us have never seen them… We did not know then, nor do we believe now, that we retained any kind of control over our sons' and daughters' right to get their original birth certificate as adults." It goes on to say, "…House Bill 6105…is exactly the kind of legacy the Connecticut General Assembly should leave on our collective consciousness as a nation reckoning with its history of shaming women into the shadows of silence and secrecy. It starts with acknowledging truth and it ends with being on the right side of history. We promise."[6]

Myth: Birth parents forget what happened and move on with their lives.

Another lie is that these parents go on to forget the child they placed for adoption. A multitude of studies have shown that to be absurdly false for both birth fathers and mothers. They never forget their child. In fact, they are permanently scarred and pay a high emotional, physical, and psychological price. It is important to understand that both men and women will say "my son" or "my daughter" when speaking of the children they have relinquished. *They are parents forever.*

One survey conducted in 1984 cited that 96% of a sample of 334 birth parents responded that they had considered searching for their relinquished child, and 65% of them had initiated a search.[7] Birth parents grieve for their child for extremely long times. One study in 2007 showed birth mothers who were twelve to twenty years post placement still experienced feelings of grief and loss.[8]

> **Renee~**
> There was very little support afterwards. I had a few counseling sessions. I had one counseling session prior to the adoption, it was one forty-five-minute session with a lady who had placed a child for adoption. She pretty much told me that I knew exactly why I was doing it, and that I was a cognitive realist. It was really something. Of course, her door was right next to the adoption agency door in the office building, so a bit of a relationship there but it was really, really tough going through all of that.
>
> The immediate effects after the adoption—the old me died. I say that all the time. I sat on my living room floor making these screams and sounds I'd never heard myself make. It was a very dark time. I didn't parent. I didn't eat. I didn't sleep. I wasn't doing anything but just dying.

Myth: Birth parents never wanted to keep their baby.

The final myth that needs to go by the wayside is the idea that these birth mothers never wanted to parent in the first place. While clearly unplanned, most of them feel bonded, quickly, with their newfound pregnancy. They want to mother. They also constantly worry about their ability to provide the best possible life for their child.

Interviews and studies all show a consistent story. The reason why an expectant couple, or woman, decides to place their baby for adoption is because they don't feel they can give their child the life it deserves. How that looks to each of these people is different. Adoption was the last option when all other avenues had been exhausted.

Reasons For Relinquishment

A study conducted in 2018 by The Donaldson Adoption Institute (DAI) surveyed 223 birth mothers who had relinquished a child within the last twenty-five years (post 1993). Of them, 79.4% knew they were pregnant within the first trimester of their pregnancy. More than two-thirds of them, 87.6%, said they seriously considered options other than adoption, the majority of which was to parent their child.[9]

In the same study it is also noted that four out of five of them listed financial stability as a major reason why mothers first considered, and ultimately chose, to place their child for adoption. The overwhelming majority stated they would have liked to have learned more about potential resources to help them parent.[10]

According to one participating birth mother, she shares, "I think if I had more help and resources, and the ability to not have the prospective parents (and my parents) pressure me the way they did, I think my life would be very different."[11]

According to a 2015 study, the factors these parents faced were unemployment, low-paying jobs, a lack of health insurance, and no parental support.[12]

An article published on The Adoption Alliance in November 2020 shares the top ten reasons why a woman relinquishes her child for adoption:

1. Cannot afford to raise a baby
2. Too young to be a mother
3. The environment at home is not suitable for a baby
4. Don't feel a strong connection with the baby
5. The baby has special needs that she will not be able to meet
6. Don't want their baby to live in a one-parent family
7. Support system of family and friends is unstable
8. Pregnancy is a result of a sexual assault
9. Abortion or being a parent are simply not options
10. Don't want to jeopardize their future[13]

After seeing this information, the most common reaction is confusion. Afterall, does America not have a social safety net that is supposed to help people?

These programs for families are managed by the Department of Health and Human Services. Annually, 15% of its budget is used for the foster care system. Only 1% of its budget is being spent to help strengthen families to remain financially stable.[14]

A report from The Brookings Institution shares that reductions in poverty for families has been shown to promote stronger educational, emotional, and health outcomes.[15] One can expand that to say when a more financially sound family is created, everyone does better. Some will say this becomes an argument to relinquish a child to a financially stronger, two-parent home. It is clearly one of the many aspects that these expectant parents are weighing with great care.

But relinquishment comes at the potential psychological expense to that now adopted infant, and with the additional emotional cost for that birth parent. Why not instead support the first family to be more financially capable of supporting itself, rather than pass around these high emotional costs? These are questions that any society who wishes to claim itself as a moral one ought to at least examine. The trauma created by separation affects generations of families.

Money does not solve all problems. What it does do is provide people with options. To afford better housing in safer neighborhoods. Better access to educational opportunities, more reliable transportation, which can lead to higher paying jobs with better benefits.

One of the most fundamental beliefs that Americans hold dear is the idea that anyone can make it. Someone can be raised in poverty and still become successful. Most people at one time in their lives have had some financial struggles, but these situations are often temporary. The decision to relinquish one's child is forever. All of this combines to create scenarios where adoption is being used as a part of the safety net that is supposed to keep people housed, fed, clothed. But is that really what its role should be?

Financial relief will not solve all the reasons why relinquishment occurs, but money changes hands to benefit an adoption agency. Which, in turn, builds a family for an adopting set of parents, created with someone else's child.

Birth parents deserve to be treated with dignity and understanding. They are the essential ingredient to a family, whether that is created naturally or by adoption. They are not selfless martyrs, nor people to be manipulated for their offspring. Adoption can be made better if, at a minimum, they receive the same care and concern every human being deserves.

1. Birth parent research. National Council For Adoption. (2023, July 20). https://adoption-council.org/pdfviewer/birth-parent-research/?auto_viewer=true#page=&zoom=auto&page-mode=none

2. Birth parent research. National Council For Adoption. (2023, July 20). https://adoption-council.org/pdfviewer/birth-parent-research/?auto_viewer=true#page=&zoom=auto&page-mode=none

3. Birth parent research. National Council For Adoption. (2023, July 20). https://adoption-council.org/pdfviewer/birth-parent-research/?auto_viewer=true#page=&zoom=auto&page-mode=none

4. 6 open adoption facts that will surprise you. Adoption.com. (n.d.). https://adoption.com/6-open-adoption-facts-will-surpriseyou/

5. https://concernedunitedbirthparents.org/adoptee-rights

6. Eileen Woebse McQuade and Karen Galarneau Quesnel. (2022, March 5). Opinion: Catholic birthmothers to legislators: Help us heal. CT Mirror. https://ctmirror.org/2021/05/12/catholic-birthmothers-to-legislators-help-us-heal/

7. American Psychological Association. (n.d.). Apa PsycNet. American Psychological Association. https://psycnet.apa.org/record/2013-42267-008?doi=1

8. Impact of adoption on birth parents: Responding to the adoptive placement. Impact of Adoption on Birth Parents: Responding to the Adoptive Placement - [[:Template:Adoption Wiki]]. (n.d.). https://adoption.com/wiki/Impact_of_Adoption_on_Birth_Parents:_Responding_to_the_Adoptive_Placement

9. Understanding options counseling experiences in adoption: A qualitative ... (n.d.). https://www.adoptioninstitute.org/wp-content/uploads/2017/03/Understanding-Options-Counseling-Experiences-in-Adoption-Qualitative-Study.pdf?

10. Understanding options counseling experiences in adoption: A qualitative ... (n.d.). https://www.adoptioninstitute.org/wp-content/uploads/2017/03/Understanding-Options-Counseling-Experiences-in-Adoption-Qualitative-Study.pdf?

11. Understanding options counseling experiences in adoption: A qualitative ... (n.d.). https://www.adoptioninstitute.org/wp-content/uploads/2017/03/Understanding-Options-Counseling-Experiences-in-Adoption-Qualitative-Study.pdf?

12. DG;, S. G. L. H. (n.d.). Adoption decision making among women seeking abortion. Women's health issues : official publication of the Jacobs Institute of Women's Health. https://pubmed.ncbi.nlm.nih.gov/28153742/

13. Johnson, J. (2020, November 25). 15 reasons why pregnant women give up their baby for adoption. The Adoption Alliance. https://adoption-alliance.com/2020/11/25/15-reasons-why-pregnant-women-give-up-their-baby-for-adoption/

14. Wendy Edelberg, M. S. K., Lauren Bauer, K. R., Wendy Edelberg, S. G., & Greenstein, R. (2023, March 1). The antipoverty effects of the expanded child tax credit across states: Where were the historic reductions felt?. Brookings. https://www.brookings.edu/articles/the-anti-poverty-effects-of-the-expanded-child-tax-credit-across-states-where-were-the-historic-reductions-felt/

15. Wendy Edelberg, M. S. K., Lauren Bauer, K. R., Wendy Edelberg, S. G., & Greenstein, R. (2023, March 1). The antipoverty effects of the expanded child tax credit across states: Where were the historic reductions felt?. Brookings. https://www.brookings.edu/articles/the-anti-poverty-effects-of-the-expanded-child-tax-credit-across-states-where-were-the-historic-reductions-felt/

Chapter 12
The Legal System, Coercion, and Religious Influences

"Before you judge someone about their anger, ask them about their pain." ~Unknown

When a parent "voluntarily" relinquishes their rights to their child, what does that look like? Most people have never considered the process or the paperwork that accompanies such a decision.

The steps that each agency or legal service takes in beginning an adoption plan are similar, even though the laws governing adoptions vary widely from state to state. In general, when a woman contacts an agency about potentially placing her child for adoption, a few things happen:

- She is assigned to a pregnancy counselor or case worker who becomes her primary contact.
- A full medical history for both her and the father are taken, along with any current medical records to date on the health of the woman, her pregnancy, and the health of her unborn child.
- There is an assessment of her potential financial needs for the remainder of the pregnancy. If financial support is available for the expectant mother and she needs it, then the arrangement for that is created. Each state has different laws

regarding how much a parent can receive.

- If she is choosing who the adoptive parents will be, then this process begins. She will look through listings of prospective adopting parents and hopefully finds one or several she approves of.
- Meetings or interviews are arranged between the two parties and the agency or legal advisors continue to work on the "adoption plan" for the expectant birth parents.

Renee Gelin, birth mother and the founder of the organization Saving Our Sisters (SOS) says, "If you're considering adoption, what people don't understand is if an [expectant] mom starts interacting with an adoption agency, she's going to end up with an adoption. That is the goal. Some may say that they are ethical, they will refer to services, but in the end that's not how they're going to survive. Everyone working there has to get paid. And they all have a salary. There is no money in family preservation. It's going to take resources to support families, that's where we at SOS try to help them. An adoption gets somebody a paycheck."

Once these basic agreements are reached, there is very little else to do other than for the expectant mother to continue with her pregnancy, including all the standard prenatal pregnancy and care appointments. The agency or legal representatives for the adopting parents are kept abreast of the health and development of the pregnancy. Often, these parties are in close contact.

Lori~

I was having a full-on panic attack. I paged the adoptive mother because she said if you ever need anything, page me and I'll do what I can. Then she basically told me that she had no time for me.

So, I proceeded to call the attorney's office and said, "I'm not doing this. They are not getting my child."

Within twenty minutes the lawyer's paralegal is at my door telling me, "Come on and pack a bag." I was going to spend the weekend with them. "Come on, let's go. We're going to have fun."

They kept me busy. There was no time for me to think. And that was the whole point.

I went back home because I had to go to work that Monday. That was the first time I'd been in my own thoughts, but I just pushed it away and said, all right, their plan worked.

Honestly, they knew exactly what they were doing. I got a call on that Monday, and they asked, "Have you made a decision?"

I said, "We'll move forward."

The mom and the dad both did apologize to me after, but it didn't really mean much. I'm a very analytical thinker most times, and in the back of my head I have these alarm bells going off in my brain but chose not to deal with them.

Waiting Periods

All states have a required waiting period that must pass before the relinquishment paperwork can be signed. That is generally 48 – 72 hours after birth, or at least 24 hours after the last pain medication or mind-altering drugs are out of the birth mother's blood system, and laws vary widely.

This sounds simple, but there is often less-than subtle manipulation happening. The agency is motivated to close out the adoption. The adoptive parents are anxiously awaiting the baby's arrival. However, for the adoption agency or attorney, they are motivated not just to see the successful conclusion of the adoption, but also for the final payments they are presumably due from the adopting parent(s). Money is on the line.

Thus, the agency will say to the expectant mother that "they will arrive to have her sign the paperwork at x-number of hours after giving birth, because that is the required waiting period in that state. But the truth is, there is no law saying she must relinquish her rights at that time. It is supposedly the soonest that legal relinquishment can occur. Not the moment in which she must complete the paperwork.

A birth mother could go home and keep her child in her care for a week or more, and then still go back into the agency or care center and relinquish later. This scenario is what everyone surrounding that mother wishes to avoid at all costs.

The timing of when the paperwork is signed is motivated by those wanting to close her rights to parent, which must happen for the adoption to proceed. The methods agencies and legal teams sometimes use to control the termination of the rights of natural parents are worth hearing.

Abbi~

I was going to get to have him for three days. I knew it was an end to the gift. My time at the hospital comes to a close and they're bringing the relinquishment papers in and I'm trembling all over, pure dread.

I literally say to the agency worker, "I'm crying so hard, I can't see the paper." With the way I'm trembling it won't even look like my signature. "How am I supposed to do this?"

I can see her eyes looking back at me, this deer in headlights, no empathy. "It's okay. You can do it, just put pen to paper. It doesn't matter what the signature looks like."

My mother's standing to my right, rubbing my arm, not saying anything different.

I signed the papers because I literally didn't know I could chuck the pen across the room and say, absolutely not. I didn't know I could do that. Then the foster mother takes my baby, and we're all wheeled out together. I see her put him in her car and she drives off.

I fell to the ground wailing and sobbing. My mother picks me up and says, "You need to hush and pull yourself together before your father pulls around."

Katie~

The agent was there off and on for three days. She would come in. She and my mom would just sit there next to the bed waiting for me to have [my daughter].

Mom said, "Do not breastfeed her. That's when she'll get attached to you. That would be cruel knowing she's going to be placed for adoption. I'm having this battle in my mind since they told me not to do that. I didn't want to hurt my baby, so I bottle fed her.

On Saturday the agent came in. None of the doctors, none of the nurses ever asked me, how are you doing, how are you feeling?

They all come in and surround my bed, standing over me. It's my mom, my dad, the agent. And she's got all the papers. It's time to sign. I did not read the paperwork.

I can't even see. I have my daughter in one arm and I'm signing with the other arm, and I'm just looking at my daughter. These are the last few moments of us together and then I'm going to die.

I don't hear a damn word that the agent says, besides sign here, sign here, sign here. I'm signing 'cause I'm about to die. None of this matters.

I didn't read my paperwork for nineteen years. They scratched out my revocation window. It's scratched, like it's omitted. I have a copy that has my revocation window when my time is up, but on the paperwork I signed, it's not there.

They have a little note that says they gave me $500. I didn't want money, but they didn't give me money. It says that I had the right to counsel and an attorney. None of this was ever told to me. What I would have given for counsel. I had no idea. There was no notary there. But it was notarized. They were the only three people in the room.

I didn't even know at the time that Georgia had a ten-day revocation window. I don't know if I was aware of that. I don't remember anybody telling me you have ten days to

> revoke your consent to this.
>
> I can't believe I sat there on the hospital bed sobbing, in obvious pain, but not one nurse, not one doctor, nobody came. There wasn't a social worker sent in. Nobody came in to say, "Are you okay? Do you want us to tell these people to leave?" They're doing business on hospital property. I'm crying, and they just sat there and watched it. Then one of the doctors called it beautiful.

These stories reflect a consistent theme told by all birth parents interviewed for the book. One can find similar information in online forums such as Facebook and TikTok, blogs, birth parent conferences, retreats, and other support groups. Some key takeaways are:

1. Birth parents have no independent legal representation in the relinquishment process, and most states do not stipulate a requirement that it be offered or provided.
2. Birth parents often won't receive final copies of the paperwork they sign. There are stories of them contacting their agencies and attorneys decades later to try to retrieve them—often without resolution.
3. The expectant birth parents will not see or be allowed to read through the relinquishment papers in advance of when they are presented to them post-birth for signing.
4. There are a few states that allow the relinquishment papers to be signed prior to the birth, before a mother gets to see or hold her child.

In 1987 the American Bar Association Standing Committee on Ethics and Professional Responsibility stated in an informal opinion, "an attorney may not ethically represent both birth and adoptive parents." This opinion, which would apply to both agency and independent adoptions, is not binding. However, the laws on dual representation vary throughout the country.[1]

In 2006 a similar opinion was made by Elizabeth Samuels from the University of Baltimore School of Law, saying that "many state laws appear to value an increase in infant adoptions over the goal of encouraging careful deliberation."[2]

To date, these recommendations have only been written into law prohibiting dual representation by ten states, while others either specifically allow dual representation or remain completely silent on the topic within their statutes. Only sixteen states require that birth parents be notified of their rights.

Ponder the experience of giving birth. The changes a woman's brain and body have undergone are profound. During her pregnancy progesterone and estrogen surge, but both of these plunge after the delivery of the placenta. Oxytocin then flows into the body creating a strong parenting instinct. However, it also commonly causes the "baby blues" when it recedes. Prolactin encourages the milk production that is assumed a mother will need to feed her baby.[3]

Larger than just hormones, a study from 2016 shows that pregnancy creates substantial changes to a woman's brain and can last up to two years after giving birth. It shows reductions in a woman's gray matter in her brain in areas relating to social cognition.[4] The hippocampus, which is an area related to memory also loses volume. This adaptive "pruning" as it is called is intended to free up a woman's brain to more effectively bond to her child. There are other dramatic changes such as a woman's blood flow levels, nutrient absorption and other physiological capabilities grow dramatically.[5] "Brain fog" has been infamously reported by women during pregnancy and can cause forgetfulness or difficulty in concentrating.

All of the changes occur naturally, and some would say miraculously, within a woman's brain to help her body successfully transition to motherhood. Now, extend this toward a woman who has self-identified to being in a stressful pregnancy and in a situation where she may be feeling increasingly out of control. Her stress hormones such as cortisol will be high, which will also negatively impact her cognition and reasoning.

It implies an inherent need for caution. A woman fresh from giving birth is vulnerable. She is placed in circumstances where her ability to reason is compromised by the natural biological changes raging through her body that create the profound instinct to mother. This woman is then surrounded by the pressure for her to relinquish, often with no independent representation.

Revocation Window

The revocation window was created to try to give some distance around the act of relinquishment and surrendering one's rights to parent. Each state has their own laws. In New York for example, there is a thirty-day revocation window. However, next door in New Jersey it is irrevocable if signed before a judge in an agency lead adoption. In Utah it is irrevocable upon signing, while in Nevada there is currently a three-day wait.

A few articles document that revocations occur very

rarely. One agency quoted in an article on FamilyEducation.com cited that only four out of 940 adoptions completed in ten years had revoked consent of the adoption. Another agency shared it only happened ten out of 700 placements.[6]

However, the private adoption industry is virtually unmonitored, and the laws are assumed to be followed. There is little oversight of the agencies or attorney's actions to be sure they are obeying the rules.

Any expectant parent considering adoption needs to guard themselves carefully. Few people are looking out for them.

Coercion

Issues with coercion are not unique to the United States. In 2013 an extensive investigation in Australia revealed that for decades, thousands of birth mothers were drugged or even physically restrained when signing away their rights to parent. The government issued an official apology that can be viewed on YouTube.[7]

In Ireland, eighteen mother and baby homes were opened beginning in the early 1900s. They forced the young unwed mothers to labor in these facilities for up to four years after the birth of their children. Those youths and infants were adopted out to wanting parents, many from the US, and these institutions received a fee for the process. Even worse, as many as nine thousand of the babies and children died in these homes, found in unmarked graves. It is estimated that 35,000 young women went through these facilities, the last of them closing in 1998.[8] The government and the Catholic Church have both issued formal apologies. As of 2022, a new information and tracing service has been opened by the government to help women and their adult children reunite.[9]

In early 2023, the First Minister of Scotland also issued a formal apology to birth mothers for the treatment they received throughout the United Kingdom.[10]

In America, a survey completed by the NCFA, shows 63.3% of birth mothers and 68.5% of birth fathers said they were satisfied with their decision to place their child for adoption. The number one reason these men and women cite for their satisfaction is "not being pressured into their decision." The other major predictor was receiving "accurate information in making their adoption plan." The study also showed that birth mothers who placed their child in 2010 or later were much more likely to report satisfaction with their decision as opposed to those who placed their child in the 1970s or prior.[11]

Everyone should receive accurate information about the adoption process, and one's legal rights within it. Most people have no idea. They assume this to be the case. But shouldn't a moral society ensure that at least this is the minimal ethical standard?

The NCFA is a pro-adoption organization. Brave Love, a birth mother support organization which collaborated on the survey, is also pro-adoption and has Christian evangelical foundations. While well intentioned, both organizations ideally wish to see adoption and relinquishment be viewed positively.

When asking Renee Gelin from SOS about this survey, she explained that from her perspective, the wording of the questions made them particularly difficult to answer. Of the initial survey respondents, 2,164 started the questionnaire, but 764 of them did not complete it. Their answers were disqualified from the results because of that, which is a 35% drop rate. When speaking to educators and researchers, they state that any survey with a drop rate higher than 20-25% is an indication there was a problem with the construction of the survey questions and the high drop rate is outside the "best practices" for such surveys.

The Donaldson Adoption Institute (DIA), also explores the outcomes from birth parents, agencies, lawyers and case workers interactions. Of the types of information birth parents received from the agency, 63.7% of the 223 respondents said that they did get pamphlets or other written materials on adoption. However, very little other information was received by the majority.[12]

Of those who used the services of a private attorney, information about resources available to assist birth mothers should they desire to parent their child was not provided to 8 out of 10 mothers surveyed. "Monetary rights, expectations, and responsibilities related to their child was not discussed with 53 (63.1%) of the birth mothers. Additionally, almost as many birth mothers reported that information about monetary expectations and responsibilities for the agency and/or prospective adoptive family was not discussed (n=52, 61.9%). More than half (n=52, 61.9%) of the birth mothers also reported they were not told about options for independent legal counsel to protect their best interests during the relinquishment process."[13]

The major findings point consistently to a pattern of adoption professionals pressuring expectant parents into making decisions that lead to an adoption outcome, and negatively impact these parent's abilities or likelihood of changing their minds.[14]

Religion

Religious beliefs often influence families' views of how children should be raised or created in the first place. Religion can support a person's decision to place for adoption, but it becomes problematic if religion is used to pressure a couple into relinquishment.

Ridghaus~
Becky and I were in a strict Christian evangelical church at the time, so there was a lot of shame around pregnancy out of wedlock.

So, there was a lot of redemption imagery around that—God's will, and whatnot. Which again, looking back, felt pretty unfair for a young couple already facing a crisis, to then have eternal significance attached to their situation. But we still met with the Christian couple related to the youth pastor's wife of the church we attended.

We were desperate. She and I weren't working, we were afraid of how that would impact our child. They had been wanting children, they both had jobs. He worked for the church, and she worked for a hospital. Then, when you threw in the redemption imagery it seemed like this was a good fit. This was 1989.

As years went on, I had a largely positive, sharing, open adoptive parent experience with them.

When my son was eleven, his father left the family. So, Colleen [the mother] was raising two children by herself. I remember Becky saying, "I could have raised a child by myself."

As I look back, we were told it took two-parent families to succeed. At eleven, our child was now in a one-parent home. That was pretty disappointing. If I'd had a spy glass to look into the future, I'm sure that would have changed my decision.

Katie~

God said to be fruitful and multiply, and yet my mom's telling me this is God's plan. I was called a vessel throughout the pregnancy. That God meant for my daughter to be with this family, and he was using me as a vessel. It's the whole Romans 8:28 "And we know that all things work together for good to them that love God."

I didn't know how to fight God. I could fight my mom, the pastor, and the crisis pregnancy center, but once God got hardcore pulled into the situation I didn't, at nineteen years old, have the capacity to go into battle against God.

So, I had to come to the acceptance that this was all God's plan. My daughter was supposed to be a testament to God's glory. She was going to be a witness to how He can take a crappy situation like an unwed pregnancy and turn it around. Because, otherwise, why did this happen? Otherwise, this is a monstrous, evil, disgusting story. I could not live knowing that I was a piece of meat, and everybody was taking a bite of me, and my parents had been party to this.

Sex Education and Birth Control

Teen pregnancy rates are at their lowest levels since the 1990s, largely due to sex education programs and access to over-the-counter birth control.[15]

For economically disadvantaged persons, birth control availability has waned greatly in recent years. Clinics serving the underprivileged, often heavily made up of minorities, have reduced services or closed completely. Twenty-one states have no family planning programs within their Medicaid systems.[16] It is currently estimated that approximately nineteen million women do not live within a one-hour drive of a clinic where they can receive these services.[17]

Adults must always own their choices. This is true whether one is talking about maintaining a good driving record or the decision to have sex. However, systematic reduction in the availability of birth control to prevent unwanted pregnancy should concern everyone and defies common sense. Basic access to these medical protections should be an active part of the social safety net of American society.

Beyond the conversation around birth control is potentially the most divisive issue in America today, the access to abortion. Many birth parents are pro-life, and the decisions to keep their babies are influenced by those values. The majority want to parent. But these narratives can also be used against them.

Katie grew up in a strongly religious, politically conservative, pro-life environment, with lots of messaging around tough love. Her mother volunteered at the local crisis pregnancy center and helped other young women choose life over an abortion. But when it came to her own daughter's needs, things were different.

Katie~

It was just bizarre to me that she kept pushing adoption. I wanted my baby. This didn't make sense.

She worked in our downtown area. The crisis pregnancy center was a couple of blocks from where she worked. She ended up taking me a county over to the crisis pregnancy center there. I thought that was really weird because I knew she had been involved with the one in our town for years.

When you walk in, it was a boutique. They have baby clothes, maternity clothes, they have all this material support. The counseling room is in the back. I think I may have gone there twice.

The counselor would only talk about adoption. I kept telling her, "I wanted to keep my baby, and I needed help. That's what you're here for. To help me figure out a way that I can keep and parent my baby."

She told me. "Well, all you have is love."

Yeah, that's why I'm at the Crisis Pregnancy Center because I thought we were going to have a conversation. At this point, I had just turned nineteen. I'm not fourteen.

If someone would just invest in me, I could get on my feet in a couple of years.

"No, that's not an option for you," they kept telling me. "If you really loved your baby, you would place your baby for adoption."

Abbi~

I heard my mom on the phone doing the

> Crisis Pregnancy Care Center's hotline in the evenings at night. I would wake up in the middle of the night, listening to her talking to women. But what she talked about the most wasn't adoption. It was don't abort your baby and just come into the clinic. So, there were a lot of things behind the scenes I didn't know about. I didn't know about the next steps, but I did know that my mom was very against abortion.
>
> I know one hundred percent from my indoctrination, and it was said to me numerous times throughout my pregnancy, there is no reward for sin.
>
> You don't get the ultimate gift and blessing of a baby for sinning against God and your parents. No, we're not going to support you getting what you want. You have to atone. You must do the right thing and be selfless and give up what you want because you did not earn this gift.
>
> I had no idea how to argue that. I knew that I wanted my baby desperately, but I didn't know I was entitled to him.

Many people see adoption as an alternative to abortion. But if a woman's uterus is nothing but a "vessel" for God's good work or His will, then this dehumanizes a birth mother completely. This is not only offensive to these women, but to adoptees as well. It implies these expectant mothers should be viewed as nothing more than broodmares for children to be adopted and assumes adopting parents are part of some grand plan. This should be seen for what it is—a self-centered view that places adoptive parents at the top of a hierarchy created by humans rather than divine intervention.

Adoptions cost money, and agencies and baby brokers' profit. The average cost to adopt a domestically born infant in the US is around $45,000.

Contrast this with the fact that the most common reason a child is relinquished is financial. The implication is that if more women are denied the choice of abortion, then they can fulfill that desire for other wealthier, (more deserving) people to become parents. It is a mechanism to increase the supply of human beings to be traded and placed for profit. The adoption and child welfare industry is estimated to be worth 25.1 billion dollars in revenue in the US, as of 2023.[18] It profits mightily on the backs, literally, of the parents involved. These fees are paid by the adopting parents—who want to have a child—who often approach this process unaware of these shadier realities. They, too, are manipulated.

> **Katie~**
> I was told that I was going to carry the burden, and she wasn't going to suffer. That's what a mom does. She carries the burden so that her children don't suffer. And my own maternal instincts were weaponized against me.
>
> I also think weaponizing their motherhood is one of, if not the most cruel thing to do to a human being.
>
> That is domestic infant adoption in the United States. They weaponize a mother's love against her, and I got eaten by a machine I didn't even know existed.
>
> What is done to mothers in this country and everything that was done to me in 1999 is

done today. There has not been a change.

Many Americans have deeply held religious beliefs and view abortion as a moral outrage. They believe they are saving an innocent life that is of inherent, God-given value, and this must always be the highest priority.

What has been created in the wake of reduced access and options is that more birth parents and their infant children are fed into a system that will profit from their misfortune, which should also be seen as a moral outrage.

---

1. See ABA Comlll. on Ethics and Prof' | Responsibility. Inform,d Op. 1523 (1987).

2. Legal Representation of Birth Parents and Adoptive Parents, 9 Adoption Quarterly 73 (2006)

3. Perry, C. (2023, June 2). What to expect with postpartum hormone changes. Parents. https://www.parents.com/pregnancy/my-body/postpartum/postpartum-hormone-changes/

4. Pregnancy resculpts women's brains for at least 2 years. (n.d.-a). https://www.science.org/content/article/pregnancy-resculpts-women-s-brains-least-2-years

5. Pregnancy resculpts women's brains for at least 2 years. (n.d.-a). https://www.science.org/content/article/pregnancy-resculpts-women-s-brains-least-2-years

6. Birthmothers who change their minds about adoption. FamilyEducation. (2006, July 25). https://www.familyeducation.com/kids/adoption/birthmothers-who-change-their-minds-about-adoption

7.https://www.youtube.com/watch?v=5hVbokTpYeg&t=146s

8. Specia, M. (2021, January 12). Report gives glimpse into horrors of Ireland's mother and Baby Homes. The New York Times. https://www.nytimes.com/2021/01/12/world/europe/ireland-mother-baby-home-report.html

9. https://www.birthinfo.ie

10. BBC. (2023, March 22). Sturgeon issues apology over forced adoption. BBC News. https://www.bbc.com/news/uk-scotland-65043159?https%3A%2F%2F

11. Birth parent research. National Council For Adoption. (2023, July 20). https://adoptioncouncil.org/pdfviewer/birth-parent-research/?auto_viewer=true#page=&zoom=auto&pagemode=none

12. Understanding options counseling experiences in adoption: A qualitative ... (n.d.). https://www.adoptioninstitute.org/wp-content/uploads/2017/03/Understanding-Options-Counseling-Experiences-in-Adoption-Qualitative-Study.pdf?

13. Understanding options counseling experiences in adoption: A qualitative ... (n.d.). https://www.adoptioninstitute.org/wp-content/uploads/2017/03/Understanding-Options-Counseling-Experiences-in-Adoption-Qualitative-Study.pdf?

14. Understanding options counseling experiences in adoption: A qualitative ... (n.d.). https://www.adoptioninstitute.org/wp-content/uploads/2017/03/Understanding-Options-Counseling-Experiences-in-Adoption-Qualitative-Study.pdf?

15. ABC News Network. (n.d.). ABC News. https://abcnews.go.com/Health/teenage-birth-rates-us-reached-historic-lows

16. Usha Ranji, A. S. F. @a_salganicoff on T. (2019, October 29). Financing family planning services for low-income women: The role of Public Programs. KFF. https://www.kff.org/womens-health-policy/issue-brief/financing-family-planning-services-for-low-income-women-the-role-of-public-programs/

17. Contraceptive deserts. 2023 | Power to Decide. (n.d.). https://powertodecide.org/what-we-do/contraceptive-deserts

18. IBISWorld. (n.d.). Adoption & Child Welfare Services in the US - market research report (2013-2028). IBISWorld Industry Reports. https://ibisworld.com/united-states/market-research-reports/adoption-child-welfare-services-industry/

Chapter 13
The Cloak of Grief and Shame

"Shame erodes our courage and fuels disengagement. ~ Brene' Brown

Birth parents always grieve their loss, whether they acknowledge it or not. But what they most often experience is *disenfranchised grief*. This is any loss or sorrow that is not acknowledged due to societal norms. These emotions are often minimized or not understood by others, which makes it particularly hard to process and work through. No one comes visiting with banana bread or a casserole. They're on their own, and often alone with no one to share their suffering. Even close family will not acknowledge what has just happened. Co-workers avoid them. Friends and extended family are at a loss. Worst of all, no one wants to talk about or even see how traumatizing the relinquishment has been.

One small study from 1986 cites, "A variety of factors operated to impede the grieving process in these women. Their loss was not acknowledged by family and professionals, who denied them the support necessary for the expression of their grief. Intense anger, shame, and guilt complicated their mourning, which was further inhibited by the fantasy of eventual reunion…"[1]

Laura~

I could not talk about the time when I was there. If I tried to mention something about New Orleans or the home, my parents would physically stand up and leave the room. I left a pretty normal teenager and came back a pretty messed up young woman.

I was physically sick. I think I had some issues going on, but I never went back to a doctor. My mother never took me even when I told her I was having problems. She said, "Well, that's what happens to girls who sleep around with a bunch of men," which I never slept around with a bunch of men.

Katie~

My baby daughter flies to Canada with her new family, and that week my mom gets a pool installed and a new convertible. How the hell am I supposed to navigate that?

My mom brings me to the crisis pregnancy center to take all the stuff back that I had gotten. My mom tells them that I'm not bouncing back like I should have. Do they have anything? They have absolutely nothing to do with the adoption.

This is what I get—*Letting Go and Moving On: A Post-Adoption Workbook*. The lady at the crisis pregnancy center pulls this out and wipes off the dust. They also had a birth mom come in to do counseling sessions with me. They're just throwing this together. This other mom that comes in to talk to me placed her kid ten years ago. She's dead behind the eyes.

> It's the saddest thing. She's going through this workbook with me. I'm getting the sense that she's thinking, this is bullshit. I think I met with her twice.

Very few families, especially from the closed Baby Scoop Era, recognize or even tried to understand the devastating loss a birth mother just experienced. Its profundity is buried and unspoken. The secrecy is damaging physically, spiritually, and emotionally to them.

According to one study, "Almost all the women reported they received little or no help from family, friends, or professionals. Over half of them had used alcohol or sedative medication to help them cope after relinquishment. Almost all reported that they dealt with their distress by withdrawing and bottling up their feelings. Only one third subsequently sought professional help."[2]

Telling

The women who talk about what occurred, most especially with any new romantic partner, accomplish something important. Regardless of how well it is received, the early practice of telling, and exposing such a tender secret seems to carry forward. A story told once, can be repeated again. Speaking truth restores personal power, however small.

> **Ellen~**
> I met a guy only a few months after the baby was born. He was a sweet man. He basically picked me up out of the gutter, shook me off, and said, "Hey, there's nothing wrong with you." And he loved me. It was through him and his caring that I was able to get on my feet.

> **Laura~**
> I did tell [my first husband] before we went out to California. He made me feel even worse. He said, "Don't you ever tell my parents this happened." And when I was crying and telling him how sad I was about leaving my son Jamie, that was my son's crib name. He said, "Well, are you gonna love me and our children as much as you love this Jamie?" He was almost jealous, but he was a very immature, narcissistic kind of guy. We married each other for the wrong reasons. I felt like who's going to want me? I'm damaged goods.

Eventually Laura's marriage to her first husband falls apart, although she did have a number of children with him. She then meets the man who she is still married to.

> **Laura~**
> I said, "I need to tell you something, and I hope you won't feel less of me."
>
> He said, "What do you mean?"
>
> "It's something horrible that I can't talk about to anybody, but I'm going to tell you, because you're always saying I'm a good mother. You think I'm such a good mother, but I'm not the mother you think I am."
>
> He was puzzled and nervous.
>
> So, I told him, and of course I broke down because it was the first time I had opened my mouth about it since I told the other guy.
>
> He went over to my side and put his arms

> around me, and said, "I'm so sorry you went through that."
>
> "Do you want me to help you find him?"

For birth parents from the open adoption era, some of the same considerations arise, but they take a different form. Then it becomes a matter of discerning who to share the details of their lives with and how much. This is where the difference between secrecy and privacy takes form in real life.

The Next Phase

As birth parents begin to move forward in their lives, they will tend to follow a few different paths that form visible patterns. Some relinquishing couples will continue their relationship, marry, and have other children, but they are the minority.

Many young women, and most especially from the Scoop era, will immediately seek a husband and more children which they can keep. These rushed marriages will sometimes work well for several years and produce children. A study from the Medical Journal of Australia in 1986 notes, "The relatively high instance of pregnancy during the year after relinquishment invites speculation that this represents a maladaptive coping strategy that involves a "replacement baby."[3]

> **Cathryn~**
> I found a guy who I thought was good-looking. He was the opposite of my boyfriend in every way. I thought, this will do. We got married and I couldn't wait to have a baby. I wanted to make a good home that would be

happy and welcoming, and there wouldn't be secrets like in my home.

I was pregnant a few months after our wedding, and again two years later. I think most new mothers can relate to this, just feeling like I'm so lucky and I love them so much, just overflowing. And it struck me like a bolt of lightning that I have another one somewhere. I have another one who is mine as much as these two. By then it was 1974, five years later was the first time that I thought of that child and how she was mine and she wasn't with me. It just hit me like a ton of bricks because I had thought of her as somebody else's.

Barbara~

I'm wishing I had my baby because I wanted little arms around my neck. Sometimes when I babysit for a friend, those hugs from my little buddies always made me feel good.

The next thing I knew I was pregnant again, but this time it was on purpose. I gave birth to another boy. This one I kept. He was my savior. I didn't marry his father because he went off to work. But I met a man named John, and I married him. We had a daughter and another son, plus he adopted my son I already had.

Other women will take the reverse course. They may marry, but will not feel entitled to bring another life into the world, when they have already set aside their first child.

An unknown portion of these women face secondary

infertility. This is anytime a woman who has already had one child but cannot, for whatever reason, become pregnant or carry to term, again.

Women's nervous systems are tightly wrapped around their stress hormones which control pregnancy in ways that are still the subject of much study. For a birth mother, her relinquishment is traumatizing to her nervous system, which can have the reverse effect, making her body less inclined to perform as it once did.

The rates surrounding secondary infertility in birth mothers have had almost no formal study. In Nancy Verrier's book, The Primal Wound, she cites statistics of between forty and sixty percent. But this was based on the anecdotal secondary infertility rates within a birth mothers support group she interacted with in writing her book.

There is one small study done in Australia in 2010. It surveyed a total of thirty birth mothers who returned a questionnaire. Of them, eighty percent had gone on to have subsequent children. The survey does not weed out those who aged out of their childbearing years or those who never found a suitable partner.[4] However, what is surprising is that within the researcher's support group at her agency in Perth, the birth mothers happen to have the same anecdotal secondary infertility rate of forty to sixty percent.

Anger

The anger that so many birth parents feel, mothers in particular, cannot be understated. They will often spend their first several years after relinquishment numb, disassociated from their pain, or will hide in drug and alcohol use. Too few will get help.

Two therapists who specialize in childbearing loss, Butterfield and Scaturo (1989), have documented a series of stages grieving mothers' process: denial, shock, disbelief, numbing, guilt, anger, yearning, depression, disorganization, despair, and integration. They also emphasize this is not a linear process—several or many of these experiences may be happening at once.[5]

These impacts run across all areas of a mother's life. They will affect her relationships with herself and others and resurface throughout her life. These feelings often intensify over time, rather than diminish.[6] A common phrase is, "time heals all wounds." This does not appear to apply to birth parents. They will go on, most of them, but integrating their feelings and finding healing takes decades or may never fully resolve.

Shayanne~

I was not okay for a long time. I was really, really not okay, and I am proud of myself because I almost didn't make it. I realized that my kid was gone and I was not going to get a visit no matter who I asked or what I did. I think becoming a foster parent subconsciously helped, as if by being a foster parent I was as good as these other people. I was going to be as good as his adoptive parents and then they won't be afraid of me anymore. They will let me have a visit.

They will do this and that and the other thing and it'll be like I proved to them that I'm good enough. And I still wasn't good enough, even after raising these other kids and becoming a foster parent. I was a shell. I just laid in bed and cried because of the devastation from realizing, "Oh my God,

> I don't have a choice. There's nothing I can do." I have never been able to not help myself before. And it was so infuriating for me to realize, "I can't do anything."

The Impact of Shame

Postpartum depression impacts many mothers. Maternal suicide is not a nationally reported issue. However, it is listed as one of the leading causes of death in the US, Japan, the UK, and Ireland. Suicide accounts for up to twenty percent of all postpartum deaths and is listed as the leading cause of death in the first year after childbirth. In a CDC review of data from fourteen states, suicide is listed as the sixth leading cause of pregnancy death.[7]

According to commentary from an article, Birth families: Living with the Adoption Decision, "Exiled parents who surrender children for adoption are expected to live a lie the rest of their lives. The adoption eliminates the public record of the child's birth, and the exiled parents are counseled by family, friends, and social agencies to go on with their lives as if the pregnancy never occurred. This socially sanctioned denial not only interferes with the resolution of grief but intensifies the parents' poor self-image by reinforcing the idea that what they have done is so heinous that it must be concealed forever."[8]

Dr. Lynn Zubov, a birth mother and researcher at Winston Salem University, has a study cited earlier which paints a much more disturbing picture. When she began, she was initially doing a survey on reunions. However, the responses came back from many adoptees that their parents had died young. Still ongoing as of the fall of 2024, she surveyed 900 adopted adults and 400 birth parents and found the following statistics."[9]

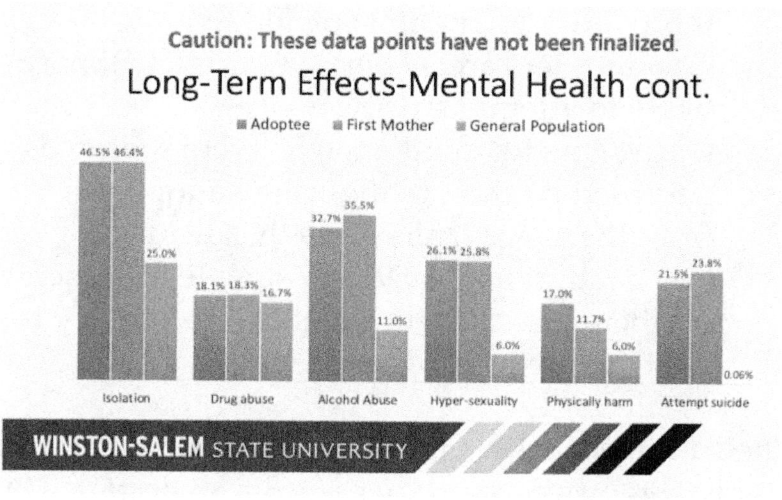

Source: A Preliminary Exploration into Adoption Reunions. Data on when adoptees knew they were adopted. Facebook, 7 2024, 3:19PM, https://www.facebook.com/profile.php?id=61555968231690, Accessed14 Jun 2024.

The graph compares adopted adults and birth parent answers and then shares these rates of drug abuse, suicide and other data measured with the general population. Even more concerning is the rates of suicide or attempted suicide by both birth parents and adoptees.

According to her preliminary findings on the long-term effects from relinquishment, Dr. Zubov reported that 21.5% of adoptees and 23.8% of birth mothers attempted suicide. According to the American Foundation for Suicide Prevention, 0.6% rate of attempted suicide is the national average. These results when calculated show the following:

- Adoptees are roughly *36 times* (36*0.6=21.6) more likely to attempt suicide
- First mothers are *39 times* (39*0.6=23.4) more likely to attempt suicide
- Of the 245 first mothers who were reported deceased by their relinquished adoptees from the survey, nine died by suicide.
- The death rate of 3.59% by suicide for first mothers makes them roughly *511 times* more likely to die of suicide.[10]

When adoptees taking the survey reported that their birth mother was deceased, the average life expectancy for these women was between the ages of 65 and 70. The national average life expectancy for a woman is currently 80.[11] This is showing these birth mothers died of disease ten to fifteen years before their counterparts. For adoptee suicide statistics, these numbers are far higher than the previously quoted study that adoptees are four times more likely to attempt or commit suicide.[12]

Clearly more information should be gathered. If the consequences of relinquishment mean such potentially high rates of addiction, suicide, and other negative or self-harming behaviors for these women, should this not be disclosed to expectant mothers beforehand? Or, how about a potential reduction in overall life expectancy of ten to fifteen years. Should this be disclosed? What about the unknown and largely unstudied rates of secondary infertility many birth mothers have experienced?

Disclosures are made routinely about the risks of smoking, alcohol use, or driving without a seatbelt. Riding a motorcycle without a helmet is illegal in most states, but adoptions happen daily in this country and often no one has been informed of the risks.

Cathryn~

I can't think about this. I can't ever think about this again or I'll lose my mind. So, I didn't. I pushed her down and away. I thought, I have to keep going—there's no choice. There's nothing I can do. It was as if she was dead.

I held a gun. The girls were young teenagers. My husband was a hunter, and he had bought a handgun for small game hunting. I've always hated guns. I considered taking my life just because I was in so much pain, and I didn't know what was wrong.

Debi~

Afterwards, I drifted. I couldn't figure out life. I didn't know what I wanted. I felt vulnerable. I felt abused and had no ego. Everything was broken down.

I'd just turned twenty. By this time, I was already shooting heroin in the streets, dealing heroin in the streets.

One night, I couldn't find any heroin. I drank Old Grand Dad and ate Quaaludes and tried to drive home and went off the road. Praise the Lord, I didn't have a seatbelt on because I was thrown out. I broke my back in three places, both my ankles, my shoulder, my jaw, and landed on someone's front lawn.

I spent a long time with braces, crutches, and bandages. I didn't live at home, although I did go home right after I got out of the hospital.

I met this beautiful man. We used to sit and talk for hours and hours and hours. He was a psych major, so what do you think he told me? That this wasn't normal, and that I should seek help. Thank God, I sought help.

Honoring The Lost Mothers

The shame for some women who relinquish consumes them. They continue to make bad choices or meet unkind people who further abuse them in a cycle of self-harming behavior that reinforces their shame. Others never learn to tell even one person and remain isolated and alone with their secrets to their graves.

For the ones who don't make it back into the light of day, may they be heard from now through the eyes of those who survive them.

Donna Marie honoring her birth mother Elizabeth~

I have done a bit of research into the timing of my mother's death. I know I was around twelve when she was found. This was 1984. There's no way of knowing what exactly happened, but everybody that I've spoken to in the past have always said it would have been suicide. She wasn't in a good way. She wasn't with a good man.

There was such a huge search for my birth mother, when in fact, many people go missing all the time. When we learned about her death, there was a whole page article [in the newspaper]. I saw the picture of my birth mom and knew, and was being told, that she was potentially dead.

When she relinquished me, she was more

or less a functioning, relatively mentally-well person. She was staying with friends at the time who had said they would take care of me, rather than me being adopted, just in the interim. I would love to meet them to find out for sure. But in the pictures that I can see of her holding me, she was twenty-seven-years-old. She looks absolutely fine, and she doesn't look like she's falling apart. But obviously she was in a situation where she was on her own and needed help.

She was back and forth, you can see it in the paperwork. She kept changing her mind and the social workers kept convincing her to get back on the right track of adoption. So, there's coercion in the paperwork that I have seen.

I think that's why it's easy for family members to cast it off as a suicide because she was in that state. She married in 1982. I've heard rumors that she had a black eye when she got married. That's just two years before she dies.

Fred, honoring his birth mother Maureen (not her real name)~

My birth mother—she never let it go. She had a hard time with it—went to her grave with it. I wasn't allowed to go to her funeral. She told her daughter specifically, "You don't let them come. I'm afraid people are going to find out."

My kids, I hate to say it, they were kind of the bait—she wanted to see them. If we met in a restaurant, she was afraid to go in with us so we would have to go in through a side door and meet in a back room. I got mad at her a few times for that, "Why can't you just acknowledge me?"

[After having me] she moved out of state, got married, and had three kids. She didn't tell her husband that she ever had a kid before that. Even when I found her, she told me, "If you'd have come five years ago, I would not have allowed you to find out who you were because my husband didn't know. He was never going to find out."

I understand the impact that holding secrets like that can have on relationships. How is that relationship with your husband? Probably one of the biggest events of your life. Not even from the standpoint of me but from the standpoint of what you went through—a nine-month pregnancy, giving birth to a baby, fighting like hell as you gave it away. And then you're supposed to pretend it never happened. Then you're going to hold that secret from your husband.

When she agreed to let me know, she did make that conditional. "I'll tell you, but you have to swear nobody finds out." I wanted to find out, so I agreed. Even when I wrote and published my memoir—she is cloaked. Was that a good idea? I don't know. It took its toll on me. I think it took its toll on her.

---

1. Condon, J. T. (1986). Psychological disability in women who relinquish a baby for adoption. Medical Journal of Australia, 144(3), 117–119. https://doi.org/10.5694/j.1326-5377.1986.tb112233.x

2. Condon, J. T. (1986). Psychological disability in women who relinquish a baby for adop-

tion. Medical Journal of Australia, 144(3), 117–119. https://doi.org/10.5694/j.1326-5377.1986.tb112233.x

3. Condon, J. T. (1986). Psychological disability in women who relinquish a baby for adoption. Medical Journal of Australia, 144(3), 117–119. https://doi.org/10.5694/j.1326-5377.1986.tb112233.x

4. Andrews, I. (2009). Secondary infertility and birth mothers. Psychoanalytic Inquiry, 30(1), 80–93. https://doi.org/10.1080/07351690903200184

5. Effects of adoption on the mental health of the mother: What professionals knew and didn't tell us. Supporting Those Separated by Adoption. (n.d.-a). https://www.originscanada.org/adoption-trauma-2/trauma_to_surrendering_mothers/effects-of-adoption-on-mental-health-of-the-mother-what-professionals-knew-and-didnt-tell-us/

6. Condon, J. T. (1986). Psychological disability in women who relinquish a baby for adoption. Medical Journal of Australia, 144(3), 117–119. https://doi.org/10.5694/j.1326-5377.1986.tb112233.x

7. Policy Center for Maternal Mental Health. (2023, September). Maternal Suicide in the U.S.: Opportunities for Improved Data Collection and Health Care System Change [Issue Brief]. https://www.2020mom.org/issue-briefs-and-papers

8. Effects of adoption on the mental health of the mother: What professionals knew and didn't tell us. Supporting Those Separated by Adoption. (n.d.-a). https://www.originscanada.org/adoption-trauma-2/trauma_to_surrendering_mothers/effects-of-adoption-on-mental-health-of-the-mother-what-professionals-knew-and-didnt-tell-us/

9. A Preliminary Exploration into Adoption Reunions. Data on when adoptees knew they were adopted. Facebook, 7 2024, 3:19PM, https://www.facebook.com/profile.php?id=61555968231690, Accessed14 Jun 2024.

10. A Preliminary Exploration into Adoption Reunions. Data on when adoptees knew they were adopted. Facebook, 7 2024, 3:19PM, https://www.facebook.com/profile.php?id=61555968231690, Accessed14 Jun 2024.

11. Centers for Disease Control and Prevention. (2024, March 21). *Products - data briefs - number 492 - March 2024.* Centers for Disease Control and Prevention. https://www.cdc.gov/nchs/products/databriefs/db492.htm#section_1

12. Keyes MA, Malone SM, Sharma A, Iacono WG, McGue M. Risk of suicide attempt in adopted and nonadopted offspring. Pediatrics. 2013 Oct;132(4):639-46. doi: 10.1542/peds.2012-3251. Epub 2013 Sep 9. PMID: 24019414; PMCID: PMC3784288.

Chapter 14
Open Adoption – is it working?

"It's a wedding and a funeral at the exact same moment, at the exact same time."
~Jennifer Joy Phoenix

Open adoptions have been hailed as the great new social engineering in modern adoption. There are things it does well, or at least potentially better than the closed system. However, as with any ideal, there are pitfalls because the practice is up to individuals with their own motivations, challenges, and frailties that affect the outcomes.

Adoption is supposed to be about the welfare of, and what is best for, the child. Birth parents often surrender their rights because they believe it is the best decision, but in doing so they give up the privilege of access. There are always consequences attached to that, which will be paid by both them and the adoptee.

> **Luna~**
> This was an unplanned but beloved human that I delighted in creating. I would talk with her [in the womb]. I just did it with the framework of, "I'm doing this for you, and then you're going to go be someone else's." I would fear, "How is she going to know that I have this great and immense love for her if I can't be in her presence to express it, ever? Do I need to give up not only parenting her, but also visits? Do I have to be willing to give that up too, so that she can have what I believe she needs?"

Few people realize the "agreements" between the adopting and birth parents are *not legally binding in most states.* The entire process has an inherent power imbalance, all of it in the hands of the adoptive and not the natural parents. This is not "co-parenting." The birth parents have relinquished their rights, and the adopting couple has total legal authority as primary guardians.

Ridghaus~
Open adoptions baffle the outside world unless they're a member of one. They're a very challenging concept, I think, for a lot of people to wrap their heads around.

I was glad to see Zach, and I'm glad that Brian and Colleen fulfilled what they said they would do for me. But even in our open adoption, the fragility of it, was evidenced in that Becky [the birth mother] didn't have all of the same chances.

[The adoption] closed for her. She had no recourse to compel anything else.

While I had a positive experience and don't advocate for closed adoptions, I think open adoption is a lie that can be used to overcome the objections of a young couple in crisis and fail to fulfill the actual objection they had. Why is adoption the severing of one relationship? Why is it the exclusion of one?

And obviously there are situations where a child's welfare is critical and legitimately in danger. I don't know if that's the case with ninety percent of them.

I would say that I had a moderately decent experience and I'm glad that Zach was able to have those mirroring moments and biological contact. But, overall, open adoption is not the answer either.

Open Adoption 101

Below is a table that shows some of the advantages to each of the three primary styles of adoption: closed, semi-open, and open:

Open Adoption, Closed Adoption, and Mediated Adoption: Pros of Each

	Closed Adoption Advantages	Mediated (Semi-Open) Adoption Advantages	Open Adoption Advantages
Birth Parents	• Privacy • Some feel this provides a sense of closure and the ability to move on	• Allows for some information transfer between birth and adoptive parents (and perhaps the child) • Some privacy	• Increased ability to deal with grief and loss • Comfort in knowing the child's well-being • Potential for a more fully defined role in the child's life • Potential to develop a healthy relationship with the child as they grow • Less pain and guilt about the decision • May make the decision to place the child up for adoption easier (compared to a contested termination of parental rights trial)
Adoptive Parents	• No need to physically share the child with the birth parents • No danger of birth parent interference or co-parenting • Increased sense of having the "right" to parent and increased ability for confident parenting	• Greater sense of control over the process • Roles may be more clearly defined than in either confidential or open adoptions • Increased sense of entitlement compared to confidential adoptions • Enhanced ability to answer the child's questions about his or her history	• Potential for an authentic relationship with the birth family • More understanding of the child's history • Increased empathy for birth parents • Less fear of birth parents reclaiming the child because they know the parent and their wishes.

Adopted Persons	• Protection from unstable or emotionally disturbed birth parents	Only applicable if the relationship is "shared" with the adopted child: • Genetic and birth history is known • Birthparents are "real," not "fantasy" • Positive adjustment is promoted in adoptees	• Direct access to birth parents and history • Eliminating the need to search • Identity questions are answered (Who do I look like? Why was I placed?) • Eases feelings of abandonment • Lessening of fantasies: birth parents are "real" • Increased circle of supportive adults • Increased attachment to the adoptive family (especially if the birth parents support the placement) • Preservation of connections (e.g., with siblings and relatives) • Lessens loyalty conflicts • Exposure to racial and ethnic heritage • Ability for an evolving, dynamic, and developmentally appropriate account of the adoption

Source: Gilmore, D. J. (n.d.). Open or closed adoption: Advantages of each type of adoption - findlaw. FindLaw. https://www.findlaw.com/family/adoption/open-or-closed-adoption-pros-of-each.html

Adoptees

Open adoptions accomplish many things for the adoptees. They often struggle in a closed system, and some level of openness appears to be inherently good. Their birth parents are real people and not ghosts, and they gain the benefits of some genetic mirroring, if direct contact is allowed.

They can also receive age-appropriate answers to their questions about why they were placed, know their kin and their heritage, and have real-time access to medical history. It also removes the frustrations of searching for relatives later in life. Also, some control is given to the adolescent adoptee over whom they wish to spend time with. It is the only scenario that adoptees get some say in their parenting.

Open adoption fails to eliminate attachment issues. As infants they will still be separated from their natural mothers, and that pre-verbal trauma still exists. These arrangements don't address adoptees' feelings of insecurity or being someone's "second choice." They may still have feelings of fear, obligation, and guilt. Children always want to please their parents. Now they have two sets to navigate.

Birth Parents

Open adoptions were created and "sold" to birth parents initially for them. They have pretty pictures in their minds of play dates and school functions and birthday parties they are invited to. The ambivalence created by closed options is often a living nightmare for birth parents who wonder for the rest of their lives how their child fares. Open adoptions ease some of those pains.

But birth parents still suffer. Their grieving process is continual, and may prolong their feelings of shame, guilt, and unworthiness. A natural mother will grieve her losses again and again, even while contact remains, yet still feel it is the best option as opposed to a fully closed situation.

The power imbalance cannot be understated. The adoptive couple can minimize or severely reduce contact, regardless of the terms created in the agreement. They can also close the adoption at any moment, and there is little to no recourse a birth parent will have if that happens.

This creates scenarios where natural parents feel like they are "walking on eggshells." They worry constantly if something is not handled as well as it could be, a standard set by the adopting parents, they risk losing access to the child. The security of these bonds between the parents is precarious, delicate, and needs all the adults to bring their best selves.

Jean~

They agreed that they would send me one

letter a year about Katie, just to make sure that she was okay. I got a letter a year from them until she was around nine. I didn't hear anything for three years.

I reached out to the agency, and I asked why the letters had stopped coming. It's been several years. Is she dead? Did something happen and they're just not wanting to tell me?

The woman we worked through called me back. She said, "Would you like to talk to Debbie, Katie's mom?"

I remember feeling so excited that I could speak to the woman who was raising Katie, and I could ask her anything I wanted to. I could ask her what she likes to eat for her favorite snack and what time she wants to go to bed. Her daily life and what she was like, what her personality was.

When Debbie and I finally talked, it was like connecting with an old friend that you hadn't spoken to in a long time. It was so natural for us to speak and share and be there for each other and Katie.

She said that she wanted to protect the relationship she had built with Katie, and that's why she'd stopped writing. Then she said she read a book called *The Spirit of Adoption*, and it talked about the birth mother and how much they love their kids.

She thought, "Did this woman desperately love this child? How can I withhold that from her life?"

So, she decided that it was time to bring me into Katie's experience because she knew how much I loved her.

Plans Versus Realities

Current studies say openness in adoption is better than a fully closed structure, even though it creates additional challenges. From one study in 2003, "disquiet arises from the recognition that it is not a panacea but a complex phenomenon that brings its own potential risks and difficulties."[1]

There are a variety of factors, but one way to break them down is:

1. Setting and understanding clear expectations from the beginning.
2. Managing the mechanics and levels of physical interaction between the child and their birth parents.
3. Understanding the likely, gradual shifting of decision-making over to the adoptee, meaning choices about contact will be less in the hands of their parents.

Expectations

Clarifying, communicating, and setting boundaries between the parents is critical. This step cannot and should not be skipped or taken lightly. The ethics of everyone involved is key, and adoption counselors, case workers, and legal professionals can get this right, or, in some cases, horrifyingly wrong.

> **Luna~**
> When we started talking about openness, all the counselors said, "We're going to just all talk together at the exact same time to avoid any misses."

The parents said, "Let's have three visits the first year, two visits the second year, a visit the third year, and we will remain in contact. We don't know what your life is going to be like, and we don't want to speak about agreeing to something five years from now, ten years from now, if it's not a healthy thing to do."

Lori~

I found out they were not necessarily the most ethical of attorneys, and still, to this day, they are not. Once I made the decision on the parents, we met the following day. It was very awkward. They tried to find out as much information physically about my background and stuff like that, but there really wasn't much other conversation.

I went with this attorney—that was part of why I went the private route—because I'd never heard of any other type of adoption that would allow it to be open.

It's 1995. There was no Google, so I couldn't exactly look things up. Open adoption wasn't even legally allowed. There was no legal construct to even make it happen in Florida then.

Many years later, my husband and I met with my daughter and her adoptive family, and they brought her baby book with them so I could see pictures. The mom says to me, "Oh, you should have received these."

I said, "Receive what?"

"These pictures, you should have gotten them."

"I never received anything. The last thing

> that I received from you was a lovely necklace that you purchased from London on your last trip. I never received anything else."
>
> So, we found out at that point that the attorney had told them that I didn't want anything to do with them after the first three months.
>
> And then I was told that it was the parents who had changed their mind, and they didn't want an open adoption. So, you'll never hear from her again.

Managing Access and Decision Making

Parental egos need to take a back seat to the child's best interests, which is easier said than done. From a study published in 1988, "Professionals generally agree that the child is least confused about loyalties to either parent when the open relationship between the adoptive and biological parents is clear and positive."[2]

The agreements are generally negotiated at the time the adoption plan is created. Families of children who had formal arrangements for contact have over five times increased odds of connecting with the birth family after the adoption.[3] A typical flow will be that it may first only happen via an intermediary such as the agency or attorney. Eventually, in-person meetings will take place. Birth parents, as one might imagine, are thrilled to see their children. But this does not mean they "want to take them back." In one in-depth study of twelve open adoptions, the researchers found that the more frequent the interactions, the *less* adoptive parents worried about the natural ones feeling entitled to the child.[4]

Another study in 2023 surveyed 223 birth mothers, 155 of whom had contact, showed birth mothers who regularly spent time with their child reported significantly more satisfaction with their decision to relinquish and improved emotional well-being.[5] Those who had never arranged post-adoption relationships, or those who did, but the adoption became closed later, showed no differences. In other words, if these interactions begin, but are stopped, it is painful, as though these meetings had never been allowed in the first place.

The more time the two sets of parents have with each other—improved familiarity and trust is more likely to form between them. If meeting dates are set and then canceled, especially if done repeatedly, then uncertainty festers. This harms the delicate balance of the relationship.

Another factor adding to the complexity is the presence of additional siblings in either family. If a birth mother, for example, is already parenting a child and then relinquishes—this becomes another layer in the situations that need to be managed.

> **Renee~**
> I don't have the actual paper that I signed so I don't really know, but I do remember them saying something like there was going to be pictures and updates for five years. We had started out so open and sharing a lot of things. I realize now that's what's done. The reassurance is there, but the actual promise doesn't have to be followed through.
>
> We did have a visit at five months. Then we had a devastating cancellation of a visit. That first Christmas they were supposed to come and spend some time with us. I had decked out the house, got all the presents wrapped, everything. Then, I got a text four days before they were supposed to be here that they weren't coming.
>
> We had been planning for months, and my

oldest daughter is eight then. For that to come through as a text, after crossing the Xs off on the calendar for them to arrive, the planning. [My daughter] knew instantly that something was wrong.

I went through all those emotions and had a really difficult conversation with them. I don't know if they would call it a conversation.

We eventually did get another visit when he was sixteen months old. He didn't know me. He didn't come to me. How do you act? What do I say? That was a tough visit.

And then, three months later, the adoption agency called and said they were going to close the adoption, because of some negative comment I'd made.

It was tough to watch all that. I tried to protect my oldest as much as possible. But when the Skype visits didn't come or the calls wouldn't come, it was just kind of this thing I had to deal with. What I realized through all of this was I always had to be the bad guy. I had to tell her this was going to happen. Then I have to tell his father, my then boyfriend. I mean it was just one thing after another, and it was horrible.

There can be amazing and heartwarming levels of grace and generosity that emerge from parents toward one another, or the alternative can be witnessed. In this story there are other children who end up caught between the power struggles of the two sets of parents.

Abbi~

I knew from the very start I had to be

hypervigilant. They could cut contact with us literally at any point with no explanation, for no good reason.

We got pregnant with our second child, our daughter, who is two years younger than my eldest son that they were raising.

I'm nearly due, I'm seven-ish months pregnant. We went down for a visit and their eldest adoptive son, he's four years old. He looks at me and says, "Do we get to adopt that baby when she's born too?"

And the adoptive mother just laughs it off and doesn't address or say anything to me about it. I move on. Kids say things.

The years progress. We work hard to teach our children very careful language. I won't get into how complex it is trying to raise my younger two children. For them to wonder, "Could I be given up?" or all these confusing, terrifying things. I see them curious and confused and then also feeling abundantly loved by me.

I asked the adopted mother at one point, "I want to let you know that I let my kids know that Jake is their brother. They're very aware of all the details of our story. And I just want to let you know that they might occasionally refer to him as their brother. I just wanted to say that out loud to you to make sure that I was honoring our agreement and had a conversation with you about it."

I was trembling. I was so afraid to have that talk with her.

She looks at me and says, "Well, I guess that's okay because we're all brothers and sisters in the Lord."

> We went down for a visit, and my daughter is about seven. Despite my best efforts, things still go wrong. I think we had a good visit. The kids really bond and play and have a great time, which is all I could hope for. We go home, it's 11:30 at night, and I get a text from the adoptive mother saying, "We've just spoken with Jake, and he let us know that [your daughter] told him that I'm not his real mother, I'm just a stepmother and that you're his real mother. If you can't teach your children the correct truth, then we're not going to allow visitations anymore because this has been traumatizing for Jake."
>
> I said, "I didn't even know that she would think to use the word stepmother. I've been going over this with her for months and she's never used that phrase before. So, I didn't even know that was one to address and make sure she didn't say something specifically like that. I have been working so hard for nine years to make sure that we made you guys feel safe and that we never jeopardize the ability to have visits.
>
> If you want to have a conversation about that, I would be happy to. But, please, please don't reduce visits or say that you don't trust us. I'm doing my very best and I'm sorry."
>
> She didn't respond to me.

Extreme religious narratives can be problematic in adoption in general, but especially so if the view is one where this is all God's plan.

> **Abbi~**
> They wanted my baby and felt deserving of

> my baby. They wanted to be chosen. They'd been praying and begging God for their second child to adopt for a long time, and they knew that He was working on their behalf to make all things come together. A lot of paperwork came through just in time, which was God's way of showing them that this was His plan for my son to go to them. They were always meant to be his parents. It was all about a woman's body being used by God to get them their child.
>
> We had a phone call, the four of us, my husband and hers. We begged them to hear our story and point of view. We'd never been able to tell it. They never allowed us to share any of our feelings about what happened. Why we lost Jake. How voiceless we had felt. How deeply we desired to have a real relationship with our son, to be able to share the things we believed he needed to know.
>
> They literally said to us, "We do not need or want to know your story. It's not pertinent to who Jake is. It's not relevant. God ordained that we be his parents. The fact that you don't understand that is evidence of your lack of a healthy relationship to God. And you are in no way spiritually connected to Jake because he is in no way your son."
>
> So, my husband wrote a letter and told his story. That's when they cut us off and said, "You're both clearly outside of God's will for your lives and we can't allow you to have contact with our family anymore."

Open adoptions can be done well. Some enter these arrangements with the best intentions and then grow and surpass even the most positive expectations. Here is a final example of what can happen when all parties truly show up for each other.

Luna~
We had our first visit when she was two and a half months old. It was very tentative. Alia was being held by her adoptive mom, Susan. I didn't want to take her from her, but at the same time I yearned for her. Then Susan handed her to me, and I was so thankful.

I believed that I cannot show them I'm hurting. I do not want to cause them harm by showing any of my pain.

I came away from that first visit, and it felt so incredible. Then three months later, we went and had another visit. After I left that time, it felt like Alia died, just as painfully as it had at the hospital. I hadn't even fathomed it would be like that again. It became like a twisted game of "Grief Russian Roulette" after every visit. I couldn't do it. I'm ashamed to admit, I didn't take all my visits.

When she turned two, I said, "I don't think I can take this. It's just too hard." And I did share with them, "I am not okay, and I've never shown you my pain, but I'm a broken, broken human being." I had to take all her pictures down in my house. I said, "Please don't send anything until you hear from me. I just need to figure out how, because what I've been doing, and just accepting this, is not working. I need to figure out something else."

They honored that. We had a phone conversation about it on her second birthday because they called me, so I could talk to her.

Then her third birthday was coming. They let me come to their home.

This couple continued adopting. Now they have three girls adopted through domestic infant adoption, and then they have four boys adopted through foster care. Three of the four boys were kinship placements because their biological mother continued to have children. So, they're homeschooling and they're living their lives.

I'd gotten therapy, and I did feel better. They let me drop presents off on Christmas Eve for all the kids. They sent me videos, and we are communicating now via email.

Then three weeks before her fifth birthday, I got an email from them that said, "Here is something that we talked about when we first met you. Once she started asking questions or showing curiosity, we wanted to champion that in our kids. We don't feel like their stories should be kept from them. She has started asking about you." They had a picture of me. On her birthday they would look at photos of me, "That's your birth mom." They've done so much of what they could to make it so that there were no dual loyalties.

Susan said, "I don't know where you are. I know there have been times that it's been harder for you, but if you would like to come over for a little birthday party for Alia, we would love to have you and your family."

Alia is being cute and coy, and she asks if she can sit on my lap. To her mom she says, "Mama, this is my birth mom. I'm sitting in my birth mom's lap." And we all died. Every single one of us lost our soul in that moment.

I wanted to spend time with all the kids. The girls wanted to give me tours of their rooms. We brought presents for everyone. Her parents made Alia wait to open hers after the other kids opened their presents.

[Her parents] said, "We don't really know what this means, but we're going to see how this goes for everyone. There's no map. But we all fiercely love this child." I was able to dispel a lot of the myths of the crazy birth mom because I respected their boundaries. I was so careful. I didn't want to do anything to step on any toes, or offend anyone, or ask too much, or be too needy, or impact them in a negative way.

From ages five to eight, they would invite me about twice a year to come see one of the kids do something.

Years passed, and I got married to my best friend from high school, and all seven of the kids [from Susan] were junior bridesmaids and groomsmen in our wedding. We tried to have kids. I ended up having secondary infertility. I'm calling Susan weeping. And we're weeping together about infertility grief.

Susan said, "At one point, I realized this is the only other woman on the planet who loves my child as much as I do." And what mother wouldn't want more people to love their child?

---

1. Wrobel GM, Grotevant HD, Berge J, Mendenhall T and McRoy R, 'Contact in adoption: the experience of adoptive families in the USA', Adoption & Fostering 27:1, pp 57–67, 2003

2. Linking families in preadoption counseling: A family systems model ... (n.d.). https://www.semanticscholar.org/paper/Linking-Families-in-Preadoption-Counseling%3A-A-Bradbury-Marsh/d850250976d0ea30aff2140008b13ad5f4a0a9f0

3. Monica Faulkner mfaulkner@mail.utexas.edu & Elissa E. Madden (2012) Open Adoption and Post-

Adoption Birth Family Contact: A Comparison of Non-Relative Foster and Private Adoptions, Adoption Quarterly, 15:1, 35-56, DOI: 10.1080/10926755.2012.661333

4. Risks and benefits of open adoption - JSTOR. (n.d.-b). https://www.jstor.org/stable/pdf/1602407.pdf

5. Donna M. Aguiniga, Elissa E. Madden, Bonni Goodwin & Scott Ryan (2023): Post-Adoption Contact Experiences of Birth Mothers, Adoption Quarterly, DOI: 10.1080/10926755.2023.2228772

Chapter 15
Agencies, Marketers, and Manipulation

"Parents are looking for care.
Agencies are looking for supply." ~Ridghaus

Privacy is a myth in the modern world. Most people are aware that wherever they are, they are tracked by their phones and other electronic items. Online browsing history is also followed across all platforms and devices. What any person clicks on, watches, or types into Google is recorded and fed into databases that marketers use to present products and services someone wants them to see.

An expectant mother in crisis looking for resources will undoubtedly turn to the internet. She is seeking help and solutions to her problems if she can find them.

What she will see if she types in anything related to "adoption" as a search term will be hundreds of thousands of results. As with any other search, the top responses will all be paid sponsored ads from the adoption agencies in her area bidding the most money to display their name at the top of the list. Below that will be organic, unpaid results. However, these too are competed for. Marketing agencies charge large sums for coordinated campaigns with paid ads, social media ads, search engine optimization (SEO), and a variety of tools to get their agency highly ranked in the listing. Those who are willing to spend the most, win.

This mother in need will not see government programs for financial help, better health coverage, or more affordable housing. What will also be much harder to find are smaller firms, those without large advertising budgets.

They may or may not be more ethical. However, they are not spending as much money to create a larger supply of infants to place with prospective parents.

The Big Agencies

As in any industry, there are always a few companies that are significantly larger and generate higher revenues than their smaller counterparts. In infant adoption in the US, they are The Gladney Center For Adoption, Bethany Christian Services, and Holt International Children's Services. These three deserve special review, simply because much can be learned by looking at the industry leaders.

Gladney

Started by Edna Gladney, the roots to this agency go back to the 1880s and the first Orphan Trains to stop in Texas. It is a non-profit, 501(c)3 in good standing and tax-exempt since 2008.[1] By the 1990s and to the present day, its administrative offices house educational and counseling centers, and facilitate domestic, international, and foster care adoptions.

Gladney is based in their original home in Fort Worth, Texas plus six additional offices in Texas. They also have locations in six other states and facilitate international adoptions in ten countries.[2]

This agency is unique in that it quotes up front to adopting families that the fee they charge for their service is $55,000.

In a quick look at their financials, for the fiscal 2023 year they received $4.2 million in domestic adoption fees. They also have an endowment worth $23 million and earned another $21 million in grants this year according to their tax return.[3] In their fiscal year, 2023, they completed 133 adoptions (valued at $7.3 million) but not all fees are received in a single fiscal year. Gladney talks about their core goals of providing post adoption support services. They spent $589,000 on those programs which is less than 3% of their total annual expenses of $19 million.[4]

Gladney has an assortment of different websites it owns, including:

- Adoptionsbygladney.com
- Adoption.org
- iAmGladney.org (Gladney University)
- GladneyAdoption.com
- Adopting.org
- Adoption.com
- App.Adoption-Education.com (AdoptEd)

Gladney's labyrinth of websites is extremely smart. They utilize both .org and .com URLs in their assorted site structures. Google recognizes a .org site as an "organization" primarily used for nonprofit websites such as open-source projects, charitable organizations, and educational platforms. From an SEO strategy that means a .org is what is called a "top level domain". Meaning Google gives it additional authority, or "weight" as being a credible source as compared to a .com, which is a commercial enterprise. When a .org site links to pages, articles, or other information on a .com site, that website's rankings improve.

What that means is that within those seven sites owned by Gladney, the three .org sites are using the additional credibility or SEO weight to lend to the rankings of their .com sites. These, along with dozens of "subdomains" or specific sales pages around a particular topic, are what are known in the industry as "feeder sites." Meaning this structure is built entirely to improve Gladney's organic rankings in *all* search engines, and their pages will be found more easily and quickly than others because they are ranked higher, and with more "authority."

Bethany Christian Services

Founded initially as a nonprofit in 1945 in Grand Rapids, Michigan, Bethany became a licensed adoption agency in 1951. It is a 501(c)3 in good standing.[5]

In a quick bird's eye view of Bethany.org one sees they are transitioning out of domestic infant adoption and are more focused on international adoptions and the foster care industry. They are currently accepting domestic infant adoption applications from wanting parents only in three states: Michigan, Iowa, and Nebraska. In 2022 they completed 350 adoptions.

They are also, by far, financially the largest of the big three institutions. For 2022 they show $172 million in revenue with $152 million of that coming from "child support" which is not defined on their website.[6]

Expenses for 2022 show the largest amount as $78 million in refugee and immigrant services, foster care in the US at $31 million, and with just under $20 million listed as "management and general." Also, $11.4 million for adoption, and $8.8 million for family preservation and strengthening programs.[7]

Holt International

Started by Bertha and Harry Holt in 1956, Holt International is the founding institution for international adoption into the US. In fact, it was the first international adoption agency created and pioneered the practice overall.[8] It is a 501(c)3 nonprofit in good standing and has been tax exempt since 1972.[9]

According to the 2022 Annual Report on their website, they received $25.9 million in revenue. $16.5 million is from sponsorship contributions, $5.4 million is from "other contributions and grants"and $5.6 million is from adoption fees received.[10]

Their total expenses are listed at $30 million, with $22 million going for programs and services. $5.2 million was spent for fundraising and $2.5 million is listed for "management and general." The agency serviced 190 international adoptions into the US and 147 of them joined new families in their home country.[11]

Online Marketing Tactics

Every non-profit organization must survive on donations, dues, memberships, or fees for its services or programs. Fundraising mostly involves getting the word out about their organization, its goals, who they serve, or the good work they do. This is universally called marketing.

Setting Holt and Bethany aside, given their international focus, a quick review of what online marketing methods utilized in the US by Gladney seems prudent. All organizations, whether for profit or non, do what works best for them. If a particular marketing or fundraising strategy wasn't successful, it would not be used for long.

A reminder on the size of the domestic infant adoption market: at any given time in the US there are about one million couples seeking to adopt (demand) and only about 18,000 domestically born infants available (supply).

For this examination, the author used personal resources to run a standard paid media analysis via SEMRush and Ahrefs keyword search tools, which are prolifically used in the online marketing industry. Several SEO/paid ad experts assisted, without compensation, in evaluating the data.

For paid rankings, there are online tools that can see what individual companies are spending per month on pay per click ads—those you see as sponsored ads on the top of any internet search. The cost per click (cpc) is a marker that indicates the value of a keyword at a given time. Much like the housing market quotes the value of a home, (it is worth what someone is willing to pay) the cost per click of a particular search term is displayed in the same way.

In a review done on December 21, 2023, the following results show for Gladney. The top keywords they are spending money on are:

1. Pregnant and considering adoption
2. Open adoption agencies near me
3. Adoption agents
4. Adoptions agency
5. Gladney center for adoption Fort Worth
6. Adoption attorney in Houston
7. Adoption lawyer Los Ageless–they are not a licensed agency in the state of CA
8. 1800 adoption–a variation of "dial 1-800..."
9. Louisiana adoption agencies–not a state they are licensed in

These costs per click are relatively high ranging from $9.11 to $13.21 on the number one spot (pregnant and considering adoption). Gladney is ranking in the top 3 for all these search terms, meaning the paid ads they placed and are bidding on will have them displayed in the top 3 spots when searched for. These results are all going to the same click through URL: https://adoption.gladneyadoption.

com/you-dont-have-to-parent.

What this shows is they are willing to spend a lot of money on these search terms and this drives up the price of that same search term for everyone else in the industry.

This analysis was done only on one subdomain of their site listing—Adoption.GladneyAdoption.com. Meaning this list is all driven around a landing page, (or sales page) that is geared around a woman looking to potentially relinquish her child. When this analysis was run, there were a total of 96 search terms, spending $6,464 during the period of November to December 2023. According to their 2023 tax return, Gladney spent just shy of $900,000 on program advertising and promotion during the 12 month period.[12]

If a woman clicks through to the pages they are sending her to, she will see offers for her to learn more about adoption and be shown options for her to select: "currently pregnant" or "I'm already parenting." On the following pages depending upon her circumstance, the messaging is "not ready to parent—adoption is the answer," along with additional slogans, "your heart has no limits," "your bravery has no limits," and that "YOU are in control. You make the adoption plan that feels right for you and your child."

Manipulation, Brokers, and Money

There is no national agency responsible for tracking how many adoptions happen and what the sources are, whether domestic or international. Any laws or rules governing the practices are handled by the states and few allocate significant budgetary infrastructure or personnel to oversee if the rules are being followed.

When there is little accountability, no one should be surprised that problems emerge. They appear to be widespread according to a Time Magazine article from November 2020.[13]

The disparity between the supply and demand for infants has created a murky subculture of adoption facilitators who function as for-profit middlemen between parents, agencies, and adoption attorneys. Some of them charge tens of thousands of dollars for their services.[14]

The National Council for Adoption (NCFA) quotes that of the approximate 18,000 adoptions occurring annually, only 1,000 of those are with public agencies, the balance are handled by private agencies and attorneys.

"The money's the problem," says Adam Pertman, President of the National Center on Adoption and Permanency. "Anytime you put dollar signs and human beings in the same sentence, you have a recipe for disaster."[15]

One birth mother interviewed shares a story about being caught in the middle of the money spent by prospective adopting parents, the broker handling the adoption, and her wishes to potentially change her mind:

> **Shayanne~**
> [My adoption counselor] answers the phone. She asks, "What's your question?"
>
> When I called previously, I had been asking if I could buy a blanket or get food with my gift card? What am I allowed to buy?
>
> She would say of course you can buy a blanket. Of course, you can buy food, do whatever you want. So, she's thinking I'm going to have an easy question.
>
> "Well, what would happen if I kept my baby?" I asked.
>
> She got really quiet for what felt like a century, but it was probably a second or two.
>
> She said, "Well, the adoptive parents can

take you to court and sue you for the money they've already put into this baby and given you for all this other stuff."

I said, "Okay, thanks." And I hung up the phone.

My roommate, a friend from high school, was standing there during the whole conversation, and he remembers it happening.

After that, he also said he remembers me just shutting down.

At the time of this phone call in 2010, the laws in the state of Oregon protected Shayanne from this scenario. Her adoption counselor likely knew that, given it was her job to understand the laws in any state the agency was licensed to practice in.

A Corrupted System

Paige Knipfer is an adoptive parent and former owner of the firm Love Grown Adoption Consulting, who gave an extensive interview and shared her wisdom about what is right, and wrong, with the adoption industry. Since the time of this interview, she has now closed down her consultancy.

Paige ~

There's no perfect way to do adoption. It's hard because websites look beautiful, and agencies promise they're doing all this amazing post-care for birth parents, or that they continue to provide therapy. But then they don't. They fall short, and they don't follow through.

There's this whole gray area of consultant, facilitator, and agencies. Consultants don't need to be licensed. They don't need to have a degree. They can just start their business and start consulting families. Some of these companies, especially the first ones that came out, have exclusive deals with certain agencies. Meaning they get a kickback when a family of theirs is chosen with that agency. So, there's a lot of unethicalness that's been going on for years. Some of these people make millions a year.

The United States is by far the only country that still does it this way. If you look at other countries, this is not how adoptions occur. The whole premise of a prospective adoptive family taking a financial risk and paying lots of money to a private entity who, whether they're for-profit or not, are a business trying to make money. They're competing with one another for these expecting parents. No cap on expecting parents, no cap on any of these expenses. No regulation if all her options have been explained to her. What are the factors of why she's making an adoption plan? And are they setting her up for success if she did want to pursue parenthood? We really fail in a lot of ways. Plus, properly preparing prospective families of all that adoption entails.

The unevenness in state laws around waiting periods, revocation windows, and how much money, if any, a birth parent can receive invites corruption.

In the aforementioned Time article, they asked all 50 states for adoption statistics. Of the 41 who responded, disturbing trends appeared.[16]

Nine states, in particular, stand out as having an outsized number of outgoing adoptions compared to live births, even when accounting for variables in regional birth rates. They are: Arizona, Indiana, Louisiana, Oklahoma, Utah, Florida, Kansas, Nevada and Texas.

Combined, they showed 34% of the births surveyed, but 60% of the outgoing adoptions. This is because these are known in the adoption industry as "favorable" states for the agencies and prospective adoptive parents. Meaning they have shorter windows for waiting periods or revocation times, or allow for more favorable compensation for the expectant mother.[17]

> **More from Paige Knipfer~**
> In Utah, a birth parent's termination of parental rights happens in 24 hours, and it's irrevocable. Irrevocable meaning, she can say, I was coerced, I was high on meds from my C-section, and she can't go back on it. That's what irrevocable means. Families pay more, typically, for a Utah agency to do an adoption, and they may not know that. Utah agencies charge more because that termination of parental rights is irrevocable at 24 hours. It's the quickest adoption that occurs.
>
> I caution families. The agencies are known for flying parents into their state to skirt these laws. So, if she resides elsewhere and comes to Utah to make her adoption plan, she now is following the 24-hour law.
>
> Also, if she crossed state lines and she's on

> Medicaid, that doesn't come with her. They are paying higher adoption agency fees and they're now also footing the medical bill for the expecting parent.
>
> In Florida there is no cap on expecting parent expenses, and her rights are terminated in 48 hours. It is revocable though, at least.
>
> I'll also say this, more adoptions aren't happening in Florida or Utah, more women aren't getting pregnant in these states. They are being transported or relocating to that state because of these laws, or because there is no cap on expenses.
>
> I don't fault the expecting parent for that either, because oftentimes there are so many factors on why she's making an adoption plan, but often finances are one of them. So, if she's offered more money during her pregnancy to relocate to Florida, I don't fault her for that. I fault the agencies and the fact that this isn't being federally regulated. Until then, we're going to keep seeing these loopholes.

Bias and poverty intersect with adoption and child welfare routinely. In Gretchen Sissen's book, *Relinquished,* she interviewed over 100 women who gave birth between the years 2000 and 2020. She says that 80% of the women interviewed said they financially could not keep their child and was their sole reason for placing them. In these interviews, Sisson reports the mothers repeatedly told her they just needed a few thousand dollars to financially meet their initial needs, and that if they would have had the money, they would have parented and kept their babies.[18]

The 2023 tax credit for adopting a child is $15,950 for a

family to help offset their expenses for an adoption. This credit is available as long as their modified adjusted gross income is below $239,230.[19] This tax credit was likely created to encourage middle to lower income families to adopt, most especially from the foster care system. Yet it's available for what most would consider wealthy people and applies if they are adopting from foster care or if they have paid an attorney $75,000 for a private infant adoption.

Both private and public money is involved. Beyond that are the human and mental health costs.

This mother needs only a few thousand dollars but more than $15,000 as a tax credit is offered to a much wealthier family. Many will argue against the creation and expansion of "the welfare state" and say everyone needs to be responsible for themselves. However, the prospective adoptive parents are also making choices. These are the financial paradoxes of adoption.

Adoptees should not have their personhood or placement tied to money or marketing strategies. Adopting parents are generally not at fault for these practices. However, this country and its culture may need to wrestle with the ethics of how it fulfills the "demand" for a child and the natural desire to parent.

1. https://projects.propublica.org/nonprofits/organizations/750917409

2. https://annualreport.iamgladney.org/

3. https://projects.propublica.org/nonprofits/organizations/750917409

4. https://projects.propublica.org/nonprofits/organizations/750917409

5. https://projects.propublica.org/nonprofits/organizations/382822017

6. https://bethany.org/About-Us/Annual-Report/2022-1#financials

7. https://projects.propublica.org/nonprofits/organizations/382822017

8. https://www.holtinternational.org/about/

9. https://projects.propublica.org/nonprofits/organizations/237257390

10. https://www.holtinternational.org/wp-content/uploads/2023/03/Annual-Report-2022-small.pdf

11. https://www.holtinternational.org/wp-content/uploads/2023/03/Annual-Report-2022-small.pdf

12. https://projects.propublica.org/nonprofits/organizations/750917409/202411949349300331/full

13. https://time.com/6051811/private-adoption-america/

14. https://time.com/6051811/private-adoption-america/

15. https://time.com/6051811/private-adoption-america/

16. https://time.com/6051811/private-adoption-america/

17. https://time.com/6051811/private-adoption-america/

18. "Relinquished': Gretchen Sisson presents a clear-eyed look at Adoption - the Washington Post. (n.d.-g). https://www.washingtonpost.com/books/2024/03/06/relinquished-sisson-review/

19. Topic no. 607, Adoption Credit and adoption assistance programs. Internal Revenue Service. (n.d.). https://www.irs.gov/taxtopics/tc607

Chapter 16
Healing and Activism

"Without courage, we cannot practice any other virtue with consistency. We can't be kind, true, merciful, generous, or honest." ~Maya Angelou

For this book, nineteen total birth parents were interviewed. Two of them were men. One third of them come from the Baby Scoop Era while the balance of the placements happened in 1973 or later. Fifty-three percent of these men or women come from an abusive or dysfunctional household. Three of the women or girls were sexually assaulted resulting in the relinquishment. Two others were in abusive relationships at the time of their pregnancies.

Seventy two percent of the women went on to have other children, while three experienced secondary infertility. Three others consciously decided that they did not wish to have subsequent children.

More than half, eleven of the eighteen, were severely controlled by their parents in the relinquishment process, six of whom are post-Scoop Era placements. For two birth mothers in particular, their mothers so dominated the decisions happening around them that they gave their children to adopting couples who were *not of their choosing*. Neither of these women are still in contact with their parents, and while both adoptions were initially open, one of them has closed. Of the eight open adoptions, five were closed by the adopting families, one of them re-opening later.

Four of these birth parents are also adoptees, one a late

discovery, and one coming from the foster care system. Most of the birth parents interviewed are twenty years post placement or longer, except for three whose children are still minors.

Of the thirteen birth parents whose relinquished children are now adults, all have found one another and had some amount of communication. However, less than half have stayed in touch or been able to continue a relationship for longer than ten years. A few have only recently found each other. However, in two cases the adoptees terminated contact, and in one instance the adopted adult committed suicide.

Own It

Birth parents must make peace with their decisions, even if they don't feel they were listened to or were railroaded into relinquishment. Owning their part in the events that unfolded is essential if they are to heal and move forward with their lives. They haul around the burdens and internalized shame that must find release somewhere.

Birth parents often live in fear of their decisions because they are terrified of the judgment and stigma of others. Society does not understand their choices, or the lack of them. Beyond that, their greatest concern is that their grown adopted children will *hate them* for their actions.

These fears are in some ways valid. Adoptees, even when fully grown adults who understand the world, its pressures, and intellectually "get it," can struggle to fully accept being relinquished. Deep inside them often lies a very wounded inner child. What remains are two people who want to bond but have complicated feelings underlying these desires. For an adoptee to truly understand, their birth parents must first take ownership, working through the heavy emotional acceptance of their past choices.

Jennifer~
I did that to her [my relinquished daughter]. And I think that is a part of my motherhood I have had to forgive myself for. *I did that to her.* And she's right. She read The Primal Wound. I couldn't even read the whole thing. I'm an adoption and trauma therapist who tells everyone, "If you want to understand the depths of things, read *The Primal Wound.*" I couldn't finish it because it's true.

All parents mess up. All parents make decisions that end up impacting their children in a negative way. But my decisions changed who she was as a human being. It's not better. Her and I talk about this all the time. It's not better. It's just different.

Ellen~
Every adoptee needs to understand that any woman who makes the decision to give up their child, regardless of why, was probably the best decision for them as a human being. I honestly don't believe any woman wants to give up their baby. If they're forced into making that decision, for whatever reason, that child needs to understand it was the only decision the woman could make. You cannot blame that woman for the choice she had to make.

Laura~
For all those years, I kept that secret and beat myself up constantly. I had to shed the skin of that young woman who thought she was less, who thought she didn't deserve this child. She

had really screwed up, and this was going to follow you the rest of your life and look at what you've done. I had a child, and I gave my child up for adoption. Not something that I would ever have wanted to do.

I didn't make any excuses for it. Even to this day, it's something that hurts and haunts me. But I had to be the adult that realized life goes on. I had to learn to live for the moments we have together, instead of constantly beating myself up about the past.

Healing and Support

Ellen~

That kind of a situation brutalizes a woman for the rest of her life. We never get to have a normal life after that. Any woman who goes through what we went through never gets to be who she could have been.

Some birth mothers have sought therapy, although too few of them do. Often it is much later in life. However, even if decades have passed, it is still helpful. Writing is also powerful and increasingly embraced by first mothers. Memoirs have cropped up over the past decade as the option to self-publish became common. Many traditional publishers are also supporting these much-needed stories.

Cathryn~

I discovered I had symptoms of PTSD. I was jittery, I had nightmares and trouble sleeping. I was on an antidepressant. I worked for the VA and was aware of PTSD but thought that was only a military thing.

I ended up going to a therapist who special-

> izes in PTSD. When I went in to see her, I said, I don't really know what to talk about. I'm a happy person. I don't know why I'm like this. I don't know why I get irritable and cry for no reason. And honest to goodness, I had no idea.
>
> It didn't take long before I started talking about the baby. Getting pregnant, the experience of going away, etcetera. I went through the whole thing, crying every visit. Eventually, I had a visit when I didn't cry, and I said, "I feel like I'm getting better." She said she thought so too. I said, "I think I want to write."

The first support group to fulfill their specific needs was started by CUB (Concerned United Birthparents) in 1976, when founder Lee Campbell placed a personal ad in the Boston Globe to find other birth mothers. The first meeting was held in July of that year.

Since then, dozens of other groups have sprung up for birth parents across the nation. At first, small in-person meetings were all that happened. By 2020 there were a few online gatherings, but one good thing that came out of the pandemic was most meetings moved onto the internet. Now people could connect beyond their geographic locations—and the number of support groups exploded.

Some address a particular member of the triad and stay focused on their needs for expression. Others invite members from all sides of the constellation to gather and share their stories.

> **Ridghaus~**
> I think most of it centers around the idea of truth. And in "truth," I mean also understanding what happened, even if from a biased perspective, 'cause everybody's got their side of the story.

Yvonne~
I refuse to accept the shame. The whole thing of being an unwed mother. Some will even say because you placed your child, you didn't love your child. But people believe what they do based on what they grew up in.

I was in a grief support group. It wasn't about adoption. And someone said to me, "Well, you gave your baby away. You didn't love your baby."

It took all I could to hold myself in the chair, to not come across the table. "Let me educate you, because I don't know your background or whatever. I placed my son. And it wasn't because I didn't love him. It's because I couldn't raise him *at that time*."

Laura~
When things come up, a lot of times we think it's better to hold that inside because it might really mess up this relationship if I tell them the truth. But that is not the case.

Every time I finally opened up and told the truth, it helped not just me but the other person. And if it did destroy a relationship, well, it wasn't meant to be.

CUB has grown steadily over the past forty-plus years. Its mission has evolved beyond just birth parent support. The organization now actively participates in campaigns to help adopted adults gain access to their birth records, and advocates for birth parent rights within adoption processes.

Amy~
When I first started getting involved with CUB,

> I was so taken by the character and the quality of the women. These are warriors. These are women who've lived and triumphed over horrific traumas. They're movers and shakers. They're delightful, and they're fun.
>
> I don't want to be the poster child for being a birth mother. But if I have to be, I think we should understand who we're talking about. These are not women who just leave their baby on the side of the road because we don't care. It's because we thought this was the best opportunity we could give our child.
>
> One of the writers from *This Is Us* came to a CUB retreat and she said, "I want to see who comes to these kinds of meetings." She took all our suggestions and took notes. I really appreciated that she wanted to hear from birth mothers.
>
> But one of the things somebody said during that meeting was "None of us were told that our child would be traumatized by our choice. We were told that we would have trauma." And all of us said, "That's okay. As long as the innocent baby is going to have something better, I'll do whatever it takes."
>
> Nobody said, "Your baby is going to be traumatized and miss you and have a hole in their heart and have identity issues and struggles with self-esteem." Go down the list—nobody ever said any of that to us.

CUB has now been joined by other coalitions such as Bastard Nation, the On Your Feet Foundation and many others—one of the most important being SOS or Saving Our Sisters.

Activism

Renee Gelin started the organization SOS after relinquishing her child in 2011. When she tells her story, she talks about how she wasn't able to make rational choices.

> "Fear was absolutely the underlying thing of how I got here. This decision was made completely on fear and misinformation and omitted information. I was just in such a state of panic. I had lost faith in myself."

She started connecting initially with other moms online through birth mother blogs and eventually met a search angel. These are people who donate their time to help mothers and adoptees from the closed adoption era reunite. But she realized this was too late in the game. The adoption had happened, and she knew she wanted to be out in front of the situation. To prevent others from making what was essentially an unnecessary adoption placement like hers.

Then, while participating in several Yahoo groups formed by mothers, she interacted with a mom in New York who said, "I'm considering [adoption] and I have a car and I'm pregnant with my third, and the dad isn't around anymore. He doesn't want anything to do with the baby and I don't have space in my car for three car seats."

Renee explained, "The mother was connected with an agency, and they were courting her right along, had her matched with a family, the whole bit."

We said, "What else?"

She said, "I just don't know how I would get everybody around." That was her main reason—she didn't have room in her car for three car seats.

Renee and a few other women pooled together and sent her a car seat, and they made sure it fit in her car. The woman ended up keeping her son. "She has continued to parent to this day and recently completed her degree in social work. She just needed someone to tell her to pump the brakes. That's how it got started."

Eventually SOS formed its own formal 501(c)3 organization and has been assisting women in crisis pregnancy situations, or post placement, for nearly a decade. They help explain the process and women's rights prior to relinquishment or providing consent to an adoption in their state. They also share with them the longer-term consequences of relinquishment both to themselves and their children. They have even helped women get their babies returned when attorneys or agencies had not honored revocation windows or ignored the mother's requests for the return of their infants.

They estimate that since their founding, about 1200 to 1500 women, and a few men, have contacted them before relinquishment, seeking help via phone, email, or social media. Of that, only *eight* continued to move forward with their placement.

A Few Words to Adopting Parents

Birth parents and their views toward adopting parents vary widely and are heavily influenced by the way they were treated by the process both before and after placement. Closed adoption circumstances are also vastly different from open ones, but all have strong messages to share.

> **Ellen~**
> About adoptive parents: They opened their home. They opened their hearts to a human being who may not have had another life. I think adoptive parents are to be commended. Not everyone can have children. If people want a child, if they want to raise a family, adoptive parents need to be commended and

thanked.

Now, having said that, not every parent, not every family is going to end up being good. We're all flawed humans, and it may not be a happy ending, but give them the grace of a thank you for wanting to give another human being a place to be loved. To be loved is something that too many people don't get to experience.

I did not grow up in a household where there was any love, and that breaks a human. It leaves permanent damage, so any adoptive parent that wants to give a child a chance, I say kudos and applause.

Lori~
Birth parents are not on this earth to give anybody a child. And I'm sorry that you can't have children for whatever reason, but it is not my purpose to fix it for you.

Yvonne~
What adoptive parents need to understand is that a child came from somewhere before you got there. They grew in someone—they have the DNA of someone other than you. I will always say that I wanted to place my son in a good home. It was not my intention to provide a solution to a couple who couldn't have their own. Big difference.

There's a lot of brokenness and hurt and pain on all sides. And everyone has to deal with it. My constant phrase is, everyone needs to do their work.

I call it mirror work, and consistently do it. Your mirror work is the fact of who you are,

> what you bring to the table, and how open you are. How can you meld and understand and build with someone else without recognizing the brokenness we all come from. I call it drama trauma, and we need to eliminate it as best as we can. So, to anyone in the triad, just make sure you do your work, get help, do your reading, get connected with other people.

Adoptive parents hold the keys to the way their child will feel toward their birth parents. Their children learn a frame of reference for their natural family, which carries forward into adulthood. This is true in a closed, fully open, or semi-open adoption. If shame or secrecy is prevalent, or if the adoptee feels there is a loyalty test attached to their desire to know their birth family, they sense that, which can have the effect of shutting them down and lead to rejecting their birth parent(s).

Alternatively, if there is the willingness to be expansive and give grace, much beauty in these relationships can occur. It often means doing a lot of hard, but worthy, internal work.

Openness may not be a physical thing, but rather an attitude or expression of the heart. An open approach to the nuances and complexity of emotions within the adoption experience benefits everyone in the constellation.

Part IV - Adoptive Parents

Chapter 17
The Path to Adoption

"Your children are not your children. They are the sons and daughters of life's longing for itself. They come through you but not from you, and though they are with you, yet they belong not to you." ~Kahlil Gibran

Parents are not born—they are made. Forged through the power of will, they endure sleepless nights, endless worry, and humbling experiences they pray result in happy, healthy adults. All parents make sacrifices and are often brought to their knees by the overwhelming needs of their children.

How they parent, what they teach their children, both formally and through unconscious behavior, becomes the model for how *their* children will parent. From one generation to the next, all men and women are first informed by how they were raised.

Parenting is considered the hardest and most fulfilling journey that exists. When adoption is added to the creation or expansion of a family, the complexities increase.

Couples choose to adopt for a variety of motivations. Whatever their reasons they may not have a great deal of information before beginning. Adoption *is* different. A great many parents interviewed lament they wished they had understood the additional nuances created by adopting a child *before* beginning their journeys.

Understanding the unique fundamental needs of an

adoptee is the first and highest priority. Creating a thriving adopted adult requires parents who are attuned to their adoptee's specific needs.

What improves the experience for adoptees makes life better for everyone. This premise must be the starting point for all conversations about the practice.

The Journey Begins

The decision to have children is not a trivial one. Many women know from their childhood or teen years they are drawn to the role of parenting. They are the girls who babysit early and tend to be the neighborhood caregivers looking after little ones. Maternal instincts fully in place, they know they want to be mothers.

Other women are the opposite. They appear to be highly uninterested in the concept and may maintain this attitude throughout their lives. Most are somewhere in between.

Men also run through this same spectrum. They may know they wish to be fathers and have a family, while others will not pursue these goals.

For parents who adopt, there is a clear decision. Whether an individual or a couple, it is assumed they want to parent and are willing to walk through the doors of an agency.

Two separate influences are in play. One is the desire to be a mother or father, and adoption becomes the solution to a problem they didn't expect. Others, influenced by personal reasons, want to adopt. Sometimes, these reasons intertwine.

> **Ken~**
> I had this latent longing to be a dad. I always knew it would be something that would make me happy, but it was not something conscious.
>
> I was with my good friend and he and I

went to see this movie, which was beautiful and amazing. When it ended, I had a really funny feeling inside. I went to the bathroom and closed the stall door. This deep stirring in me became clear. I realized I wanted to become a father, and I knew it.

I went out and I said to my friend, "Guess what? I want to be a dad."

A few days later I'm visiting my parents and I said to them, "Just because I'm gay does not mean you're not gonna have grandchildren."

It felt very important to me to be able to think about giving them that gift. And then I began my journey.

Lori~

I finally met the man of my dreams and imagined making babies with him. Then things didn't go the way we expected. And so, like many before me and many after, we left behind the arduous trail of infertility and got on the trail of adoption.

Once we got onto the adoption trail, everything seemed to go smoothly until we became parents.

I thought I knew adoption because my best friend growing up was an adoptee. One of my high school friends was a girl who went away [to have her baby and relinquish it]. I don't recall if I knew any adoptive parents, but I certainly knew Disney movies and Hollywood stories of adoption separation and reunion, and happy ever after stuff. Adoption seemed so doable compared with infertility at the time.

The Different Methods

In the United States there are three legal mechanisms to adopt a child:

1. Adoption from Foster Care: Administered by public agencies, parents file their desire to foster to adopt and begin the home study, education, and screening process. This is typically the least expensive option in the US and also the faster path to an adoption.

2. Private Domestic Adoption: Handled by a for profit or non-profit agency or lawyer, couples meet with a professional and begin the home study and screening process in their state. Private adoption is often the most expensive and lengthy route.

3. International Adoption: Handled by a for profit or non-profit agency or lawyer, all the same procedures occur as with a domestic adoption. The international laws and requirements are reviewed, and the parents create a plan with the agency. Most, but not all, will travel into the country to complete the adoption. This is often an expensive and lengthy process.

A Look at the Numbers

When researching infant adoption in the US one of the surprising hurdles becomes finding accurate annual reporting of the exact numbers of private adoptions. While general numbers are published, they may not reflect all that occur. Currently not all states are required to report. Some do gather data, but private agencies and attorneys are not universally compelled to report the number of private adoptions completed. The National Council for Adoption (NCFA) is the representative of the adoption industry in Washington DC, and they are seeking to improve this accountability. As of the spring of 2023 a new bill (H.R. 6700) known as the Adoption Counts Act, would require states to report private adoption numbers to the US Department of Health and Human Services.[1]

Over the past 20 years, adoption from foster care is the most dominant form practiced in the US, and international and domestic infant adoption are both in decline. However, the demand for infants remains high in the US, and it is estimated for every one child that is placed and available, at least thirty-six families are waiting to adopt.[2]

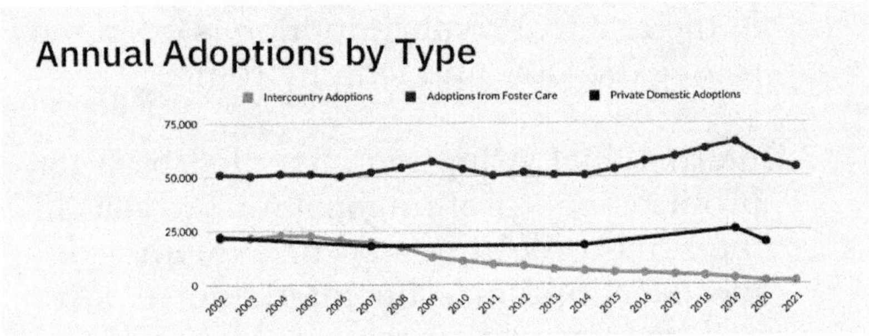

*Source NCFA website: https://adoptioncouncil.org/article/adoption-statistics/

Adoptive parents tend to be affluent and well educated in general. Historically this may not always have been the case, but it appears to be so, now.

Income levels of those adopting from private domestic adoption are the wealthiest. 24% report annual income between $75,000 - $100,000 and 20% make more than $150,000. Those adopting from foster care, 28% report their family income as between $50,000 - $75,000 and 25% between $75,000 - $100,000. 11% of foster care families make less than $50,000 per year.

Education levels are high in all three adoption method categories. 34 to 40% have a bachelor's degree and 23 to 32% a masters. The motivations for adopting greatly influence the type they pursue. When infertility is the primary motivation, those parents chose the route of a private domestic adoption more frequently than the other two options. Those who adopt internationally were influenced by their extended families or religious motivations most frequently. Foster care was the most specifically motivated method. The reasons those parents adopt is primarily to give a permanent home to a child in need.[3]

These statistics show that the couples who become adoptive parents exude and represent the values American society rewards most. They are well educated and have invested in maintaining successful careers. Presumably, this privilege will benefit their children, regardless of their source.

Different Motivations in Detail

As researchers have started to study the motivations of adoptive parents, they have broken these down into three main considerations: those centered on the self, the child, or both simultaneously.[4] Issues surrounding infertility or the desire to have a certain number of children, for example, center on the self, and the parents are making decisions around adoption for their own desires. Those wanting to help a child are more likely to be looking at adoption from foster care, or this could be a combination of motives.

Infertility

Among heterosexual couples, infertility is the root cause and most research has been done around this as the primary motivation.[5]

Grief over infertility is an invisible wound. These

couples are mourning someone who was real to them, or what they imagined or hoped would be, but isn't tangible to the outside world. It is disenfranchised grief. Family and friends may miss or fail to understand its depth.[6]

These scenarios and their pain go back centuries. What is more modern, is the idea that adoption is a solution to the emotional loss. But is it?

According to a study conducted by H. David Kirk in 1964, "Adults who failed to have children naturally were labeled abnormal and experienced discrimination. Adopting other people's children, Kirk found, did not relieve their pain. The agony of infertility followed them into parenthood."[7]

Prior emotional losses are not cured by adoption and should never be seen as a cure for the couples' grief. "When parents do not work through their emotions, unrealistic expectations about the adopted child, a tendency to reject the differences between adoptive and non-adoptive families, [and] difficulty in engaging in adoption socialization and higher levels of parenting stress may arise."[8]

If couples have struggled with infertility or have childhood experiences they need to heal from, this is work they will want to do separately—preferably before bringing a child into the middle of these troubled waters.

Adoptive parents divorce at a slightly higher rate than the general population, including non-adoptive families. The reasons for this are speculative, but include the stresses caused by infertility, financial strains from the costs of the adoption itself along with any prior infertility treatments, and the additional needs and struggles that may come with an adoption.[9]

From a study done in 2015, the researchers conclude, "...prospective adoptive parents would benefit from extensive pre-adoption preparation regarding the array and severity of child problems they might encounter, as well as post adoption support and services aimed at helping them to effectively handle child and parenting-related difficulties."[10]

Julie~

We got married. We knew we wanted to have kids, that was never a question. We kind of knew we wanted to adopt but had no idea we were going to have trouble having children. But adoption was something that interested us.

Then, after seven years of trying to have a child and multiple miscarriages, I think it's either nine or eleven—we kept thinking *this* is going to be the time.

And after lots and lots of testing and procedures, it was really an unexplained case. So my doctor, who had walked through all of this with me said, "I don't have an answer for you. If you want a child now, the best thing I can tell you to do is adoption." Because IVF and things like that really weren't on the table, because they didn't know why I was miscarrying.

So, we started talking about adoption. For me, it brought a little bit of peace because it finally gave me a goal. I could put trying to carry a child to term behind me.

One can hope that wanting couples who will or have faced these issues, take the time to reflect. They deserve the space to honor their losses. Receiving guidance from professionals and most especially an adoption informed counselor is an excellent idea if they are considering this path.

Religion

There is very limited research examining religious motives to adopt and the outcomes among adoptees. Theological beliefs have a long-standing history with parents willing to raise non-biologically related children. A study in 2003 of a large sample of white adoptive parents showed twenty-four percent listed religious influences as a prime reason to adopt.[11]

Going back to the original suggested motivations, those being centered on the self, the child, or both, religious reasons are more closely aligned to the "child-centered" or "both the self and the child" interests. The altruism of creating a better life for someone or doing good works for the benefit of society, pair easily with religious informed positions on adoption. It can be seen as a moral act, but it is not without self-interest even when motivated by theology or the fulfillment of God's will.

One way of viewing the topic is to discern and discuss the difference between intrinsic and extrinsic motivations. An intrinsically motivated couple may adopt because they believe scriptures direct them to do so or they were led by God to help a child. Extrinsic motivations revolve around using religion to adopt for improved personal stature.[12]

One study published in 2017 engaged a group of self-identified Evangelical Christians who are all adoptive parents, overwhelmingly to children adopted internationally. The researchers divided their commonly held theological motivations into the following groupings:

- **Adoption due to biblical mandate:** The biblical requirement to care for orphans as documented in numerous bible passages. The researchers noted the "underlying posture of the parents citing this theme was one of obedience."
- **Adoption viewed as ministry:** Adopting a

child was seen as evangelizing and discipling a child to the Christian God and way of life they would unlikely have otherwise. "...the church should be adopting all the time..."

- **Physical adoption as a result of spiritual adoption:** Many Christians view their relationship with God as though He has "vertically" adopted them. Practicing adoption to children in need is "horizontally" adopting them on earth.
- **Adoption due to blessings:** These parents feel blessed by what they have or achieved, and wish to share this with others. The biblical theme of "to whom much has been given, much is required" reflects this concept.[13]

The researchers also noted the consistent romanticization of adoption through the Christian viewpoint. The heart-warming and appealing aspects of the practice, regardless of their reasons, were easy for these parents to find.

The researchers also stated religiously motivated parents are an important resource. They are often willing to raise children with special needs or who are older. Such children are often harder to place, so these parents' willingness to take them in has become something social workers rely on, especially within the foster care system.[14]

Child Centered Motivations

Hundreds of thousands of children in the US are in the foster care system. At any given time, there are over 100,000 children available to adopt, and approximately 50,000 to 60,000 of them will be adopted each year. Another 25,000 young adults will age out of the foster care system annually.[15]

The need for families to adopt older children or those with the presumed trauma they may have experienced due to abuse or neglect, is huge. "Very little research has focused on factors that influence foster parents' decisions to adopt." Kinship foster care has been associated with longer stays in the system, but kin foster parents appear less likely to formally adopt because they already see themselves as family. These foster parents also at times cited their struggle to adopt may be financially related.[16]

Regardless of the hardships and troubles these couples and families may experience, most view their sacrifices as well worth it, and do not regret their decisions to adopt.

> **Leah~**
> We hear a lot of times, "I don't know how you can love a child that's not your own." And I want to shake them and say, "But they *are* mine." I can't explain it, but *they are my children*. I wish they understood you can love another child as much as you love your own. There is no difference if your child comes from a rough background and has issues or if a child born to you has issues. The root cause may be different, but you love them the same.
>
> A lot of times, people say, "Oh, I can't do what you do. I would get too attached." Yeah, that's the point. You know, I'm not some saint. I'm not, *"Oh, I'm so great and grand and wonderful, because I did this."*
>
> Anybody can do this. It's a choice. And it's hard. It's the hardest thing I've ever done. But anyone can do it if they're willing to love kids.

Everyone within an adoption experience may find themselves grieving. They all experience losses. Birth parents surrender their blood and treasure to another family. An adoptive parent may also be grieving. Lastly, a great many adoptees will face their own emotional turmoil.

Regardless of the motivations, once adoptive parents bring home their little one, their journey has begun.

---

1. https://adoptioncouncil.org/advocacy/action-center/#/

2. Adoptions, A. (n.d.-a). https://www.americanadoptions.com/pregnant/waiting_adoptive_families#:~:-text=While_it_is_difficult_to,who_is_placed_for_adoption

3. https://adoptioncouncil.org/wp-content/uploads/2022/07/Profiles-in-Adoption-Part-One.pdf

4. Why and how do parents decide to adopt? A study ... (n.d.-c). https://onlinelibrary.wiley.com/doi/full/10.1111/cfs.13001

5. Why and how do parents decide to adopt? A study ... (n.d.-c). https://onlinelibrary.wiley.com/doi/full/10.1111/cfs.13001

6. Webmaster, C. (2023, March 23). The invisibility of infertility grief. Counseling Today. https://ct.counseling.org/2019/09/the-invisibility-of-infertility-grief/#

7. Adoption history: Shared fate: A theory of adoption and mental health, 1964. (n.d.). https://pages.uoregon.edu/adoption/topics/sharedfate.htm

8. Why and how do parents decide to adopt? A study ... (n.d.-c). https://onlinelibrary.wiley.com/doi/full/10.1111/cfs.13001

9. https://www.thechaosandtheclutter.com/archives/adoption-marriage#:~:text=Though_the_actual_statistics_seem,present_in_many_adoptive_homes

10. Goldberg, A. E., & Garcia, R. (2015). Predictors of relationship dissolution in lesbian, gay, and heterosexual adoptive parents. Journal of Family Psychology, 29(3), 394–404. https://doi.org/10.1037/fam0000095

11. Emily J. Helder , Marjorie L. Gunnoe & Hannah Timmermans (2020): Religious Motivation to Adopt as a Predictor of Adoptive Family Structure, Parental Discipline, and Outcomes, Adoption Quarterly, DOI: 10.1080/10926755.2020.1790451

12. Emily J. Helder , Marjorie L. Gunnoe & Hannah Timmermans (2020): Religious Motivation to Adopt as a Predictor of Adoptive Family Structure, Parental Discipline, and Outcomes, Adoption Quarterly, DOI: 10.1080/10926755.2020.1790451

13. Firmin, M. W., Pugh, K. C., Markham, R. L., Sohn, V. A., & Gentry, E. N. (2017). Perspectives regarding motivations for adoption by Christian adoptive parents: A qualitative study. Journal of Psychology and Theology, 45(1), 58–68. https://doi.org/10.1177/009164711704500105

14. Emily J. Helder , Marjorie L. Gunnoe & Hannah Timmermans (2020): Religious Motivation to Adopt as a Predictor of Adoptive Family Structure, Parental Discipline, and Outcomes, Adoption Quarterly, DOI: 10.1080/10926755.2020.1790451

15. Bramlett, M. D., & Radel, L. F. (2017). Factors associated with adoption and adoption intentions of nonparental caregivers. Adoption quarterly. https://www.ncbi.nlm.nih.gov/pmc/articles/PMC4774051/

16. Bramlett, M. D., & Radel, L. F. (2017). Factors associated with adoption and adoption intentions of nonparental caregivers. Adoption quarterly. https://www.ncbi.nlm.nih.gov/pmc/articles/PMC4774051/

Chapter 18
Essentials for Adoptive Parents – Attachment

"I thought adopting was the end, but I found out it was the beginning." ~ Lori Holden

What now? However long they have waited and whatever the circumstances, many of these parents believe nothing could be harder than what they just went through.

The First 1000 Days

Beginning pre-birth, the first 1000 days of early development are more crucial than most parents understand. The Primal Wound outlines the possible effects of maternal separation. But could a distressing pregnancy influence an infant's development before birth? According to a study in 2006, researchers found "Maternal stress and trauma exposures during pregnancy are associated with maternal reports of increased infant distress in response to novelty, poor recovery from distress, fearfulness, and difficult temperament."[1]

Much of this research is relatively new. However, more and more science is showing the prenatal environment an unborn child develops within appears to affect it later in life.

Pre-Birth

Within the formation of the human brain, the amygdala is conventionally referred to as the human "fear receptor," and it is considered to be particularly sensitive to adversity during development. Prenatal stress has been shown in several studies to increase its volume in certain conditions, such as mothers with chronic depression or women showing higher cortisol levels during their pregnancy because of stress.[2] This same study concluded higher stress during pregnancy may result in "brain network reorganization patterns". The researchers also theorized, "This may, in turn, reflect a diminished ability to regulate fear and anxiety in young adults exposed to more prenatal stress."[3]

Jen Winkelmann, adoption competent therapist and the founder of Inward Bound, shares similar information from her own study and experience in more common terms:

> "Psychological processing starts during the second trimester of pregnancy, and even though there's no language associated with intra-uterine experiences, babies still have them. Whatever the birth mother is experiencing, so also is the child. They're literally connected. A child feels her emotions all the time. So, if from the second trimester of pregnancy on, a baby's developmental experience is, if "life is calm", then things are good.
>
> However, maybe there's a birth mother who is wrestling with whether to parent, and the stress that goes with the weight of this decision. Or maybe there are people in the life of the birth mother who are not supportive of the pregnancy. The child having that intrauterine experience is going to have a very different foundation laid for his or her brain than the other, who got the experience

> of "life is calm." Then, there's the spectrum of everything in between.
>
> So, a child who's in an environment of trauma or of stress during the development of this structure of the brain, is going to have a quicker hair trigger on 'fight, flight, freeze, or please' than their same-age counterpart who was not bathed, for lack of a better term, in stress hormones.
>
> When we talk about the intrauterine experience, that time is basically a template for where the baby's brain starts."

After Birth

A baby's thinking brain or neocortex does not develop until around age three. Before then, what is mostly present are not thoughts, but feelings. From the book *Mother Hunger,* Kelly McDaniel lays out the importance of early childhood attachment.

In these earliest days of an infant's existence, a baby or toddler lives in a "body-based emotional experience informed by the early environment." McDaniel states this translates internally to "feelings are facts." When a baby cries or fusses and someone responds, all is well. If no one comes, nothing is well. "Separation from a familiar caregiver means danger." These emotions are stored by the body's nervous system and become the only known reality for the infant. These feelings become what are known as implicit memories.[4]

If an infant is separated from their mother after only a few days or even hours, as will often happen in an adoption, then this tiny baby's body is absorbing this disruption. Which will stay with them, stored in their unconscious memory banks. "Early emotional experiences literally become embedded in the architecture of our brain," McDaniel says.[5]

Another scenario shared by therapist Amy Barker is this:

> "In Seattle, I did a talk for a grad school for therapists who were there training. I said, 'When I say the word adoption, what comes to mind?' They all said, 'Win-win, rescued, beautiful,' all those things. Then I said, 'Okay, now I want you to give me the connotation, the words that come to mind when I say the word abduction.' They answered, 'Oh, life-changing, heinous, horrible.' I said, "To the developing brain of the newborn, the experience is exactly the same. They have been taken from their mother, and it is terrifying for them. This is how they process adoption." People were so confused. These were therapists in training, but they couldn't wrap their heads around it. But I think that's the work we still have to do. There can be positives in this story, but there is trauma at the base, at the core."

The nervous system of an infant is very vulnerable, and if they sense distress from separation, what occurs is the triggering of a natural fear response. When this happens the baby's brain will be flooded with adrenaline and cortisol which can be damaging to these regions of the brain still in development.[6] If this happens regularly, where a baby is stressed in their environment, and then is soothed, but the pattern repeats, an infant's nervous system will adjust by creating a body built to tolerate that stress response.

Research also indicates infant temperament has significant developmental consequences long term.[7] These types of traumas can cause developmental delays, mental and physical health impacts, and create behavioral problems and difficulty in forming healthy relationships.[8]

This all begins to paint a very concerning picture of what has happened inside this tiny baby's brain and body. But there is hope.

Neuroplasticity

A much more holistic view is needed to give parents better tools and help their adopted children adapt.

If couples can understand their baby has also experienced a loss it cannot process or verbally express, this is a good first step to helping their child heal.

> **Therapist, Jen Winkelmann~**
> "If I've had a traumatic event right after my birth, and my amygdala is going to continue to be shaped through the first eighteen months of life - how my caregiver steps into a place of helping to calm my fear receptor is going to play a significant role around my emotional regulation going forward in life.
>
> Does this mean as I grow, I can't work with my fears, because everything is "locked in" after eighteen months? No. One of the things we've learned about the brain in the last ten to fifteen years has to do with neuroplasticity. The quality of our experiences and the repetition of them can change the wiring of our brains.

> An example of this is what we call 'the attachment cycle.' I think of it like a clock: twelve is "need", three is "signal", six is "gratification", and nine is "regulation." Every time we make it around that clock, we're laying down a file in another structure of the brain. This helps to regulate the amygdala, which is our fear receptor, in the hippocampus. It all fits together, but we're not all taught these things about the brain and its wiring.
>
> How can we make sure everybody has the information they need and are open to learning it? Because the stakes are high!
>
> It plays out in a major way with adoptees for sure. But guess what? This applies to all humans—not just adoptees. Understanding the brain and regulation can help you in every single relationship you have with another human being for your entire life."

Science backs up much of what is shared above. But there is no "one" adoption experience.

The early stages of brain development lay the groundwork for human adaptability and resilience, yet they are not without their challenges. Given the significant impact experiences can have on brain development, children are particularly susceptible to being negatively affected during this critical period. However, this phase also presents a prime opportunity for parents to make a positive impact. Favorable early experiences wield meaningful influence on children's prospects for accomplishment, fulfillment, and overall well-being.[9]

"There is considerable evidence that sensitive parenting plays a causal role in recovery." Parenting styles can have a positive effect. Those who encourage and reinforce secure attachment with warm, sensitive, parent-child relationships can create better developmental outcomes.[10]

Parents need to show up expecting *anything* other than a blank slate. The structure a family sets up around adoption needs to reflect emotional safety and security and provide an environment where they can thrive.

Yes, And...

Adoptive parents may be asking what happened to their beautiful adoption dream and picture postcard family. That's understandable, and it can still happen, but this needs to be based in an environment of truth.

Yes, it *can* be beautiful and ultimately the right decision, creating a positive experience for the adoptee—which should always be the goal. *And,* it also has some inherent trauma and loss involved by separating a baby from its mother. The child may, in fact, be grieving this pre-verbal loss but have no ability to find the words to communicate their feelings.

According to Robert Allen Hafetz from Adoption Education & Family Counseling, "There is a disconnection in adoptees between their emotions and their ability to identify them. This is the core issue in adoption, and it is the foundation of most of the problems that occur in adoptive parenting."[11]

Yes. And... It gives parents a framework to be able to attune to the needs of their child. If parents can allow for a wide variety of emotions their children may need to express but not see it as a personal failure of theirs, this can become bedrock to build upon. To meet their child where they are in the moment. Acknowledge their right to feel as they do before responding. This goes a long way to establishing a bond that lets openness and talking flourish, so healing can begin, and their children can thrive.

1. Brand SR, Engel SM, Canfield RL, Yehuda R. The effect of maternal PTSD following in utero trauma exposure on behavior and temperament in the 9-month-old infant. Annals of the New York Academy of Sciences. 2006;1071:454–458. [PubMed] [Google Scholar]

2. Mareckova, K., Miles, A., Liao, Z., Andryskova, L., Brazdil, M., Paus, T., & Nikolova, Y. S. (2022). Prenatal stress and its association with amygdala-related structural covariance patterns in Youth. NeuroImage. Clinical. https://www.ncbi.nlm.nih.gov/pmc/articles/PMC8938327/#:~:text=In%20humans%2C%20all%20the%20major,Jones%20et%20al.%2C%202019)

3. Mareckova, K., Miles, A., Liao, Z., Andryskova, L., Brazdil, M., Paus, T., & Nikolova, Y. S. (2022). Prenatal stress and its association with amygdala-related structural covariance patterns in Youth. NeuroImage. Clinical. https://www.ncbi.nlm.nih.gov/pmc/articles/PMC8938327/#:~:text=In%20humans%2C%20all%20the%20major,Jones%20et%20al.%2C%202019)

4. McDaniel, K. (2021). Mother hunger: How adult daughters can understand and heal from lost nurturance, protection, and guidance. Hay House, Inc.

5. McDaniel, K. (2021). Mother hunger: How adult daughters can understand and heal from lost nurturance, protection, and guidance. Hay House, Inc.

6. McDaniel, K. (2021). Mother hunger: How adult daughters can understand and heal from lost nurturance, protection, and guidance. Hay House, Inc.

7. Enlow, M. B., Devick, K. L., Brunst, K. J., Lipton, L. R., Coull, B. A., & Wright, R. J. (2017). Maternal lifetime trauma exposure, prenatal cortisol, and infant negative affectivity. Infancy : the official journal of the International Society on Infant Studies. https://www.ncbi.nlm.nih.gov/pmc/articles/PMC5624542/#R11

8. The invisible wounds: Understanding the long-term effects of pre- and perinatal trauma. Red Beard Somatic Therapy - Madison, WI & Boulder, CO. (n.d.). https://www.redbeardsomatictherapy.com/post/the-invisible-wounds-understanding-the-long-term-effects-of-pre-and-perinatal-trauma

9. Baby's brain begins now: Conception to age 3. Urban Child Institute. (n.d.-a). http://www.urbanchildinstitute.org/why-0-3/baby-and-brain

10. David Brodzinsky a, a, b, c, group, A. a very heterogeneous, Crosbie, J., Demers, L. A., Hodel, A. S., McLaughlin, K. A., Merritt, D. H., Meyer, M., Nelson, C. A., Peñarrubia, M., Raby, K. L., Sheridan, M. A. v., Tottenham, N., Dries, L. van den, Bij, J. van der, Askeland, K. G., ... Gunnar, M. R. (2021, September 17). Adoption and trauma: Risks, recovery, and the lived experience of adoption. Child Abuse & Neglect. https://www.sciencedirect.com/science/article/abs/pii/S0145213421003781#preview-section-snippets

11. Parenting the adopted child Robert Allan Hafetz MS/MFT Adoption Education& Family Counseling LLC. (n.d.)

Chapter 19
Outdated Advice and the Importance of Openness

"Blood can help make family, but family often transcends blood." ~DaShanne Stokes

For most of the last century, adopting parents were told to take the child home and raise it as if they were their own. There was no notion the process was traumatic for the baby.

This dominant opinion came from both medical and mental health professionals—therefore, parents never questioned it. Compounding the effects of this was the Baby Scoop Era where a massive wave of adoptions took place while these attitudes prevailed.

Unfortunately, what this created was a vast unwillingness for the psychological community to listen to and fully understand the needs of adopted individuals, or their parents.

A study done in 1970, "How They Fared in Adoption", surprised researchers in multiple ways. It focused on the outcomes of one hundred adopted adults whose placement occurred between 1931 and 1940. During that time, no serious thought was given to how the adoptive couple fared after facing infertility.[1]

The researchers used markers such as school performance, the quality of past and present child/parent relationships, physical health, vocational outcomes, and divided the adoptees into low, medium, or high problem groupings. When most of the parents were interviewed, what astonished the researchers was the type of parenting or the strictness of their style had little to do with the outcomes. Also, seventy-three percent of the parents insisted the problems they had encountered with their children had nothing to do with their being adopted.[2]

Only one thing did appear to affect the outcomes: "... adoptees who expressed more curiosity about their natal backgrounds were more highly clustered in the "high problem" group. This finding confirmed a view that was widespread at the time. Indifference to genealogy was a sign of success. Adoptees who gave little or no thought to the facts of their birth had turned out well."[3]

Indifference to Genealogy

Genealogy is currently an industry worth $3.5 billion in the US. People have always valued knowing where they came from and kept photos, letters, and memorabilia. They enjoy sharing artifacts with their children and grandchildren so they could pass these stories on to future generations.

But adoption was intended to be the systematic erasure of a child's familial history. Their original identity and surname are subjugated to their new family and overwritten. Fifty years ago, when the above study was written, the prevailing attitude was, in general, children were to be "seen and not heard." Their lives were secondary to the adults around them. Many youngsters felt tolerated rather than celebrated.

Every adoptee is a walking, talking experiment in nature versus nurture. If their nature is denied, a paradoxical existence is being forced onto that young person.

If indifference to one's physical DNA, identity, and

personal or cultural history is deemed a "success" in adoption, then what does this say about the process? The study directly states that compliant adoptees who didn't question their circumstances made it easier on everyone around them.

One should wonder if this "indifference to their genealogy" was real or feigned. Adopted children have often felt muzzled by the assumption they should be happy and are unable to acknowledge or process their feelings. If one understands there is innate trauma to adoption, then this also feeds into whatever is happening psychologically.

How significant those emotions are varies for every adoptee. Many will develop coping mechanisms to manage their internal landscape. These can manifest as feelings of anxiety, hyper-vigilance, depression, or attachment disorders. Others may show or experience few, if any, symptoms and never outwardly appear to struggle.

The price-tag for an adoptee feeling they belong to their new family should not include the denial of their inner nature or first family.

The Impacts on Behavior, Attachment, and Identity

Every adoption, if one is necessary, should be as open as humanly possible. One of the few meta-studies on open adoption shows generally broad benefits to adoptees. The more normalized and at ease the parties are with one another, the better. Familiarity breeds compassion. "Studies that have explored the experiences of adoptive parents have shown that they become more comfortable with the arrangement over time and generally believe that contact (direct or indirect) has positive repercussions for the family and child."[4] These parents also declared that maintaining closeness with the birth family was important, even through their personal discomforts.

One longitudinal study of ninety-two adoptive families showed long-term direct relationships with the birth family reduced problems of aggressiveness or rule-breaking with the adopted children.[5] The same study also found these benefits increase for adoptees who have siblings involved in their lives.

Two other studies explore how birth family contact influenced the emotional adjustment of these youths. Both found a positive relationship between emotional adjustment and interaction with the birth family. One discovered that female adoptees in adolescence showed lower levels of adoption preoccupation when there was sibling involvement. A sample of sixty-eight young adolescents, found that post-adoption contact was linked to higher self-esteem and fewer symptoms of depression.[6]

In looking at the topic of identity, five studies found a link between adoptees' identity formation and openness in communication and visitation arrangements. Personal relationships with their native family allow adoptees to acquire more information, filling the gaps in their life story. They also come to understand their birth parents' circumstances, forming a more realistic view of them.[7]

A cross-sectional survey of over 1500 adoptive parents in 2016, found that "openness in adoption was related to less distrust toward the adoptive family" by the adoptee.[8]

> **Paige~**
> Start your education journey as early as possible. My daughter was probably three years old when she was playing with a baby doll, and she told me she wanted to be a mom, not a birth mom.

So, give your kids some credit. They definitely understand a lot more than you think, and they have a lot more questions they may not feel comfortable asking. We have very open conversations and relationships. We don't reside in the same state, but we Facetime and visit as much as we can.

I can see characteristics or food preferences my daughter enjoyed as a little kid that my daughter's birth mom has. That came up organically, and I find it fascinating. I can see a mesh of all of us in her.

When we first started our adoption journey, I very much didn't understand open adoption. I think a lot of adoptive parents won't admit that, but we go into it very scared and not understanding. "Oh, are these people going to be overstepping? Are they going to be telling us how to parent? I think listening to birth parent voices has shifted how I view things. By the time we did adopt, I knew it was important. That's why I reached out to my daughter's birth mom.

Linda~

As an adoptive mom twice in open arrangements, I've learned that an adopted child can benefit greatly by knowing and connecting with their birth family—any member of their birth family. We're all part of nature and nurture, and as a kid growing up parents can do a great job nurturing. But what's in their nature? If they never have that opportunity to see through their biology, that's a void.

> If you can help fill that, it doesn't have to be the birth mom or dad—it could be a birth grandmother, an aunt or uncle. It could be any member, any kin. The real benefit is so the child can fill that void. If I could clone that mentality into every adopting parent, we would be better for it. I'm a big believer in the primal wound. However, our adopted children always knowing their birth parents help minimize the wound.

When Open is an Attitude

Sometimes a physically open adoption is not possible. In rare instances a birth mother or father may be unsafe or need to stay anonymous. In international adoptions, rarely is there any connection or communication between the two families. Regardless, parents can go a long way in creating an attitude of openness around their child's adoption story.

If adopted children are not allowed to express themselves freely when they are young, they will likely turn inward. What has come to be called "the ghost kingdom" within adoptee circles, can be a lonely place. When an adoptee feels discomfort wondering about a family they do not know or have access to, regardless of why, they will dream up their own images about who and where they come from. Create entire structures imagining what their parents are like, pretend siblings, grandparents, and other comforting characters. This may seem harmless, but what is happening is the child is building a false self. The real self is the nature piece of who they are, their native essence, biology, familial and cultural history.

According to therapists, if this self-expression is denied

it can become potentially more serious. "...there is no more consequential step than abandoning the real self. The child forced to give up the real self cannot develop feelings of belonging. There is instead a feeling of basic anxiety, of being isolated and helpless. For this reason, adopted children often try to shut out the subject of adoption. This means they are separating one part of the self from the rest of the self—a pattern known as dissociation, disavowal, numbing, or splitting."[9]

The artificial self presents as the ideal child. These children prioritize others' needs over their own, suppressing any feelings of anger. However, internally, they harbor a sense of feeling fraudulent, which can become overwhelming in adulthood if they feel disconnected from their true selves.

Conversely, the forbidden-self rebels against conformity, often displaying antisocial behavior. Throughout life, adoptees may oscillate between these two selves. As adults, the artificial self may eventually confront suppressed anger, or the forbidden self may transition into a more dutiful role as a son or daughter.[10]

How do parents prevent this dynamic from forming? Openness. Adoptive parents may also have their own "ghost kingdom's". They too have imagined prior children they may have lost to infertility. This is another reason why parents doing their own internal work can be so important for their family. There may be layers of grief to process which everyone needs to heal from.

Lori~
From day zero, whether birth parents are around or not, adoptive parents need to start carving space for them, so the adoptee doesn't have to do that work too.[11]

> What does that look like? It can be pictures on the wall, it can be comments. "I wonder if your birth dad likes this too." It can just be providing that space for your child to enter, or not, when they start to show signs of being ready to process their adopted-ness.

Adoption gives all families who enter the ultimate test. The ones who do it well embrace the process wholeheartedly and put their child at the center. As an adoptive mother and author, Linda Sexton wrote, "Putting the child's well-being at the center of the triad relationships, as the North Star, helps guide everyone."

---

1. Adoption history: Benson Jaffee and David Fanshel, how they fared in adoption, 1970. (n.d.). https://pages.uoregon.edu/adoption/studies/JaffeeHTFA.htm

2. Adoption history: Benson Jaffee and David Fanshel, how they fared in adoption, 1970. (n.d.). https://pages.uoregon.edu/adoption/studies/JaffeeHTFA.htm

3. Adoption history: Benson Jaffee and David Fanshel, how they fared in adoption, 1970. (n.d.). https://pages.uoregon.edu/adoption/studies/JaffeeHTFA.htm

4. Smith, M., González-Pasarín, L., Salas, M. D., & Bernedo, I. M. (2020). Review of benefits and risks for children in open adoption arrangements. Child & Family Social Work, 25(4), 761–774. https://doi.org/10.1111/cfs.12753

5. Smith, M., González-Pasarín, L., Salas, M. D., & Bernedo, I. M. (2020). Review of benefits and risks for children in open adoption arrangements. Child & Family Social Work, 25(4), 761–774. https://doi.org/10.1111/cfs.12753

6. Smith, M., González-Pasarín, L., Salas, M. D., & Bernedo, I. M. (2020). Review of benefits and risks for children in open adoption arrangements. Child & Family Social Work, 25(4), 761–774. https://doi.org/10.1111/cfs.12753

7. Smith, M., González-Pasarín, L., Salas, M. D., & Bernedo, I. M. (2020). Review of benefits and risks for children in open adoption arrangements. Child & Family Social Work, 25(4), 761–774. https://doi.org/10.1111/cfs.12753

8. Agnich, L. E., Schueths, A. M., James, T. D., & Klibert, J. (2016). The eYects of adoption openness and type on the mental health, delinquency, and family relationships of adopted youth. Sociological Spectrum, 36(5), 321–336. https://doi.org/10.1080/02732173.2016.1198950

9. The inner life of the adopted child: Adoption, trauma, loss, fantasy, ... (n.d.-a). https://omnilogos.com/inner- life-of-adopted-child-adoption-trauma-loss-fantasy-search-and-reunion/

10. The inner life of the adopted child: Adoption, trauma, loss, fantasy, ... (n.d.-a). https://omnilogos.com/inner- life-of-adopted-child-adoption-trauma-loss-fantasy-search-and-reunion/

11. The narrator Lori Holden wishes to credit Suzanne Bachner with this concept, from her podcast: Adoption: The Long View, episode 302, https://lavenderluz.com/how-does-it-feel-to-be-adopted/

Chapter 20
When Families Struggle

"The possibility of renewal exists so long as life exists. How to support that possibility in others and in ourselves is the ultimate question." ~Gabor Mate

Most parents put it upon themselves to be fantastic at the job. They have dreams, goals, and aspirations for being a "super-mom" or dad, and they will try to fulfill those roles even knowing the expectations are unrealistic.

This is often especially true for adoptive parents as they are indeed chosen by the birth parents to raise their child.

The Struggle Bus

Online support groups for foster and adoptive parents commonly reference the term "the struggle bus". It signals to other parents they need support, but it also keeps things neutral. No one is blaming anyone else within the family, most importantly, the child. At some time in their journey, every adoptive or foster care family takes a ride on the struggle bus.

Julie~
There's so many red flags and so many things we did not do well, but more out of ignorance. I felt like we bonded very well. If we were in a group situation, [Isaac] certainly picked me

out as mommy. If he would fall and get hurt, I would be the person he ran to.

He has always been this exuberant personality. A wonderful smile and laugh. He can hold a crowd in the palm of his hand.

Looking back now, doing that at two, probably were signs of an attachment disorder.

My husband was a high school teacher, and we would go to basketball games and Isaac would walk into the gymnasium and go up and down the stands with everyone. The cheerleaders would stop cheering and talk to him. When I think about it now, that's not normal behavior for a two-year-old who did not have any fear of strangers. There were red flags we didn't see then. We actually saw the opposite.

We had such a long infertility and miscarriage journey. I would say we probably did not realize we had some issues on our hands until around six years old.

It was during that time he started to understand what it meant to be adopted, that someone had to give him away. He had some anger. He found his adoption papers in our lock box and shredded them. We were trying to figure out how to deal with a child who was obviously grieving, but we didn't have enough training to understand what was going on. In the school world, it was all treated as discipline issues, so he was just constantly in trouble for acting out. He started to ask lots of questions and butt heads with me, and it became increasingly worse.

> When he was six, seven, eight years old we were starting to see glimpses of that anger, like he was almost ashamed of his family. Internally, it hurt a lot. I mean, I always say as an adoptive parent you've got to provide safety and security for your kids. I felt like I was failing. If he was that angry, then obviously I was failing at what I needed to provide for him. So, you start to question—does he have a better life?

This family has a special gift to share because both Isaac and his mother Julie were interviewed for the book. Here is Isaac's account of what was happening for him at this same time:

> **Isaac~**
> There was a season, especially after I found out my birth mom had kept her next child, that it was a big issue. I mean, I was struggling with depression and suicidal things at seven, eight, nine. So, for a couple of those years, adoption conversations, things coming up, nightmares, those things were happening all around my birth mother.

From their stories, clearly both Julie and Isaac were in emotional pain, and trying their best. Julie's heartache for her son is palpable. She knew something was not going well for him but felt utterly unprepared to respond. Some would say this is just the common struggles of parenting. Adoptive parents are constantly weighing, "What part of this is adoption, and what is general kid stuff?"

Isaac was adopted at the age of two. It happened very

quickly after his placement, so his parents did not receive a lot of advance preparation which may have helped them. Like so many before and since, this family found their path forward, but the professional community needs to know adoptive families could benefit from far more knowledge, training, and help than many realize.

> **Input from Jen Winkelman at Inward Bound~**
> I know a lot of adoptive families feel like they have to clear so many hurdles already. Sometimes it can seem unfair. But if these systems were working in a way that might serve kids and families better, everybody who is adopting would have a relationship with an adoption-competent therapist before they're matched with a child.
>
> That same therapist would walk with the family through the early days of their placement and be available to consult as the child grew.
>
> As a child hits new developmental stages, things may bubble up or take a different shape. How powerful could it be if the same person who was with you at the beginning is available to you when that child is five, or twelve, and then seventeen?

Crisis

Sometimes situations develop where a couple may recognize their child is struggling, but it is often so hard to decide what is "normal teenage behavior" or something more dangerous. Adoptees attempt or commit suicide at a rate that is four times higher than the general population. This is occurring within a society already confronting significant mental health challenges. Even prior to the pandemic in 2020, within the United States the "diseases of despair" had risen to concerning levels.

Deaths of despair are known as those caused by accidental overdose, alcohol-related disease, and suicide. Between 2015 to 2017 the annual life expectancy in the US declined largely because of premature deaths due to these causes. This was the largest sustained decline since 1915 to 1918. Moreover, "From 2009 to 2018, the prevalence of alcohol-related, substance-related, and suicide-related diagnoses respectively increased by 37%, 94%, and 170%."[1] If adopted individuals, excluding those from stepparent and kinship adoptions, are dealing with outsized rates of addiction and suicide at even higher rates than the general population, surely this is something adoptive parents, should be concerned about.

> **Beth~**
> He tried to kill himself. That was day zero, but there was probably a year or maybe two where things were going south. At the time I was unwilling to acknowledge it. Joey was thirteen, fourteen, but we had adopted him as a baby. Okay, he slept a lot, closed his bedroom door, didn't want to hang out. I just thought, this is what teenagers are like, because all of it is kind of what teenagers are like.
>
> My wife who struggled with substances when she was a young adult, she's saying, "Beth, this is not good. I think he's using drugs." She knew something was up and I was, "No, no, no, he's fine. My son wouldn't

do that."

But he did. He was using drugs in the house, and they exacerbated his suicidality, and he tried to kill himself. He tried to hang himself from the closet rod. He did it multiple times, half a dozen times.

He got into psychedelics, and had some great experiences with it, and some really horrible ones too. He saw his birth mother on the other side, and he just felt everything was okay. He's on the other side of consciousness and he loved it there and that's why he tried to kill himself because he wanted to stay there. It's been a struggle since then. He was fifteen, now he's nineteen. There was probably a dozen other suicide attempts or very strong suicidal actions. We had to get him help.

The first year, I went into my head and problem solved, like a workaholic, trying to fix Joey. I found him every alternative treatment, therapist, psychiatrist program. I had metrics and charts and lists, and I took him everywhere and tried to get him fixed.

Then I hired a life coach who also had a daughter that struggled with addiction. She specialized in helping parents of kids with addictions. She changed my life. She helped me so much and my wife too. She says, you have to put on your own oxygen mask first, otherwise you can't help your son. You've got to get yourself stable.

She taught me the CRAFT method (Community Reinforcement and Family Training), which is a scientifically proven better way to get your loved one into treatment or recovery, better than the tough love approach. It's staying in connection with someone, not trying to fix them, staying positive, giving them unconditional positive regard. Sometimes it's really hard to find something to be positive about depending on what's going on. "I'm so proud of you. You got outside today and took a few breaths of fresh air. Bravo." I mean, sometimes it's all I can do.

So that's the process I learned, and it is working. It really shifted our whole thinking. He noticed when I shifted, but I had to do a ton of work on myself, which started this gigantic personal growth path I've been on. It's been like getting a master's degree in letting go of control and realizing I cannot change another person. All I can change is myself. And sometimes if you do, it creates a path for somebody else to change if they want to.

Helping Adoptive Parents

Here is some additional input from adoption competent therapists, Jennifer Joy Phoenix and Amy Barker, who were interviewed together for the book:

Jennifer~
I think the most important piece adoptive parents really need to consider is what they subconsciously and unknowingly project onto their child that keeps them from being able to see and enjoy who their child is. For many

parents who adopted because of infertility, the child is the answer to a heartbreaking problem.

So [the adopted child] is the reason for this parenthood they thought they wouldn't be able to have. There is so much expectation and projection and so much desperate need for [the child] to grow up and continue to facilitate this dream. And kids get missed because their personalities or aptitudes aren't similar. There isn't a genetic connection. There are no mirror neurons happening. It's really hard, especially if they aren't secure in their parenthood. You want your child to be like you. And there can be this underlying disappointment the child takes on in their nervous system, and by default, struggles with shame and feels out of control.

Pervasive disappointment in your child will breed shame. Your child is grieving. Grief is a human experience which has similar physiological traits across cultures. Your child is grieving the death of their natural mother. We have to understand what that actually means in regards to attachment ability.

Amy~

Some parents do not get it. They do not understand, and they think the child is disobeying. They think the child is acting out from their obstinate feelings, or they're manipulating.

I had a great supervisor who always said, "How do we get our needs met?" You call it manipulation because that's got a negative connotation, and you don't like their behavior. And you feel like somebody's doing something to you, but somebody's asking for what they need. They're not manipulating, they are trying to get their needs met.

Another thing I think is super important for parents to understand is that the severed bond will have an impact on their actual bodies, not just their minds. So, we're going to see sensory issues a lot of times because trauma is an assault on the senses. The work we do with parents a lot of times is trying to peel back the layers. Your child may have ADHD because of what they've gone through in their trauma story. Your child may have an auditory sensitivity we need to address. So many times, parents are just aware of what's wrong, but they don't understand it is actually from trauma. The child isn't acting out or trying to do anything wrong. Kids really want to be liked.

Most of the time they're working really hard for somebody to love them. If you had a sensory issue where all the tags in your shirt drove you crazy, every second of every day without relent, then you would be a crotchety little kid too. Not because you want to be a crotchety little kid to your adoptive parents because they aren't your biological parents. It's because your clothes bother you."

I think parents really need a better understanding of how trauma impacts a child's body. It may be showing up in behavior that needs to be addressed. It could be pretty easy—just cut the tags out.

Jennifer~
Emotions demand to be heard. That's what emotions do. They exist to communicate from our subconscious to our consciousness something incredibly valuable and important. And yes, it is okay to be angry, but you know what? Really, there's sadness buried under the anger, almost always.

Humans don't want to feel grief because it feels vulnerable. It's scary. When we're angry, we feel powerful. We get dopamine hits off our anger neurobiology. We don't get dopamine hits from grief. So, our brain will choose for us to default to anger because it's more pleasant than devastation. But we have to feel all of it. And we have to let them feel all of it.

If the US is facing a mental health crisis, as many believe, then one more cry for help among adoptive families can get lost in the storm. They are a very small percentage of the overall population. For all of the above cited advice, stories, and statistics many families appear to be more than fine, and most hope this would be true for all.

Regardless of its source, when trauma passes from generation to generation and is not acknowledged or healed, everyone loses. More resources for help for adoptive families are included in the Appendix.

---

1. Brignone, E., George, D. R., Sinoway, L., Katz, C., Sauder, C., Murray, A., Gladden, R., & Kraschnewski, J. L. (2020). Trends in the diagnosis of diseases of despair in the United States, 2009–2018: A retrospective cohort study. BMJ Open, 10(10). https://doi.org/10.1136/bmjopen-2020-037679

Chapter 21
Multicultural, LGBTQ+, or International Adoptive Families

"I'm very sad my sons had to have me. I wish they lived in a world where I hadn't been necessary to them." ~Julie Etter

Parents who decide to adopt a child from another country, or outside of their native racial or cultural background, create a unique family. It is like taking a large billboard sign with them into public spaces as if to say, "Hey, we're different!" This has several effects. One, it causes some of the members to feel like they stand out, even when they don't want to. It also tends to make the public feel as though questioning or commenting on a blended family is okay. Even if it's not.

Yet, when talking to these family members, they have endless stories about the commentary and assumptions other people make. Most are well intentioned or merely curious. A few share judgments these families often wish they would keep to themselves.

> **Gayle~**
> One time we were at the mall, all five of us. Jacob was two. [He's black, we're white] Matt and the other two were in front of me. Jacob was in the middle throwing a two-year-old tantrum. I'm walking behind him, because now I'm a three-time mom and you just let

them have fits.

This black couple walks up and asks, "Are you okay, son? Have you lost your family?"

I'm like, "Eh, he's with me."

The husband turns to his wife and says, "See, I told you. You could just see it."

That was funny.

Ken and Greg~

Jessie is a different color. We're walking down the street, and it's complex in a lot of ways. Because the adults are two males, so that's the whole queer thing right there. We're white and Jessie is brown skinned. She feels like everybody instantly knows the whole story, so that has been very awkward for her.

Which is kind of funny because I never even thought about it.

Jeff and Melissa~

Randall is African American. Alex is Hispanic and African American. Ray is also African American. So, very clearly, when the two boys are at school together, people will say, "Wait. Why are you two brothers?" And they explain, with positivity rather than let it be this dark cloud over their life. I think the reason for that is, they know where they came from. They know it was a choice someone made as to why they are with us. The birth mom, in every situation, made a decision to place with us. We made a decision to accept that and become their parents. That part of it helps a lot.

We've had so many conversations in

> general and about our birth moms specifically. They go through some rough times. Or a birth father will relapse, and his addiction is a sickness and it affects things. [We tell them] this is what your birth mom is going through right now, and she's having a hard time, and we still love and care for her. I know it affects them.

People see the world through their own assumptions. These parents are viewing their adoptive family through their eyes. Because they are the adults and decision-makers, while unintentional, their view eclipses that of their child's. No harm is intended. But this accidental neglect of their youngster's lived perspective can leave their adoptees feeling left behind or even ignored.

These complexities mean parents cannot operate on "autopilot," and require much more diligence and situational awareness—which is exhausting. Few people can withstand that level of vigilance in their daily lives, yet it appears this is what this parenting requires. "Checking in" with their young person and listening to what they share becomes crucial.

This is on top of all the other things this family may be managing. There is already the adoption. Maybe one or several of those are open to a degree. They may have naturally born and adopted children all together. In the case of queer couples, their relationship is already viewed differently by some in society and creates yet another layer of assumptions to sort through.

LGBTQ+

Long discriminated against, queer couples in the US who

adopt also face many cultural obstacles and still do. For most of the early decades that adoption was practiced in the US, single-parent adoption was not done, and same-sex/gender parenting was illegal in most states.

In 1997, New Jersey was the first state to allow same sex couples to adopt jointly statewide, and in 2016 Mississippi became the last state to allow it.

Multiple studies over the past twenty-plus years reach similar conclusions, which is that "measures of children's adjustment, parenting approaches, parenting stress, and couple relationship adjustment were not significantly associated with parental sexual orientation."[1] This same study also noted that teachers agreed with the parents that there were no additional behavior problems.

One study from 2011 explored the concept that gay and lesbian parents added inherent strengths to their family building specifically within transracial adoptions. The researchers theorized that because of the discrimination these queer couples had already faced made them potentially stronger advocates to help their children. The findings appeared to support the idea.[2]

When discussing the topic of how adoptee identities form, it has been theorized that because gay and lesbian individuals developed their own identities as members of a minority group in society, these "parents have direct knowledge to pass to their transracially adopted child." The same study also cites an earlier one by Brooks and Goldberg (2001), noting that gay and lesbian couples are, "particularly suited for adoptive and foster parenting."[3]

Anthony Hynes, who was interviewed earlier in the book, has his own research and opinions on the topic. He was transracially adopted by a lesbian couple. He's also involved at CASE where he trains adoptive parents in complex family situations to help them navigate these realities more effectively. From his interview he shares:

> I don't feel that gay parents make good or bad parents. Gay parents are people. So, people make good and bad parents…I've heard the argument that gay people will have experienced more discrimination. So, therefore, they would make better parents to a child not of their race than somebody else.
>
> I have seen zero evidence of that in my own work with queer white families. This "whiteness" envelops everything. So just because someone has experienced discrimination as a queer individual doesn't mean they're going to understand what it's like to be a member of a racially marginalized group. And it also doesn't mean they can't be racist. So, they can be aware of bias against LGBTQ+ communities and still have racial bias themselves. I've seen it in action, enacted upon my own body in some of the queer white spaces I've walked into.
>
> I did my master's research on the psychological well-being of children within same sex headed households. I found that [for these kids], their wellbeing measures were the same or better in some cases than kids from other places and family types. I should say, there was no evidence that being raised in that type of household was detrimental to them at all. And yeah, I do think when done right, there are also potential benefits to being raised in the LGBTQ+ household.
>
> For me, I've learned a lot from growing

> up in a queer-headed household. It's helped me support the efforts of queer rights in this country in ways that perhaps I might not have if my parents weren't as open and willing to mirror for me what really fighting for civil rights for them looks like in action.

One gay couple, Ken and Greg, interviewed for the book, have a variety of stories to share. Ken adopted Jessie from Cambodia as a single man, and then later when he and Greg met, they blended their families together. Greg, having been married previously, also brought in his two daughters. Together they have been through many adjustments.

> **Ken~**
> One little story happened while Jessie was in kindergarten. We were deeply accepted, everywhere. Beloved, accepted, embraced. That never changed.
>
> But she got some homework, and it was, "Every Creature Has a Mommy." Match each baby animal to its mommy animal.
>
> I thought, Oh, are you kidding? I called the teacher and just like that she said, "I am an idiot. I am so sorry. I will never use that again." So, she handled that really well. Another time, there was a pizza party, and all the kids were saying to Jessie, "Where's your mom? Everyone has a mom. Where's your mom?"
>
> That was really hard for Jessie.

Ken is of Jewish heritage and has Holocaust survivors in his extended family. He is also a family therapist, which has likely helped himself, his partner, and their internationally adopted daughter adapt to many of the complexities of their lives.

Ken~
Jessie comes from a family with two genocides—one Jewish and the other from the Khmer Rouge. She talked about parents not being able to take care of their children and what it was like in Cambodia. We went to a bunch of adoption workshops to help her frame her adoption.

Jessie and I talked about this in many different ways, and many times. She wanted me to have a partner. She said to me once, "You know, Dad, you're not enough."

And I said, "What do you mean I'm not enough?

She said, "When I cross the street, I want one dad holding each hand. I want one dad with me in the bedroom, and the other dad cooking in the kitchen. You're not enough." But then when she got that, it was hard for her. Although, oh my God, did she want sisters!

When Greg and I married we created a whole new family. His two girls and Jessie became this blended family. It was a wonderful and complex transition for everyone, but we've thrived together.

One time, when Jessie was little, she said, "Dad, you're like a sputtering flame and Greg is like a cool breeze." That's a good balance. Greg has been too passive at different points, and I have been too controlling. I often say that together we make up one serenity prayer.

Domestic Adoptions

Some parents have actively stated they are open to any race or ethnicity in advance, while other multicultural families happen by chance. So much can be impacted by the preferences and motivations of the parents, and by the advice they receive. Sometimes they have had to advocate for their kids in a variety of scenarios at school, places of worship, or even within their families.

Melissa~
Our family dynamic is unique. Not everyone is adopted, and they understand that. And they know that they are loved by us. We also know not every problem is because they're adopted. Ninety percent of what they deal with is because they're kids. I think because we've always viewed it that way and we've always viewed the birth parents as extended family, it's helped them to navigate that easier.

Somebody said something to Randall. I think it had to do with his race and having white parents or something like that. I was able to explain to him, "Look, that person's point of view is not the same as yours. And what they're saying is hurtful, because they probably don't understand and that probably scares them." We expected this because of our family dynamic and that's okay.

Kids say things to me sometimes. "Are they really brothers?" "Yes."

"How?"

"Go home and ask your parents about adoption."

Jeff~

I don't have a relationship with my family anymore, except for my brother. The last time I spoke with my dad was 2012, and my mom was probably 2016. They had concerns about me having a child of a different race. Growing up, it was believed and sometimes even preached at churches that there's a verse in the Bible that talks about being unequally yoked, if you've ever heard that.

And what that refers to biblically is being spiritually unequally yoked with another person. It does not have anything to do with race. But it's always used as race. Growing up, I believed that it was wrong for races to intermarry. That's what I was taught. I learned the truth later, thankfully. [My parents] have never met any of our kids. I also think that we, being two white people, have a different experience, having children of different races versus if we had been African American and had children that were white.

But before we even got to the point where we were selected, in our hearts, we were open to any race or gender. Of course, we would love to have a girl, 'cause we have three boys now. But I think we're done.

Julie~

He had a name—it was Keshan. And they advised us to change his name. That's one of the things I regret. It's just part of his culture, part of who he was before us. We took that away from him, and I do regret that.

> At that time when we adopted him, the whole colorblind thing was the big deal. It worried me. I wasn't completely ignorant. I just didn't know how to fix it.

Advice to Parents

The advice given to adoptive parents by social workers and adoption professionals has evolved and continues to do so. The "Blank Slate Theory" is still believed to be the norm when discussing adoption among the general public. "All you need is love." Just adopt—it's all the same!

When talking about "color blindness" within a multicultural family, what can happen is that instead of transracially adopted children being seen as equals, they can feel invisible. Angela Tucker, a transracial adoptee, mentor, and author shares, "How do we learn to love ourselves if you're not going to see us?"[4]

There is a difference between color blindness and color evasion. Color blindness is an ideal that society strives to achieve to reduce or eliminate racial prejudice. But what often occurs instead, is "color evasion", which is the denial of racial differences, creating an inability to talk about or acknowledge a person's race, ethnicity, and culture.

Few parents are equipped to navigate these challenging cultural nuances. Most are doing their best but naturally rely on others to guide them. Many websites from various adoption agencies and other platforms give some good advice to these parents. A summary of this content is:

Ask for Help - Parents do not and cannot know everything their child will need to learn. Seek counseling for the entire family from an adoption competent therapist.[5] Find summer camps and other activities that continue to immerse adoptees in their own culture and roots. Go with them and integrate the family experience.

Surround Them – Live in diverse neighborhoods where possible, or if not then have children in social groups at school and in other venues where they are surrounded with their own, and other cultures. Have dolls and artwork mirror who they are, which lets them know they are seen and belong.

Talk About It – Parents are always setting the tone for how adoption is spoken about. Do not make the adoptee do the work of that heavy lifting. This is challenging because many parents will say their adoptee doesn't want to talk about their heritage. As that youngster grows, leave the door open. Ramya Gruneisen, MS, from an article on the NCFA website suggests initiating conversations with simple questions, such as:

- "I noticed the book you picked from the library is about an adoptee who is interested in finding her birth mom. I know that might be hard to talk about, but I am here if you want to talk about it or we can find someone that feels safer to share with.
- I noticed the summer camp you went to last year didn't have many children of col-

or. How did that feel? I want to make sure you always feel included and like you belong everywhere you go. Would you like me to look for another camp?"[6]

Support Them and Their Choices – Allow the adoptee to have as much control over their lives as appropriate. Let them decide what they want to share of their adoption story, and with who. Acknowledge the world is imperfect, and that racial biases exist. Open the door to talking about their experiences at school and with their peers and teachers. If they feel unsafe somewhere, respect that. Most importantly, *listen to them.*

International Adoptions

In addition to Ken and Greg above, several other families were interviewed who adopted children from other countries. Their experiences were each challenging in different ways.

Audrey and her husband adopted twice from Ukraine. They traveled into the country each time, the first little boy they adopted seemed to do well so they went back several years later to adopt again. Their second child struggled mightily.

Audrey~

I know all the principals of all the schools in the district because us and our son Andrei were thrown out of each of them, one after another. Thrown out or we were asked to leave.

I've tried to block out a lot, but he was

throwing things at big wardrobe closet doors that were all mirrors. There was a lot of yelling and screaming. My husband says we need to close all the windows and doors because somebody's going to think that we were abusing him. We weren't. We just didn't want anybody to get hurt.

We got counseling, and then some more. Every little bit contributed. We did a lot of body work because trauma lives in the body. Everything moved him in the right direction.

The schools were not supportive or understanding of the fact that we had a traumatized kid. They didn't want to deal with it. We had an IEP written up for special dispensation on different things.

The problem is, at least in California, there's a no bullying tolerance policy. So, there were things that happened, and we would have to say, "You're right, it's not appropriate." But is this the appropriate response?

We kept trying to tell him that it's hard as a young person. Sometimes he didn't do anything wrong. And we would try to fight it, but we were never going to win. They already had a track record of things that were not appropriate. He is super smart, he just hated school. He hated the authority it represented.

I have a very solid marriage. At one point, I said to my husband, "I'm done, I can't do this. It's taking us sideways."

My husband said, "Well, let me remind you. This is a forever deal and you're not going anywhere. Because that isn't the deal you have with me, and that is not the deal you have with him."

We worked through it. It was very challenging.

[Back in Ukraine] he was in a room with four kids. One of them was starving himself to death because he was traumatized. He remembers that.

He knew he had brothers because he remembered them. Andrei's middle brother, Nikolai, found him last year from a 23&Me test, which was a beautiful, amazing thing. We love him. He didn't grow up with us, but he's family.

He was old enough that he told us a few things that filled in a little bit of the neglect going on. We didn't understand. I didn't know the dad had died. They don't tell you anything.

The mother really suffered and had challenges with drug use and alcohol and did some crazy things to the kids, which we had never heard. Nicolai took care of Andrei. The mom wasn't capable. The kids didn't go to school.

The two oldest brothers would [do labor] to have sufficient money to feed the little one. There were clearly a lot of bonds there. Turns out they look almost identical. They have a lot of the same traits. Nikolai has been a huge blessing in our lives and it's a beautiful thing for my son.

This next family is unique in that the adoptive mother is

herself transnationally adopted from Korea and raised with a white family. Her personal journey as an adopted adult plays out keenly as she and her husband move to adopt their own child from Korea.

Carrie~

For a really long time, I refused to accept that I was Asian. All the way up until I was filling out the application for adoption for my oldest son. That changed as I adopted my son.

To be perfectly honest, I think somewhere in me, I felt called to have this experience that mirrored mine. There's also a saviorism aspect to it. There are these kids that aren't going to be adopted and they're going to end up in orphanages. They're probably not going to be adopted in Korea because there isn't a strong domestic adoption program—definitely not for older kids. There's a lot of bias toward it.

I wish I had stopped and said, "I need to do stuff for myself."

I think adoption agencies have lots of problems. But the one thing I do think they did well was they tried to educate us. I really do feel like they did.

The one thing that I would ask them to do in the future is make everyone take some sessions with a therapist first. To take some time and have someone be able to help you process.

The first time I ever went back to Korea was to adopt my son. I just didn't know what I was getting into. It was painful to see how much he loved his foster mother. He loved her so much and he couldn't stay with her.

The way this ridiculous adoption system works when you go to pick him up. They put him in a van. You go in the van with him, and the foster mother stays at the adoption agency, and you whisk him away. I mean, it's literally like kidnapping. That's what it felt like. Even when I was walking down the street toward the adoption agency, I saw him drive by with his foster mother.

I saw him in the window and obviously he knew what was going to happen.

They explained it to him, but I looked at his face. I said, "I can't do this."

I sat on the ground. "I can't go forward."

But my husband picked me up and said, "We're going. We have to do this. It's too late. We have to do this."

So, he said goodbye to his foster mom, and we took him in that horrible van and back to the hotel.

And then we were his parents.

It was the most bizarre, insane, terrible thing you could witness.

At first, he was in shock. His foster mom packed two gigantic duffel bags filled with food and snacks and clothes and toys. All the things he loves. But none of it was going to make it any better for him as he started to realize she wasn't coming back.

I remember every second of that experience. When we landed in America, it was a really hard transition. He was angry, obviously, and sad. He was hoping for his foster mom to

> come back. He would stare out the window. He would wait by the door.
>
> He had a lot of different transitions. We were the eighth family that took care of him. All those changes in his first year of life really caused some challenges. He had some delayed speech. He also had a special consideration. He has a birth brother that was already adopted by another family in America.

A few years later, Carrie and her family adopt again from Korea and welcome a child through birth. She has called her family, a "social experiment within a social experiment." It's not a bad description as she continues to process both her Asian culture, adoption, and her children's journeys alongside each other.

Adoption is not a fairytale. There is no "one" adoption story. The outside world wants adoption to be simple. As a lived experience for both adoptees and their parents, it is often anything but.

---

1. Farr, R. H., Forssell, S. L., & Patterson, C. J. (2010). Parenting and Child Development in Adoptive Families: Does Parental Sexual Orientation Matter? Applied Developmental Science, 14(3), 164–178. https://doi.org/10.1080/10888691.2010.500958

2. Ausbrooks, A. R., & Russell, A. (2011). Gay and Lesbian Family Building: A Strengths Perspective of Transracial Adoption. Journal of GLBT Family Studies, 7(3), 201–216. https://doi.org/10.1080/1550428X.2011.564936

3. Ausbrooks, A. R., & Russell, A. (2011). Gay and Lesbian Family Building: A Strengths Perspective of Transracial Adoption. Journal of GLBT Family Studies, 7(3), 201–216. https://doi.org/10.1080/1550428X.2011.564936

4. https://www.today.com/parents/family/black-adoptees-transracial-adoption-tips-white-parents-rcna68821

5. https://adoptioncouncil.org/article/positive-practices-in-transracial-adoption-parenting/

6. https://adoptioncouncil.org/article/positive-practices-in-transracial-adoption-parenting/

Chapter 22
The Online Adoption Market

"If adoption were truly child-centered – about finding families for children – we would be working very hard to prevent attachment problems and to provide transitions that are kind and loving for the infant or child." ~Joyce Maguire Pavao

The organizations that facilitate adoptions vary widely in their motivations, ideology, and business models. They can range from a solo, licensed attorney to an agency that serves a large region of the US and abroad. They can be for profit or non-profit. All are supposed to be overseen by their respective state governments and receive a formal business license to facilitate adoptions in their area.

The organizations that facilitate the transfer of a child from one family to another via legal adoption are:

1. State-run: these can be both attached to the foster care system or outside of it. They are usually the least expensive option for adoptive parents.
2. Private adoption agencies: these can include both for-profit and nonprofit agencies. Costs vary widely.
3. Private attorneys: these are largely individual legal counselors licensed in their state, operating individually or as part of a larger agency. These are often the most expensive adoptions, and the facilitators are almost always operating from a for-profit motive.

The modern adoption industry is driven entirely to satisfy the desires of would-be parents. They alone are the ones who pay the fees associated with the process and it is literally driven on the backs of their longing and often painful journeys

The Marketplace

No other country has created such a vast and organized online marketplace as the US and our rates of adoption are significantly higher than the rest of the world. Prospective couples or individuals who have signed with an agency are advertising themselves to an expectant parent on websites in an online marketplace. These hopeful parents have already paid at least one or several deposits by this time. They have met and been assigned a caseworker or agent and have also completed the home study. They are ready to be matched with an expecting parent or mother.

The agency encourages them to create enticing stories about their families, living situations, careers and education, religious orientations and other details about their lives and personalities. Hopeful couples are encouraged to build out their profiles, share their desires on social media, and some are offered independent SEO (Search Engine Optimization) or social media advertising packages. They are competing against each other in this marketplace and paying to participate within it.

This has become so normalized they no longer see it. But this is not how adoption is practiced in other countries. A few examples:

In the United Kingdom—private adoption is not legal. The only adoptions are handled by the state. If a mother expresses her desire to relinquish, after birth the child is placed into foster care for six weeks. Then the social worker assists the mother to try to improve her personal or living situation. If those attempts are not successful, the process to terminate parental rights begins, and the baby will be matched with a prospective adoptive couple who has applied for the program.[1] There are no fees charged to these adoptive parents.[2]

In Australia—open adoptions are the only type allowed in the country, and it is illegal to arrange a private adoption, and any party can be penalized for attempting to do so.[3] Due to the valid concerns about the extreme coercive practices of the past, the natural parents may only consent to relinquishment in the presence of two witnesses.[4] Adoptions can only occur through the Department of Communities and Justice or an accredited provider.

In Germany—only the guardianship court may declare an adoption, and agencies are the ones who connect the child and prospective adopting parents. There is no advertising allowed in Germany even though these are private agencies.[5]

Here is a chart compiled during the research for the book that shows the estimated statistics on the rate of adoption compared to live births. It attempts to share an understanding of the rates of domestic adoptions internationally, compared to the US. These comparisons are not done within the same years because data in some countries was sparse or is not gathered internally for review on an annual basis.

Country	Year	Live Births	Private Adoptions	Public/ Foster Adoption	Intercountry Adoptions (adoptees born in country and adopted by people in other countries)	Intercountry Adoptions (adoptees born in other countries)	Total Number of Adoptions	Ratio Births: Total Adoptions
USA	2020	3,661,220	19,658*	55,658		1,622	95,306**	~182:1 private ~65:1 foster care ~38:1 total
UK	2022	605,479		3,010			3,010	~201:1
Northern Ireland	2022	54,483					108	~504:1
Australia	2022	297,725		Unknown		28	201	~1481:1
China	2021	10,722,217* (crude estimate)		Unknown			12,447	~861:1
S. Korea	2022	249,200		Unknown	142		324	~769:1 ~1369:1 when only counting adoptions within S. Korea
Germany	2022	738,819					3,820	~193:1

**Best estimate from the NCFA*

***19,943 stepparent adoptions*

One large area not mentioned above are countries dominated by the Islamic faith. This is because adoption as it is conducted in the west is culturally forbidden. Orphans are taken in, and this is encouraged via a system of guardianship or as it is called "sponsorship." But contained within Islam is the tenant that a child's surname remains part of their identity. Thus, adoption, as Christians or those of other faiths practice it, is not done in these countries.

There are three methods an American couple wanting to adopt can use to avoid the domestic competition for infants: the foster care system, a private attorney, or adopt internationally.

Private Attorney Adoptions

When a prospective couple connects with an attorney to adopt, the process is somewhat different compared to an agency. They will still have to complete whatever state requirements exist for the home study, potentially requiring the couple to work independently with a social worker and these costs may be separate. Instead of a marketplace, the attorney becomes a "matchmaker."

An attorney attracting expectant parents to arrange adoptions with them may have several such cases at a given time. As a hopeful adoptive couple comes into their office, they will gather all pertinent information and present this to the potential birth mother. If she likes what she sees on paper, then one or several meetings are arranged between the parties. If they like one another and agree, then they are matched, and the process moves forward.

The trust all these parents give toward one another is both monumental and precarious and contains inherent inequality between them.

A paper written in 2006 prepared and presented by

Elizabeth Samuels of the University of Baltimore School of Law examines some of these implications. "Many state laws appear to value an increase in infant adoptions over the goal of encouraging careful deliberation. Most domestic infant adoptions involve powerful market forces as well as powerful emotional pressures… Infant adoption service providers' livelihoods or profits generally depend on successfully arranging adoptions for their primary clients, who, for the most part, are relatively prosperous, well-established, and socially favored married couples whose desires to bear children have been thwarted by infertility."[6]

In question are the ethics surrounding "dual representation" of the same attorney for both the expectant/relinquishing couple and the prospective adopting parents.

Currently, four states explicitly permit dual representation: Arizona, California, Kansas, and New Hampshire. Sixteen states prohibit dual representation, and the majority of twenty-nine states make no mention of the practice in their statutes.[7]

When attempting to analyze the individual state laws, one enters a labyrinth of variables that become increasingly difficult to assemble and understand. In Iowa, for example, the law states the birth parents are required to receive independent counsel. Yet nothing in the statute requires they be informed of said right, nor is there mention of who pays for the representation. Some states specifically require that if the birth parents are minors, they must have independent counsel. It is assumed the expectant parents likely cannot afford the attorney's fees, as if they could pay them, they most likely wouldn't be relinquishing their child.

Only two states say the agency involved in the adoption should pay—Kansas and Vermont. All others remain silent on the issue or say the adoptive parents should provide these fees. Lawmakers are clearly ignoring these inherent conflicts of interests, and this goes against the advice from the American Bar Association in 1987.[8]

Certainly, there are ethical attorneys who are honest and follow the law and honor the wishes of the people they represent in adoptions. The issue comes down to one where the entire industry is well aware of these inherent conflicts. But they make no attempt to improve despite knowing this for decades.

International Adoptions

The other method parents can use to adopt that bypasses the American marketplace for infants is to adopt internationally. These types of adoptions have dropped dramatically in the past decade. The peak was in 2004 when there were 22,991 intercountry adoptions into the US, but by 2021 there were 1,785.[9]

Reasons for this drop vary, but they are largely because of concerns about international trafficking and corruption. In 2015 China ended its "one child" policy and the country decided to focus on developing their own domestic system for child welfare. They had been the largest source by far of intercountry adoptions since the early 1990s.

Other countries have also attempted to build up their infrastructure to improve child welfare, with varying degrees of success. But the online world of international adoption gets murky. If one Googles "low-cost international adoptions", for example, there will be dozens of ads and articles for couples to arrange adoptions from Ethiopia, Ukraine, Columbia, Bulgaria, Taiwan and beyond. There will be both .com and .org sites sharing information and asking prospective parents to sign up and learn more.

One website, https://consideringadoption.com lists

estimated adoption costs by country. They range on the low end of $15,000 from Thailand, for example, to the more expensive countries, such as South Korea, $38,000. These listed costs do not count the couple's travel costs. The registration fees are quoted between $1000-$2000, not included in the above, and the "Adoption Program Fees" are also separate, ranging from $8000-$18,000. Home study fees as well as visas and other documentation are also not necessarily included.

What starts to be lost in all of this commercial discussion is the child who eventually grows up and is able to view this information for themselves.

The majority of these fees are going to administrative costs for the legal handling of an international adoption, some of which are certainly legitimate. Very little benefit is received from these costs by the home country. As Mikayla stated from her interview for Chapter 9, as an adoptee from Ukraine, "I saw the paperwork and the money that changed hands. Almost none of it went to benefit the orphanage I came from."

Corruption in Action

Sharon Steckler is an adoptee who also spent nearly twenty years in the adoption industry as a trained social worker and administrator. She worked extensively in the US with several different agencies. In the early 2000s, she was on a trip to Guatemala to visit some of the orphanages the agency was working with.

> **Sharon~**
> I was in Guatemala in the back of a car with somebody with a big boil on his neck. And he said, "You want a baby?" He pulled over and

he put a bill out the window to somebody on the side of the road, "I'll get you a baby. I can have you a baby today."

I said, "No, no, no, I don't want a baby."

Afterwards, I talked to another adoption professional there. She said, "Oh, don't work with that person." I wasn't going to. Then I get home and about a month or two later, I see the same person who I was in the back of that car with me in some adoption magazine. Such-and-so International announces their new coordinator in Guatemala. And it was that guy. Because they don't go down, they're not even there. They don't know these people.

I also visited an orphanage there, and these kids were coming in so malnourished, I mean starving. And it's sad. The need really was there. I've also visited an HIV positive orphanage in Guatemala. I brought my daughters to volunteer there. Poverty is really extreme, but so is the corruption.

When the Marketplace Fails

The consequences of remaining morally cavalier about adoption as an industry in the United States have broad reaching impacts. One of them is the parties involved forget these children grow up. They become adults who might feel squeamish or angry about an industry profiting from their circumstances. Even among those who love their adopting parents.

Sometimes this commodification forgets the child is a person with inherent worth and the need to be loved. There are some parents, sadly, when viewed from a distance appear self- centered. Paige Knipfer, adoptive parent, and consultant shares:

> "I would say that they feel entitled because of their journey, and often, unfortunately, it is stuff they didn't go to therapy for. I will preach therapy to no end. They have had multiple miscarriages, they've done multiple rounds of IVF, they have a whole story and my heart breaks for them. But they haven't properly processed or grieved.
>
> Adopting a child into your home will only magnify the cracks that exist in a marriage and in the trauma they have just experienced. And oftentimes too, I don't know if spouses have that deep conversation of how important biology is to them. I have terminated a contract because I found out a family was pursuing adoption for Instagram followers. So, we're in the age now where there are these influencers on Instagram who share their adoption journey and who are making boatloads of money sharing a story in the pursuit of followers and money. And, unfortunately, that is leading to, I think, other people then pursuing things for the wrong reasons. And that's creating a whole new factor into these misconceptions and misunderstandings of adoption as a whole."

Social media's influences in adoption are now very prevalent. Some adoptive parents have looked at the fees charged by agencies and attorneys and have decided to go it alone. But social media is literally the wild west in terms of arranging adoptions privately between expectant parents and hopeful adopting ones.

An article in USA Today in 2022 documents a variety of scenarios. In one instance a prospective family paid over $9,000 to a supposed expectant mother they found on Instagram seeking a family who may not have even been pregnant. There is no oversight or regulation on what is happening in these arenas.[10]

Other hopeful adoptive parents will create an Instagram page to cast a wider net to reach more prospective birth moms. Both sets of these people are operating without any professional guidance along the way. "We hear lots of horror stories from adoptive parents who have been through the wringer and have unfortunately learned the hard way about the importance of working with an ethical adoption attorney or agency," AdoptMatch.com, Co-Founder Celeste Liversidge said. "For expectant moms, pursuing adoption using the internet is very confusing… It's very difficult for them to discern between licensed and unlicensed, and then, within that orbit, who are the good guys."[11]

Adoption hashtags on Instagram, TikTok, Twitter, and Facebook are everywhere. They include not only human adoptions but those for pets acquired from a shelter. On Twitter, #Adoption mentions have increased 92% since 2018. In the same length of time #HopingToAdopt has increased by 76%, showing that this is being used by hopeful parents.[12]

There's even an App that has come out in recent years created to specifically connect expectant parents with prospective adoptive ones. Each party registers and can view one another by "swiping" as they view each other's profiles in a format not that different from Tinder, an online dating app.

Another thing that can happen is a scenario where, for whatever reason, a family is turned down by one or several agencies in their attempt to qualify to adopt. According to Sharon Steckler, the counselor previously mentioned, shares:

> There were some couples that [the agency] said, "Honestly, I don't think you're going to be chosen by a birth mother. You're on your second or third marriage, you're older." And, in one case, they were a Polish couple who put an ad in a Polish newspaper in Chicago and got a baby within a month or something. But the agency wouldn't take them because they just felt that they were not marketable, and they didn't want to string them along.

Failed Adoptions

Probably the most heartbreaking scenario can be when an adoption fails or dissolves completely. It is rarely talked about, and officials don't want to track or acknowledge it, but this is happening at an increasing rate. An in-depth investigation done by USA Today in 2022 found that there were 66,000 adopted children who ended up in the foster care system because of failed adoptions between the years of 2008-2020. The article emphasizes this number is likely lower than the actual number of failures.[13]

Many states are severely lacking in tracking these statistics and it's been something that has been a fight for many years. What is happening is that so many parents are so poorly prepared for the reality of the children they take in and the extent of their needs, they give up. This is where good intentions and creating ethical assumptions about adoption collide. From Sharon Steckler again:

> I think it was so hidden. We didn't keep any numbers of disrupted adoptions. There were all these readoptions going on in the US between parents who couldn't handle these kids. It was a mess. Kids going to these ranches, and I think that was kept quiet because they wanted to market children too, right?
>
> I think [the parents] just believed these kids were going to love them, and everything became personal because the kids were so fearful of loving and losing again.
>
> I remember this one woman said, "If you don't take him, I'm going to drop him over the city line and just leave him." She was so fed up with this kid that she had wanted so badly.
>
> I asked, "What did he do?"
>
> She said she was homeschooling him, which was such a mistake because this child loved school.
>
> It was part of their Christian values. All their kids were homeschooled. And in his very broken English, he told her that she couldn't teach anyone their way out of a box. And that was her breaking point.

Since the statistics are shaky at best, it becomes hard to discern the facts, but experts and those who work in the industry say the overwhelming number of the children from these failures were initially adopted internationally. Bereft of their native culture, language, and now their new family, they end up in the system, out on the streets, or rehomed.

Rehoming

One of the most deplorable situations that social media has created is a landscape of sketchy networks of people who will quietly and privately "rehome" their adopted child.

Rehoming is, "when adoptive parents find a new home for their adopted child without notifying or consulting the proper authorities."[14]

Second Chance Adoptions[15] is a Facebook page where children are being shown as needing a new home. Each child is staged in a lovely setting and a bit of their background is shared including why their already one-time adoptive family now thinks they need to be rehomed. The posts[16] look something like this:

"FB friends, please help us by sharing this to your FB page. To see updates on children, "like" us at Second Chance Adoptions. If you have questions or want to know more about this child, please email us at secondchanceinfo@wiaa.org."

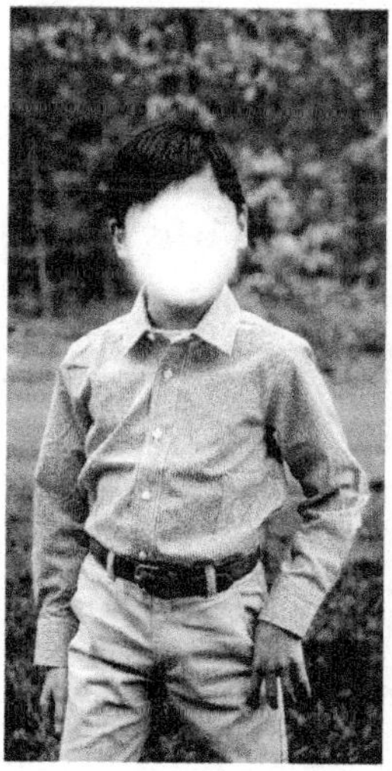

The captions for these photos describing their stories

sound similar. Overwhelmingly, the children have been adopted from outside of the US or from foster care. Their descriptions will read similar to this example (not his real name):

> "This handsome boy is Adam. He is 9 ½ years old and was adopted internationally a year and a half ago. He is very small for his age, so people think he's younger than he is. Adam is a sweet, delightful boy who has several medical diagnoses that were unknown to his family when they adopted him. He is in the 2nd grade at his local public school.
>
> Adam is a joyful, easy-going boy. He is very compliant and easy to redirect. He loves to learn and is very inquisitive. He's been learning English and can communicate quite well. He plays really well with younger children and isn't controlling or violent. He is very orderly and can easily take care of his own hygiene needs."[16]
>
> They have spent the last year and a half getting a good picture of what is going on in Adam's body, but they are struggling to meet all his needs since they have four children and two full-time jobs. The family has three other children. He has an 11-year-old brother, a sister who is the same age as him, and a 5-year-old sister. Both of his parents work full time for the government, so they have a very busy schedule.
>
> They think he will progress much quicker if he was in a family who has a stay-at-home parent (or a parent with a flexible

> work schedule) who can take him to his appointments and even potentially home-school him. They are open to families of any kind and even think he would thrive as an only child."[17]

What is so troubling about the above, is that the three other children and the parents with the "busy government jobs" are lifestyle choices they have made and were all conditions (one presumes) that existed prior to their adopting this boy. He has been taken out of his home country and is clearly doing his best to assimilate—but not well enough for this family to keep him.

Many of these listings do describe situations where the child is acting out—sometimes severely so. But these youngsters should be *expected* to have some adjustment challenges and therefore behavioral struggles. What is so devastating to encounter is what appears to be a massive systemic failure on two fronts: One, to accurately manage the expectations of these adoptive parents. And two, the lack of truly informed psychological family counseling that should be received by everyone in the family to help them progress.

Some of these children appear to survive and make headway in their lives despite this turmoil.[18] However, many do not, and worst of all, no one is tracking or even attempting to stay on top of how often it occurs. The government doesn't know. These transactions are private, and some do not have legal representatives within the process. In theory the new families have passed the home study requirements in their state, but this all needs a step back and a few additional observations.

1. Is the desire to adopt these "children in

need" even attempting to assess their needs in their home country? Are these needs being correctly and ethically addressed by the adoption? Are the prospective parents fully aware of all these essential details beforehand? Or are financial motivations taking top priority?

2. The commitment levels of some of these adopting parents and families needs to be re-evaluated with greater care. Are they truly in for the long haul or are their expectations so far out of alignment with reality that the whole scheme needs higher scrutiny?

These are painful situations and must be seen for what they are. A societal failure put into motion by a dreamy fiction sold to adopting parents about what their experiences and family life will become. That love is enough, and any child brought into their care will easily mesh with their existing family.

1. https://www.gov.uk/apply-to-adopt-child-through-council

2. Palmer, C. E., CoKey, A., & Rees, A. (2023). The motivations and decision-making processes of parents who adopt older children. Adoption & Fostering, 47(2), 211-228. https://doi.org/10.1177/03085759231174906

3. https://www.facs.nsw.gov.au/families/adoption/adopting-a-child/from-overseas

4. https://matthieslawyers.com.au/adoption-prcess-australia/

5. www.bundeszentralregister.de/adoption/english/indes_engl.htm

6. Legal Representation of Birth Parents and Adoptive Parents, 9 Adoption Quarterly 73 (2006)

7. Legal Representation of Birth Parents and Adoptive Parents, 9 Adoption Quarterly 73 (2006)

8. Legal Representation of Birth Parents and Adoptive Parents, 9 Adoption Quarterly 73 (2006)

9. https://www.statista.com/statistics/249414/intoury-adoptions-involving-the-us/

10. https://www.usatoday.com/in-depth/news/investigations/2022/06/07/social-media-influence-instagram-facebook-tiktok-adoptions-of-babies/

11. https://www.usatoday.com/in-depth/news/investigations/2022/06/07/social-media-influence-instagram-facebook-tiktok-adoptions-of-babies/

12. https://www.usatoday.com/in-depth/news/investigations/2022/06/07/social-media-influence-instagram-facebook-tiktok-adoptions-of-babies/

13. https://www.usatoday.com/in-depth/news/investigations/2022/08/22/adoptees-foster-care-adoption-help-others-child-welfare-system/10132843002/

14.Https://humantraKickingsearch.org/rehoming-adoped-children/

15. https://www.facebook.com/secondchanceadoptions (A statement from the agency at https://wiaa.org/2nd-chance-adoption/
"We are aware that our 2nd Chance Facebook Page is down. We are working on getting it restored.")

16. https://www.facebook.com/secondchanceadoptions (A statement from the agency at https://wiaa.org/2nd-chance-adoption/
"We are aware that our 2nd Chance Facebook Page is down. We are working on getting it restored.")

17. This child's profile is no longer visible. Others similar to his can be found on their website here: https://wiaa.org/2nd-chance-adoption/waiting-children/

18.http://ourfreshstart.org/?fbclid=IwZXh0bgNhZW0CMTEAAR1qI0S8XxWf93F89ertu-AqOEsGukXcropKqNf- ibog8hM0n7tBDDf5DjY_aem_Afjyf8XFO4OgV9aaWzgAVklyiUoWpGy46mK8DgvMfaPX2KWjKDR8bGZl_OOP8 C7L6LqB5SCnQzBm8aIQgdoCztL5

Chapter 23
Foster Parents

"Children that have been abused do not have 'behavior problems' that need to be addressed. They have extreme survival skills that need to be understood." ~Paula Goodwin

Content warning: this chapter contains descriptions of physical and sexual abuse against children.

Foster parents want you to know they are not saints or super-humans. They believe most people, with the right focus and commitment, can do exactly as they have–care for a young person so fiercely that they will stand beside them through anything, even though they are not their biological parents. Even though they may provide a home for only a few months.

Debbie~

These kids are great. It's not their fault they're in foster care. These kids have experienced trauma, and that affects who they are. They need extra love and support, but love isn't enough. They will also need counseling and therapy. And yes, sometimes meds. But the meds should be temporary. They love their families and want to be with them. If possible, we need to help their families become whole again, and it is worth it.

The foster care system can help build families, but as mentioned in Chapter 10, that is not its primary purpose. The central focus of all out of home care is to provide for children or youths during a time of crisis for a family, with reunification as the goal whenever possible. Filled with shortcomings, it systemically seems to fail again and again. However, good case workers, agencies, and families try to show up for their fellows in need.

Of the parents who become part of the bedrock of the foster care system, they generally break down into three different groups: kinship placements, temporary foster care providers, and those families who are actively seeking a foster to adopt situation to build their family.

When looking at the "marketplace" that exists within private infant adoption, this is the other way to bypass that system. However, most of these parents will say fostering usually has a different kind of price tag.

Interviewed for this chapter were four foster parents, one kinship adoptive parent, and five parents who adopted from within the system, four of whom specifically became care providers with the goal of adopting. Also, experiences from several therapists and allies in the child welfare industry share their valuable input.

A few generalities can be made after listening to these couples and individuals. They will certainly not encompass every possible situation, but reinforce many of the stories, statistics, and points of view shared in Chapter 10.

- Every foster or foster-to-adopt parent interviewed talked about the rampant inconsistencies between case workers and the decisions made by them, and the training they received versus the lived experiences of being foster parents.
- All of them cite how obscenely overworked and

often unprepared their case workers were, and at times, how little they knew about how to handle situations that occurred.

- None of the parents felt they received enough training to handle the youngsters placed in their care, especially regarding the way trauma would surface in their children's or teen's behaviors.
- All of them searched for information independently and took other courses, seeking instruction from other professionals or fellow foster parents, utilizing therapists, and even watching experts on YouTube to improve their personal knowledge about the situations they faced.
- Most also shared endless frustrations about the negative biases they received toward them. Supportive family and community mean the world to these folks, but they routinely expressed a lack of appreciation from their own case workers and disdain from people encountered in random social situations, or even from their children's teachers or school administrators.

Another common frustration is that the foster system is clearly full of great parents and willing families. It is also infiltrated with stories of abuse and neglect from caregivers who appear to be disinterested, abusive, or "in it for the money." One goal among many in this book is to invite the public to check their biases before making assumptions when encountering a family that is different. Good foster parents deserve respect and have earned it in ways few can comprehend. And the kids *always* deserve it.

A Temporary Home

Debbie and her husband fostered dozens of children through their sizable home in a suburb of Kansas City, until her husband, unfortunately, passed away in 2020. They had always been passionate about caring for children and their natural born ones were grown and out of the house.

Because they had a large home, they were willing to take in large numbers of sibling groups to keep the children together, and it became their "specialty," which their case workers utilized heavily, because the need was great.

Debbie~
Our first group was four sisters, and we called them our angel girls. They were so sweet. It was a good way to start off. They were thirteen, eleven, ten, and nine. After having them for about three weeks, we got a phone call to take a teenage girl. We took her too. Then we got a phone call for another teenage girl. The phone just kept ringing. So, we just kept adding more to our group.

We had the first four sisters for five months, and they should have never been in foster care. Their dad was accused of things he didn't do. It took five months to clear he hadn't done those things. He was a single dad, and the girlfriend he was living with made the accusations. She had left the home and was vindictive.

And I'll say that, after five months, if that would've been happening, I think the girls would've told us. We would've seen signs, symptoms. He was so devoted. He called them every day. He did fun things on weekends with them. He had his issues. He had been the single dad to these girls since the youngest ones were born. When the youngest one was born, she was a twin, and the twin died. The mom had a mental health breakdown and left and never came back, but he was a hands-on dad. These girls adored him. We really liked him. Now he has remarried and has another one. But they're doing good. I'm still in contact with them.

When those four left, we got a call for a sibling group of five. We took them too and ended up having nine—two sibling groups. Most of the time we had three sibling groups, but our house comfortably handled nine. So, we normally had nine kiddos.

In the beginning, we were taking more of the older junior high, high school ages. Then we got a call for a family with six kids and the oldest two were twins at fourteen. The youngest one was three months, and then they had a three-year-old and a five-year-old and an eight-year-old also. So, then we ended up having babies too. By us saying yes, they wouldn't get split. That was our goal, we didn't want to split them.

It was a lot. But they were all being reconciled, so they went to school all day. On weekends, they usually had visitation. So, they usually weren't there on weekends. For the most part, they got along really well. We didn't have any big issues. They were playmates. And I think that the trauma on the kids

> was a lot less when you have your brothers and sisters with you than when they're separated. For the most part, they were kids.
>
> One of my last ones I had, there was a baby, a ten-year-old and then fifteen-year-old girl. They witnessed their mom having a mental health breakdown. She got a gun and was going to shoot herself. Dad wrestled with the gun and got shot in the head and killed instead. When they got into foster care, it turned out that he had been raping the fifteen-year-old for years. And she thought he was her best friend because she didn't know this wasn't okay. It was horrible. Plus, the baby had been neglected and malnourished, and he was way behind. When we got him, he was more like an eight-month-old at fifteen months. He wasn't walking yet. He was thin. So, they were abused and would never be going back to mom. But after they left my home, they were split up. I don't know what happened to them after that. That's a hard one.

These parents who take on foster care youngsters grow to care *deeply* about them. Even when they get these children back with their original families, every parent interviewed could name every single child they had cared for and remember their family situation. They also often had to advocate strongly to get these youths the benefits and support they needed.

Foster caregiver Chelsea is a single person who was very much interested in being a foster care parent. She had known from a young age this was a calling for her and had a flexible job working from home as a speech clinician. She completed her training, and dove into the system. With her one major placement, she was totally committed to seeing this teenager, who will be called Alma, reunited with her mother. But this was a tough opening placement, as Alma had been in the system since she was five or six. She had been through several homes and was abused in her first foster placement.

The mother had lost all her children due to issues of neglect and substance abuse, and all the siblings were isolated from each other. However, this mother had recently gotten clean and was eligible to therefore regain custody of her daughter Alma. But Chelsea found herself in tough waters immediately, fostering this troubled teenage girl.

> **Chelsea~**
> For the entire time I was with Alma, the same social worker was there. She was new, which made it hard because sometimes it felt like the blind leading and the blind.
>
> I would ask, "Well, what about this?"
>
> And she would say, "I don't know." She would try to find out, but it wasn't someone who was seasoned and knew what they were doing. She was trying and she was very nice, but there were certain things that would happen that were made even more difficult because of that.
>
> I felt like I had to find the information. I had to reach out to the right people. The other thing I found was the services that my child needed weren't available. She was a teenager and really needed therapy.
>
> We were dealing with suicidal ideations, and they were still telling me she got to choose

if she wanted therapy. I was sitting here every night being the therapist to this child, and I don't have the training for this. I need support. I need you guys to say that she needs to go to therapy. But there are a lot of rules in foster care, and it's to keep everybody safe and in a consensual type of situation. But with that, it made parenting hard.

I told them I would pay out of pocket for her to have a therapist. She should have the support anyway. She was struggling mentally. She didn't have any diagnoses or anything. It's very scary to have a child who's talking about suicide. That was very scary for me. Often, I did feel like she was safe. They checked everything. There was a lot of communication between me and the social worker. Then the social worker would talk to her and say, "We're not in an emergency situation." But then I would feel like I needed to sleep on the couch. Everything was locked up, but a teenager, if they want to, can hurt themselves.

Finally, I was like, I can't do this. I need someone else to step into the situation. And they did eventually, but for so long they were saying "We can't force her." I think eventually I just persuaded her to say, yes, she was open to counseling. We got started immediately.

Chelsea also found something she didn't expect in her foster care journey that the training did not adequately prepare her for. She was expected to supervise the visitations with Alma and her mother.

Chelsea~

They have you monitor the visits with parents. In California, you're the person who watches if your child has visits with their parents. I don't feel I got enough training for that, because it was very uncomfortable in the beginning and hard. They can't be away from earshot. You must be able to hear what they're saying to the child and everything.

I ended up feeling like I had to parent the mother too. It wasn't just Alma. I guess that was surprising. In my head I'm thinking, okay, we're dealing with the child. But I end up dealing with the family also. I guess I didn't realize how big of a part I would play with her family in that type of situation.

Even her previous foster parents sometimes would talk to her, and it would mess with her head about certain things about her mom that we had talked about. I want her to have all the perspectives, as with any child, but it felt like there was a lot of people that had a hand in the situation. It made it hard to parent sometimes.

This story has a happy ending. After much work and many months, Alma went back to her mother, slowly transitioning with the help of Chelsea's support, to not only the daughter but the mother as well.

One sore spot for Chelsea is that other than one sister, all of Alma's other siblings have been lost in the system. All of them were adopted into other families, with their names changed so records are hard to locate. California remains a closed record state for adoptee birth certificates.

Chelsea, Alma, and her mother are all still in contact and remain part of each other's lives.

Foster Parent Training

The training that foster care parents receive varies widely from state to state. The curriculums created over time tend to follow similar teachings, but with slightly different emphasis and acronyms attached to them.

In Michigan, foster parents participate in the GROW program, spending 20 – 25 hours of training prior to licensing. The topics covered in the program include attachment and loss, the effects of neglect, abuse and sexual abuse, discipline, and how fostering and adopting affects families.[1]

Texas has a program titled PRIDE: Parent Resource for Information, Development, Education. The program trains both foster and foster-to-adopt parents together and covers the issues surrounding child attachment, loss, grief, the various types of abuse and their effects and behavior interventions. They require 50 hours of training for fostering parent couples, and 30 hours for a home with a single foster parent.[2]

In Oregon there is a 27-hour-long curriculum which does include ongoing training requirements of 30 hours every two years.[3]

One study conducted in 2013 reviewed the requirements in 47 states and found the following:

- 19 states do not have any minimum required hours for training
- 13 states only required 6 -12 training hours
- 7 states required 13 – 21 training hours
- 8 states required 22 – 30 training hours[4]

Some require additional training every few years to maintain the license while others do not. All programs are developed and managed by that state's Department of Social Services (DSS) or an equivalent. Most areas of the country have age and health requirements that must be met by fostering parents, and standards for the conditions of the home and the transportation the family uses. Some states also offer in-home training on top of the home study review process.[5]

One of the interviewed parents was a special find, in that Tom was not only an active foster and foster-to-adopt parent with his wife and existing children, but he also assisted with foster care policymaking in his home state located in the Southeast. He is therefore a wealth of information others may not have.

> **Tom~**
> Our state legally requires all foster parents to attend 40 hours of pre-service training. We have about 10,000 to 12,000 foster parents that are licensed currently. And, of the new parents that sign up on an annual basis, we lose about 50% of them.
>
> Given our backgrounds in the healthcare industry, and I worked in mental health, we felt very prepared. We felt we had resources to be able to deal with a lot of the things. Even through our research, we knew we were going to probably encounter kids, even if they didn't outwardly have a lot of trauma, they would still have that from their biological experience.
>
> Entering foster care is traumatic in and of itself. I think a lot of folks aren't as educated

on the topic as we were, and there's a lot of things that arise out of that. We had kids that we treated just like they were any other kids. But anything that came up, any emotions that arose, we would take the time to recognize those and talk through them. I think a lot of parents just discipline emotions out of a kid. So we try not to be that way.

Tom and his family's journey through their fostering came with surprises and unexpected pressures, some of which came from the structure of the way foster care is often administered in their area. Tom's state is part of a growing national trend to outsource or privatize foster care services. Which means a private entity is managing the system, training the parents, and supervising the casework instead of state employed workers.

Tom~
Our first placement, we had a young African American girl. She was eighteen months at the time. The biological mom was working diligently to get her back. Her situation was unlike a lot of the ones we are used to, because a lot of the parents we encounter have had some kind of drug or other involvement with DSS.

But this young lady's situation was centered more around medical issues, and she eventually got her daughter back. We were able to see her and her daughter, which was always good.

Then, we got a call for our first long-term placement. It was two young girls who were two and three at the time, brought into care because DSS had been involved almost since they were born, mostly due to drugs.

There was suspicion of sexual abuse too, just because of the behavior the children were showing. DSS had tried to place them into a kinship placement with a neighbor, but the neighbor very quickly became overwhelmed because of the sexualized behavior the two little girls were showing.

We met mom at the Department of Social Services when she surrendered her children to DSS and basically gave them to us. Both children tested positive for multiple drugs. Both girls had lice. Although overall, you could tell the kids were happy because they didn't know any different.

We had them for a total of sixteen months during that time. The visitations with the mom went pretty well. As time went along, mom was granted more ability to spend time with the kids, which was going well.

The father wasn't really in their lives. Didn't live with mom, wasn't married to mom or anything like that. But DSS got the father involved.

The first eight months we had the kids in our care, things were progressing well. Mom was doing well though she had some weird things that went on. She had a suspicious house fire, and a few other strange things happened in her life. It was kind of weird, but okay.

Then their dad got involved. The dad

> hadn't been in the kids' lives at all since birth. And DSS basically gave him unlimited, unsupervised visitation from day one. At the time, we didn't know any better as foster parents.

However, the complications of the outsourced administration of the state's system became a factor in how Tom was able to report on and affected what was happening to the children in their care.

> **Tom~**
> There are a hundred counties within our state. There's DSS who manages foster care. Basically, DSS works as the state level department of social services. And then there are county level departments of social services.
>
> The county level of DSS is the one who has full authoritative right over how they administer child welfare. The state basically just creates guidelines for the counties, and then the county can deliver them however they want. So really child welfare is delivered 100 different ways in the state.
>
> Then those counties can contract out their foster care to private agencies. We have a good handful of private agencies across the state, like Children's Hope Alliance and Children's Home Society, and a lot of other big names.
>
> As far as the foster parents go, we can either choose to be licensed directly with the county, which means you're only taking kids from that county and you're working with social workers from that county. Or, you can go through a private agency, which a lot of

> folks do because those are the ones advertising most of the time.
>
> And as a foster parent, if you go with the private agency, the private agency holds contracts with many counties. Which creates a whole different dynamic, because the money comes from the county to the private agency and then flows to the foster parent.
>
> Now the private agency doesn't want to look bad because the county is their customer. And so, they hide stuff. They do stuff that's not necessarily in the child's best interest because they don't want to affect the contract.
>
> But we had grave concerns when those children went back to their biological parent(s) because of some of the stuff that was going on, and we brought up those concerns. And as a foster parent, we were *disciplined* for bringing up those concerns because they did not want to jeopardize the contract.

The story of the little girls does not end well. After Tom made many reports of what appeared to be ongoing sexual abuse, none of their warnings were heeded. After sixteen months, they went back to their mother for about a year, and then ended up back in the foster care system, where they remain.

The Privatization of Foster Care

As of 2021, twenty-eight states have some level of privatization within their foster care systems. Two states, Kansas and Florida have all of their services now provided by private agencies, with Kansas having made the move nearly twenty years ago. The selling point to the public and lawmakers is these organizations can streamline care at more affordable costs. What is disturbing is that these agencies or companies are not always non-profit, but for profit.[6]

In 2013, a tragic case of a two-year-old little girl, Alexandria Hill, sent shock waves through the system when she was murdered at the hands of her foster mother. The private foster care management company, for-profit National Mentor Holdings, oversaw her care. The girl had initially been removed from her home due to marijuana use by her parents, one of whom was using the drug to help manage grand mal seizures. There was no evidence of other neglect or abuse mentioned in the report.[7] In the first foster home placement, her biological father complained of the care she was receiving because she was filthy. The Mentor case manager moved her to the second home where she was later killed.[8] According to an article in BuzzFeed published in 2015, they share the following data:

> "Mentor's profit margins vary state by state. In Ohio, according to a 2012 spreadsheet obtained by BuzzFeed News, its profit margin, as measured by the common Ebitda method, has been as high as 44%. In Alabama, the document indicates that the margin has hit 31%. That would mean that only 69 cents of every dollar that the state government paid to Mentor was spent on caring for the child and on overhead. Mentor's overall profit margin, according to its financial disclosures, has been a little over 10%."[9]

According to the records provided by BuzzFeed, at the time of Alexandria's death in 2013, Mentor was charging the state $39.52 a day (approximately $1185 per month) and paying the foster parent $22 a day for the care of the little girl ($660 per month). The case made national news, and the foster caregiver is in prison serving a life sentence for the murder, although that is little consolation for the parents who arguably should have never lost custody of Alexandria.

Further review shows these incidents do not appear to be isolated. Regarding Mentor specifically from the same article, reporters found that in Texas Mentor received reviews from state inspections showing they had more "high-ranked deficiencies", the worst kind of violations, than any other care provider of its size. In fact, they ranked third from the lowest of the twenty-three-state-outsourced foster care providers.[10]

Mentor Network is now operating under the name of Sevita Health, providing specialty healthcare in the fields of elder and special needs, as well as foster care services. It is privately owned by the equity firms of Centerbridge Partners, Vistria Group, and Madison Dearborn Partners.[11]

One single company's failings does not represent the entire industry, but the lack of accountability is disturbing, especially when looking at care providers potentially driven by profit. Just as the privatization of prisons is now being rolled back, lawmakers are beginning to look at the consequences of privatization in foster care.

A 2017 bi-partisan congressional report released by former Senator Orrin Hatch(R), and Senator Ron Wyden(D), showed that, in general, "children who are under the legal authority of their state, yet receive services from private for-profit agencies, have been abused, neglected and denied services. The very agencies charged with and paid to keep foster children safe too often failed to provide even the most basic protections, or to take the steps to prevent the occurrence of tragedies."[12]

Calls for reforms mount, but states continue to work with these agencies, and as more adoption providers offer services to these often-underfunded state social service departments, they may continue to prioritize efficiency over the quality of care received by desperate families and children.

Foster to Adopt Parents

Barbara is the only kinship adoptive parent interviewed but has a very special story. She is also a birth mother mentioned briefly in that previous section of the book. She relinquished in the 1950s, when she was very young and had become pregnant from a sexual assault. Quintessential of the time, the social worker bullied her into giving up her baby, which she had wanted very much to keep.

Her granddaughter from the boy she relinquished all those years ago was now a volatile young adult, convicted for murder but pregnant. Barbara stepped in. The baby needed a home, and Barbara was not going to let this baby go under *any* circumstances.

> **Barbara~**
> I called the social worker, and I explained that I'm the baby's great-grandmother. I want to know where she was at, and if she was okay. And she says, "Oh, she's fine. She's in a good foster home and she's got two brothers to play with."
>
> I said, "No, she ain't got two brothers to play with. She ain't got nobody in a foster home. Let's get that clear right now."
>
> She says, "Oh, what are your intentions?"

> I said, "My intentions are to get that baby. That is now my baby. Not my granddaughter's baby, not anybody else's baby. This is my baby."
>
> She says, "But you're the great grandmother. How old are you?" I told her, and she went, "What?"
>
> And I said, "Yeah, I'm fifty-five. I was fifteen when I had the father of the grandchild." I told her I was going to fight her every inch of the way to get that baby.

Barbara won the fight after many months and several trips to Montana where the child was born. She is now a happy fifteen-year-old girl living near Las Vegas. Barbara is one of tens of thousands of grandparents who take in their children's children to help raise them, either formally through adoption or via more informal arrangements. They should be supported and applauded for their efforts in preventing their youngest kinfolk from ending up without family.

Some adoptive foster parents begin with the goal of building out their families and start with first the foster care certification process. Their stories are worth listening to, as they often do take in children that appear to have no one else to care for them.

Doug and Carol already had four mostly grown children who were on their own when they decided they wished to foster and potentially adopt more. They signed up initially as foster parents, and Carol's sister had already adopted a special needs baby girl with Down Syndrome. So, they were open to many different situations.

After several temporary placements, the first of two phone calls came that changed their lives. First, they adopted a set of twins, both of whom had fetal alcohol and/

or drug addiction. Then three years later, they took in another set of twins in a similar situation.

Doug and Carol~
When you have a child with fetal alcohol or drug exposure, they will not think before they do something. They'll do it and then realize, "Oh I shouldn't have done that." or not care at all. And they really don't. It takes them longer to learn because the average child will touch something that's hot and learn it's not a good idea. But these kids won't, they'll do it again and again.

So, it's a different dynamic in the house. You commit to being around. Going out on a date by ourselves stopped. We couldn't leave our children with somebody else because they're a little different. Instead, we committed to doing family date night, and we still do it. It gets them out of the house too.

You're doing two or three appointments a week just for their therapy and care. Then somebody would get sick. We're splitting up right and left. The hardest part, I think, is that these children wouldn't sleep. So, we split a twin each.

Carol had Jamie, who was so much easier. Jacob couldn't sleep. When they're born so early, their lungs aren't finished. To get them to sleep, you have to pat them to help get everything going. They call it cupping.

For the first two years at least, I probably slept in a chair with Jacob because he really had breathing issues. Then he moved to the couch. We would do breathing treatments. We really didn't know any different. We had a couple of our own grown children who had pretty bad asthma. So, we were used to late nights and being in the shower or having a nebulizer. We were doing nebulizer treatments every three to four hours. It's a lot. I probably got four hours of sleep a night during those two years.

And then we got the next set of twins when they were three. And they were smaller. To terminate parental rights, it's quite a long process. And with Ellie and Amy, it was initially temporary. The parents were working their case, but then mom dropped off. I think I only met mom on her weekly visits, twice, I think. And then she took off, and we've never seen her since. Her kids are now fourteen.

We kept our license until the second set of twins were adopted. Then we closed it.

With fetal alcohol, they've lost so many brain cells but they have all their creative side. So, if you can help them learn using their creative side, then you can teach them around their brain. It was an incredible process, and we're still learning tons about that, but it's how we can interact, and we don't have to be as challenged.

We're getting more out of our relationship together as a husband and wife. There is way more communication because, if you're not a team doing this together, you'll never survive. You have to be 100% in it together. Because when I'm having a really bad day over something, I just turn it over to Dad. And if he wasn't all in, then everything would have failed.

But we still have our moments.

Jacob is our hardest one. He's missing a part of the front lobe of his brain. Quarter front, from the drugs. And he is very defiant and outspoken. He won't stop when he's doing something, so we do butt heads. He'll get really upset when I say, "Jacob you can't do that."

He'll eventually calm down. It just takes a little bit where his twin sister Jamie is the total opposite of him. She even gets mad at him when he struggles more in school than she does.

That was another learning thing, because we had never had a child with an Individual Educational Plan (IEP). That was why they got to start school at age three. They went into the preschool program and then rolled into kindergarten.

The schools here were amazing. Somebody will say something about one of our kid's IEPs, and I'm looking and saying that's not in there or that's in there. I know exactly what's in my kids' IEPs. I've done them for fourteen years now, for all four.

The younger two did not go into early childhood education because somebody dropped the ball, and we didn't know any better. They went right into school. Ellie and Amy had a [social] worker with them.

When they were about two years old, our

> case worker gave them back to the dad. And it was like somebody sold my children.
>
> I mean, we'd had them since they were two months old. And us knowing that the dad was still an alcoholic just made us sick to think that you're willing to put these children into a home where they could be harmed. They were with him for two and a half months. I think by then he was on meth.
>
> They still have night terrors because of those two and a half months. Now they're fourteen. So, twelve years.
>
> One thing that we did for years was take their bedroom door off and put up a baby gate. So nobody could shut their door. One of them slept with Doug and I, until they were six. When they finally slept through the night I was like, "wow, that's magic."

Tragically, Doug died of heart troubles just a year after this interview. The older set of twins graduated high school, and Carol and the kids soldier on, surrounded by other friends and family in their small community.

Lisa is an exception in that she is an adopted adult who along with her husband adopted two children out of foster care.

> **Lisa~**
> I wanted kids. Yeah, I get that I'm thirty-nine and I've waited too long. My husband had grown children from his prior marriage and had a vasectomy. We tried in vitro twice and it failed. By this time, we're in so much debt because of that, we decided to do foster care.

The first time we went through classes, my mom was dying so we didn't finish.

My husband went to Iraq and then came back. We went through classes again and got our first placement, which was two little girls. The older one was three and a half. The baby they thought was five months, but it turned out she was eight months, but she was so tiny they didn't have her age right.

It was rough. We made it but it was really rough. My husband retired from the military during then and was working some time in a nearby state. The original family were still working the plan officially. We did visitations twice a week with the dad and his mother.

We had all sorts of therapy for the oldest daughter, five or six appointments a week. She was sent back a couple times to her home, but I think sometimes they wait a long time to get things done.

It depends upon the situation, and this family did not need to have these kids. The house was infested with roaches. It was so bad that one of the kids would go to school and they would crawl out of his backpack. There was a lot of domestic violence. It was a big drug flophouse where people would be stoned out of their mind and passed out on the floor. When they took the oldest daughter initially everyone in the house tested positive for meth. She was in the system from the time she was sixteen months old. In her case, I feel like it was the right decision.

In this final story with Leah and her husband, they are now parents to six total children, including one sibling group, all from the foster system. All of the children are affected by drugs present in their systems at birth or ingested later. In listening to them you hear their fierce love and advocacy for their children, as well as their frustrations with the foster system.

Leah~
I'll be honest, adoption had kind of always been in my heart since I was a teenager. I had a cousin that was adopted, and I was fascinated by the whole process. I always had a feeling adoption would be in my future. I anticipated that it would be after we had some biological children. My husband and I got married, and he had been through chemo treatments as a teenager.

We knew that it may cause problems with us having children. And sure enough, after five years of trying it was not happening. After looking at private adoption where the costs were $40,000 to $60,000, we didn't have that kind of money.

So, in 2016 we opened our license. And over the course of the last seven years, we've taken in ten children. We ended up adopting six. The first one was a two-year-old boy, and then six months later, a newborn baby boy.

We had three others who were a sibling set who ended up leaving us, which was a very difficult experience. Then four days after they left, we got a call about a little baby boy who was the brother of our last baby. And then we got his two sisters about four months later. We thought we were done and adopted all of them.

Everything was good at that point and then in July of 2022, we took our last one and we just adopted her. Now we have officially closed our license as of May 2023. Their ages are ten, nine, seven, six, three and sixteen months.

The oldest boy had been in two kinship placements with families that didn't work out. He was basically dropped off at Child Haven and they were told to find a new place for him. For the oldest girl, she had been in five kinship placements, and the second girl had been in three placements. They failed for reasons, let's say, that were not the kids' fault, that's for sure.

The system needs an overhaul. The calling of foster care and providing for these children that don't have homes or places to go is a noble endeavor even as far as the system is concerned. But we found out very quickly that the kids are not kids. They are numbers in beds.

When we went through our initial class, we had one instructor that we really connected with, and she was very real with us. And then we had another instructor (they team taught) who was very much unicorns and butterflies and painted this picture that was not reality.

When we got licensed, the initial licensing worker was a godsend for us. She taught us a lot of the ropes of the system at the very beginning, things not to get caught up in, things to do and not to do, which saved us from a lot of heartache.

She taught us to document everything, every interaction with case workers, every interaction with biological family members, everything, write it down, write it down, write it down. Which ended up saving one of our little boys, quite frankly.

There are times when you feel like the system is in your corner, but they will turn on you on a dime. And that's what we have experienced.

Our first case worker was fabulous. She didn't play into the bureaucracy of it. She was there for the kids. When you're working with a caseworker like that, it's as good as it can be. I don't say foster care is never easy because of the drama that comes with it. But she was at least forthcoming with what was going on. We knew the progress that the bio parents had made or not made. We knew what was coming down the pipeline.

Like for instance, with our first son. We were told if you meet the biological grandma, she's not in a place to take him, but she's afraid of losing him. If you just meet her, maybe it will change things. Which in the DFS world is not generally the way they like to have you operate, but, for us, she saw that he was okay and that she could have contact with him and then she was okay with it. She's in all our lives regularly and loves all the kids.

But, transitioning into our next case, which was just horrific, it caused a lot of trauma within our lives as well as our sons. DFS is so focused on reunification they're almost willing to overlook even things that could possibly harm a child, putting children back in dangerous situations because they are just numbers. If we can get rid of this child, then that's an open bed for another child whose situation is much worse, and not actually looking at the situation.

With our next group of kiddos that ended up leaving, that case worker told us nothing. We were not allowed to know anything that was going on with the biological family. So we were in the dark, completely. Suddenly, one day we get a phone call and good news. You're losing the three kids. They're going to California. We understood that we may not be a permanent family, but we are a family for these kids at that time. And so breaking that up was not good news. [That case worker] was very difficult to work with and I still have some hard feelings on that one.

You have two polar opposites. You have social workers that are really there for the kids, and then you have the ones that are there because it's a job, and they just do what they're told, and they don't care who they hurt. Then you have the ones that are kind of hands-off. Our last one was good enough, and because there wasn't much drama in the case, she was, "Oh, okay. You don't need anything. See you next month."

> But foster parents are overall kind of viewed as the enemy. There's always something wrong with a foster parent. You're too invested. You love the child too much. You're too attached. Or there's the, "Oh, how dare you just doing this for the paycheck!" But it feels like DFS is never happy with their foster parents. They don't treat us with a lot of respect. By the time we hit two years [as foster parents], most of the people that we knew were already out. One lady in our class lasted eight days and closed her license.
>
> It's rocky terrain. And I think that for every individual it's going to be different. I honestly don't know how we survived as long as we did, but I would go back and walk through it again.

Leah's closing sentiment was echoed by all these parents. This is the hardest thing they've ever done, but it's the most rewarding, too. At least, that seems to be what good foster parents embody. Misunderstood by most of society, they want people to know how sincerely and completely dedicated they are to the wellbeing of their children, no matter how long they are with them.

The truth is everyone within the adoption constellation often feels misunderstood by society around them. This is true for adoptees, birth parents, adoptive parents, and foster parents as well as the people who support them.

---

1. https://www.judsoncenter.org/child-family/foster-care/

2. https://www.dfps.texas.gov/Child_Protection/Foster_Care/Training.asp

3. https://www.oregon.gov/odhs/providers-partners/foster-care/Pages/training-renewal.aspx

4. Beltran, A., & Epstein, H. R. (2013). The standards to license kinship foster parents around the United States: Using research findings to effect change. Journal of Family Social Work, 16(5), 364–381. https://doi.org/10.1080/10522158.2013.832463

5. Beltran, A., & Epstein, H. R. (2013). The standards to license kinship foster parents around the United States: Using research findings to effect change. Journal of Family Social Work, 16(5), 364–381. https://doi.org/10.1080/10522158.2013.832463

6. Robert Fellmeth and Sandy Santana, opinion contributors. (2021, March 25). Privatization of foster care has been a disaster for children. The Hill. https://thehill.com/opinion/civil-rights/543963-privatization-of-foster-care-has-been-a-disaster-for-children/

7. https://www.documentcloud.org/documents/1672123-alexandria-hill-mother-marijuana.html#document/p1/a204352

8. Bloomberg. (n.d.). Bloomberg.com. https://www.bloomberg.com/news/articles/2018-06-15/why-more-states-are-privatizing-foster-care?embedded-checkout=true

9. Roston, A., & Singer-Vine, J. (2015, February 20). Fostering profits: Abuse and neglect at America's biggest for-profit foster care company. BuzzFeed News. https://www.buzzfeednews.com/article/aramroston/fostering-profits#.cdVyY3Qgp

10. Roston, A., & Singer-Vine, J. (2015, February 20). Fostering profits: Abuse and neglect at America's biggest for-profit foster care company. BuzzFeed News. https://www.buzzfeednews.com/article/aramroston/fostering-profits#.cdVyY3Qgp

11. https://pitchbook.com/profiles/company/11639-35#faqs

12. Robert Fellmeth and Sandy Santana, opinion contributors. (2021, March 25). Privatization of foster care has been a disaster for children. The Hill. https://thehill.com/opinion/civil-rights/543963-privatization-of-foster-care-has-been-a-disaster-for-children/

Part V – The Constellation Comes Together

Chapter 24
Reunions: Hopes for Healing and Identity

"How do you develop an identity for yourself if you don't get to know some of the fundamentals about yourself?" ~Joy R.

From a very young age, almost all adopted children are asked, "Do you want to find your *real* parents?" It is a universal experience, and every adoptee crafts their own answer, which may change over time.

Searching for one's birth family is one of the biggest decisions an adopted adult may make. Some are certain by their teen years they want to know their first family, and never waiver from this desire. Others only come to it much later, and many don't allow this conscious consideration into their minds while their adoptive parents live. Some adoptees never want to seek their origins. A few are found by their first parents or other extended family relatives.

Liz~

One day out of the blue, I finally had a somewhat close Ancestry.com DNA match of a second or third cousin. So, I logged in for the first time in years and realized I had several of these. Not only that, but they were what appeared to be matches on both my birth mother's and father's side.

It's 2020, and I was born in 1965, and it's Thanksgiving weekend. The whole world is shut down because of Covid. I sat with my husband talking about what I should do. Do I search, finally? Both of my adoptive parents were gone, and I had been an only child. There was no one else to consult. It was just me and him now.

He says to me, "Babe, if you're even thinking about searching, no one in this scenario is getting any younger. Your mom would already be somewhere in her seventies. So, if you're going to do this, you'd better get after it." That was all it took. I began that weekend.

Joy~

It's been a long journey, there's been a lot of twists and turns and pivots and highs and lows. It's hard for the people who end up with a story they can't know the end to. I know that's a really hard thing. I want people to know that they're worthy and to keep going. Even if the story doesn't end with a positive outcome.

Putting the pieces together really has brought me peace. It's not something I think about all the time anymore. It's little closures of all these open and outstanding items. And granted, I know I've got the open door to go back to the people to ask questions, and that's not always an option for some. But I think it's about perseverance. Finding my identity

> may not have been an easy path, but getting to put some of the pieces together has been profoundly satisfying. Even if the story wasn't great, I am better for knowing what it was.

Adoptees finding their truth. Knowing and understanding their roots. Feeling a sense of closure. Learning about their families, their stories, and their medical history. These themes resonate and are discussed frequently throughout "adoptionland," and dominate the conversations with adoptees from the closed era. Almost all adoptions sealed the original birth certificates in the years between 1917 through the middle of the 1990s when open or semi-open adoptions first started to be practiced. Even when an adoption is fully open, in some states, records are still sealed.

According to a great many adoptees and birth parents alike, it is one of *the* most painful side effects. Individuals in both groups seek to repair the collateral damage caused by their separation. Some can find healing, while others do not. It is also one more reason why open adoptions should *remain open* whenever possible. If the parties have access to one another over time, then none of this drama is necessary.

The baby scoop era impacted America and a great many countries worldwide, creating millions of adoptees and their birth parents who should have the right to locate one another. However these birth parents are aging and rapidly coming to the end of their expected life cycles. Many will take their secrets with them. Adoptees who find only a gravestone can feel devastated.

Adopted adults do not have the right to a relationship with their birth parents, nor do the birth parents have a right to a relationship with the child they gave away—

that is a bonus some will have while others will need to make peace without it. But all adoptees deserve to at least have some knowledge of their heritage and surname, an understanding of what led to their placement and as much medical history as possible. Likewise, all birth parents deserve some peace from knowing their child is alive and how they have fared.

These should not just be seen as adoptee rights, or birth parent rights—but human rights.

It all begins with a family. And the tone set there builds the stage for how these searches and reunions evolve.

Adoptive Parents Set the Framework

An estimated 35 million people have taken a DNA test[1] and the industry is valued at $5.4 billion.[2] Why should adopted individuals be less curious than any other human about knowing and understanding their roots and historical family ties? Why should disinterest to their heritage be something they should feel in order to fulfill their parents or society's expectations of them?

The framework around adoption and how it is discussed in the family when children are young sets a tone that carries forward into adulthood. Parents often see their child's relative silence on questions or conversations about adoption and mistake it for indifference. But that is often not the case. If one rationally evaluates this, how or why should someone expect an eight-year-old or a teenager to have the verbiage to discuss personal or challenging topics—especially if the adults in their lives don't have the words? But this is often what happens. No one knows exactly what to say—so nothing gets discussed. Not talking about adoption can translate into the mind of a child as feeling as though the topic is taboo.

According to the NCFA survey on Adult Adoptee Experiences cited earlier:

> "A majority of adoptees expressed desires for enhancing parent-child communication when it came to discussing adoption. Key feedback highlighted the necessity of open and honest dialogue, continuously initiating discussions from an early age, and providing comprehensive information. Adoptees also discussed the importance of creating a safe space for children to process their emotions and offered guidance on appropriate messaging. Adoptees expressed additional desires for their parents to have acknowledged trauma, discussed issues related to race, and supported their preferences regarding birth family search and contact."[3]

In this survey, adoptees share their desire for their parents to make a concerted effort to help them learn more about their birth parents, and to also be open to helping them search.

This is where the motivations to adopt, and all the lessons and good advice from the prior chapters come together. One study conducted in 2005, exploring adoptive parents' experiences when their child was approaching reunion with a birth parent, particularly noted that if infertility was present, that pain would resurface. "For both adoptive fathers and mothers in this sample, the process of reunion rekindled grief around their infertility. Participants talked about the lack of opportunity to address the losses...at the time prior to the adoption."[4]

If parents have done their own internal work, honestly

evaluated and sought help when needed for their own pain, insecurities, struggles, or expectations, they will do a better job of showing up for their children. If they are uneasy about the subject of birth parents, the adoptee will know this too.

> **Sharon~**
> When I told my mother I was searching, she almost had a nervous breakdown. She cried for days. And also my father, "How can you do this to us?" So, not talking about adoption made me believe it was something you couldn't talk about. They also told me that people who searched were like delinquents. It meant something didn't go well with their adoption.
>
> **Melissa~**
> I was talking to my cousin's wife, and she's been around for a good ten years or so. And a few months ago, I said, "You know I'm adopted, right?" From her eyes I could tell it was a "no." But her head was nodding "yes." She had a thousand and one questions for me at that point.
>
> But my adoptive parents don't want to talk about any adoptive issues. I would bring up my birth mother and, you could tell, you could feel the tension in the room. It was not a good subject to bring up. I think they kind of felt like we're a great family. Why do you need another mother? You have a mother and a father. They didn't understand. They weren't educated on that stuff.

Commonly acknowledged within adoptee support groups are their struggles talking with their adoptive parents about their desires for these connections. What it comes down to for many is how much emotional capital a person is willing to spend to have the conversation. When parent's insecurities around these discussions rule the day, their children, even if fully grown adults, will predictably keep their thoughts to themselves.

The decision to search, is alone a major declaration to oneself. If the adoptee then must do more emotional heavy lifting to manage not only their own feelings, but those of their adoptive parents, they may not bother. This widens the potential divide between them even further.

According to an ongoing study from Dr. Lynn Zubov from Winston-Salem State University, her early results reflect similar outcomes. From her survey, when adoptees were asked about their levels of comfort in talking about reunion with their adoptive family, the results broke down this way:

- 43% of the adoptees felt extremely uncomfortable
- 21% reported they were somewhat uncomfortable
- 15% said they were somewhat comfortable
- 21% said they were extremely comfortable[5]

With well over half of the respondents saying they felt discomfort in talking to their adoptive parents about these desires, clearly there is room for improvement. This issue points to one of the most significant truths of all, which is that adoptive parents need to own their role. *They* adopted the child, and not the other way around. Infants do not ask to be assigned to a new family. This happened *to them.* The parents created this reality.

Their fantasy that love is all a child needs comes home to roost *at this moment.* Yes, their adoptee needs their love. But when that love feels conditional that is painful. There are few dynamics that bring these issues to the surface as much as the conversations around finding their first families. It is the moment when they begin to take charge of their own story and their chosen path. This alone deserves celebration, and is what adoptees are often craving.

Sometimes an uneasy peace is created, while other times these events can spur amazing growth in their relationships.

> **Rae~**
> When I told them that I had connected with my biological mother, it was uncomfortable for them for sure. That was obvious. But weirdly enough, their language around me changed and it was very hurtful. They started referring to their sons as the kids. [These are] my brothers. Instead of using their names or saying, "Your brother came down the other day," they said, "The kids came down the other day." And instead of referring to their parents, my adoptive grandparents, as "my grandparents," they would say, "Well, I'm visiting my mom for Labor Day Weekend."
>
> There was this shift where they "othered" me very suddenly with their language. That didn't last for too long. But for a solid month, I was scared to call them because I knew the conversation was going to be weird and awkward. Thankfully it didn't last.

Brian~
When I was in grad school, my birth mother came out to visit me. And my adopted mom said, "Why is she coming to visit you?"

I said, "Well, she wants to spend a little time with me, to get to know me."

"That's just weird. Why are you doing that? I just thought you wanted medical information..."

I never said that, but she thought I wanted information, and that would be it. But I was developing a relationship with my mother, and so my adoptive mom was becoming defensive.

Then I invited [my birth mom] to my wedding. My mom has a way of poking at you. Like, "Oh, how's Beth? How is she?" I hated it.

Thanks to my support groups, they gave me courage. I felt so guilty bringing it up, and I called her up and I said, "Mom, I have to talk to you about this. I am done walking on eggshells around the subject of my birth mother. I'm done. I can't do it anymore. It's killing me. I need you to know that I want her in my life, and she's going to be in my life. I want my kids to have her in their lives. I need you to be my mother and support me in this. I love you. I'm not going to leave you. You're my mom. You parented me, but I'm done with your passive-aggressive little stabs."

She started crying. "Oh, thank you. I'm not going to leave you either. I hope you know that." It turned into a great conversation, and we were very honest, but we adoptees are so frightened of this conversation. Most people wait until their parents have passed on for all this. So, it is a wild experience to have these two things going on at once and trying to navigate them. It's painful. It's difficult. It's complicated. But once you face all that, it's very liberating as well.

International Adoptees

International adoptees have the same desires and want to know their origin story and medical history. But for these individuals it is virtually impossible or significantly less likely they will be able to locate their original family.

It is yet one more reason to call out the concerns about deceitful, coercive, or corrupted practices. International adoptees may have no or few records, and too many have been falsified. Some can find relatives in the US via DNA searches, and a few have found each other in what feel like miraculous coincidences.

Jessie was adopted from Cambodia and lives in Long Beach, NY, and got a surprise that one of her best friends growing up was actually her cousin.

Jessie~
In high school, we were always referred to as, "You look related. You look like cousins." I didn't know what to say, 'cause I knew that we weren't, but we called each other that because we were both adopted from Cambodia and were good friends. In reality, we do look alike. It turned out that we were genetically related cousins all these years, and I didn't know it until three months ago.

They moved upstate. He's more like a

> brother to me, and I will always call him my older brother as opposed to my cousin, 'cause we grew up together.
>
> Having that sense of community... I have two cousins that live in New York. I had one that lived in Chicago. Unfortunately, she passed away from an overdose. I have one in Ohio. I have a lot in Colorado, some in Hawaii, a lot in Cambodia, in England, all over. And it's just great to know that I have all this family everywhere. It brings me a sense of comfort and it makes me feel whole.

These international adoptees and their stories of connecting with immediate or more distant relatives are rarities. DNA testing certainly improves their potential. Consultants and travel organizations that specialize in helping adoptees locate family members and to travel back into their home countries are expanding. Jessie, as a young adult, has already made two trips back to Cambodia.

But even with all these efforts, the overwhelming majority have found no close relatives or connections to their heritage.

Medical History

A person's medical history includes both their personal history and their familys' history. "This information gives your doctor all kinds of important clues about what's going on with your health, because many diseases run in families." It also indicates what risk factors should be watched for in the future.[6]

Most adults take knowing their medical history for granted, however for a great many adoptees, that information is completely unknown. Not only is very little information taken at the time of the placement, if the process is closed, the adoptee loses out on everything that continues to develop in their biological family over time.

From the scoop era over one and a half million children were relinquished to adoption. Any medical history provided, even if it was asked about and some record was kept, was minimal, at best.

Adoptees from a closed adoption go to a new doctor for the first time and when filling out the forms and the section on medical history, they often scrawl in large letters, fully across the page, "ADOPTED."

What is more, this gap carries forward to *their* children.

Dana~
My aunt Jill had given me the names of cousins that I had. I reached out to one of them and then his dad. But my aunt Suzanne passed away from ALS. I found out that's something that runs in my family on that side.

Joy~
I got to get to know a little bit about my dad. He ended up dying of a stroke. So, there's definitely a component of his health that I still stay mindful of for myself.

Pam~
The agency that handled my adoption called to tell me my natural mother just had a bilateral mastectomy, and that cancer runs in my family. And [my birth mother] wanted me to know about it. Apparently predominantly because her sister had it, her mother had it, her

mother's mother had it.

An adopted person seems fine for most of their life and then has trouble in some way. Genetic health testing can potentially help, but it does not give a full picture. According to the Mayo Clinic website, these tests are not always sufficient as predictors to disease because every individual has variations of the way genes appear.[7] The same article also notes that testing may not be able to detect all genetic defects. Medical information and not only the desire to know who they are might be motivating a search for their birth family. But the need is one of the few unifying points parents, adoptees, and lawmakers agree—the situation deserves to be improved.

You're All Like Me

One of the most meaningful and consistent stories adoptees in reunion will share is how much similarity they find between themselves and their blood relatives. They may or may not particularly favor their birth parent(s) in appearance, but characteristics will come to life in so many unexpected ways.

> **Kate~**
> I was drawn to police work and law enforcement. No one else did that in my family who raised me. There's no lawyers or cops anywhere in that tree.
>
> Then I'm reunited with my birth father. I'm a cop. He's a cop. So are my grandfather and some of my uncles. We're all cops!

This is nature versus nurture in action. It's the subtle mannerisms, the toss of the hair or head, the cadence of voice, odd or unusual food preferences. Similar interests in hobbies or education, and career choices abound, as well as artistic or athletic talents. The list of shared traits is both wondrous and endless when talking to these reunited individuals.

It is also where adopted adults, in particular, will for the first time truly understand what they have missed. Those genetic mirrors that were denied them, which the rest of the world enjoys without conscious effort. Personal contact with their birth families brings their losses into clear view.

> **Joy~**
> I think the rewarding part was getting to see people that look like me, getting to see people who thought like me. I was with [one of my sisters] and went to her house and we were making eggs. I had cracked the eggs, and she came running over. "Oh, we got to dig the little white thing out."
>
> And I say, "I'm already going to dig the white thing out. It's the thing I do. I don't eat the white thing."
>
> **Kris~**
> I grew up adopted by my Scandinavian parents. They don't touch. I think you get points taken away. There's a chart, you know, you'll lose a star if you touch somebody.
>
> There was not a moment in my life where I felt like I belonged. When my kids were born, I told them they were my little clues. And my son was born very dark. He looks more Italian

than my [biological] brothers. So, I knew there was probably some kind of Mediterranean background.

In 2019, my daughter gave me a DNA test for Christmas. The following September, my husband called and said, "There's this guy who says he's your half-brother." I called him and apparently a niece had done a DNA test and he found he had a half-sister. That's the bucket-list for an adopted person—to be found.

He sat me down and said, "In an Italian family, you are one-hundred percent part of our family and you come back at the same place of respect that anybody in your position is. The daughter of Paul." That was pretty cool.

I've met them all at different gatherings. There was a birthday party that was just for the first cousins. And they're huggers. My brother David still has to remind me when I meet people, they throw their arms up.

When I see people I knew before they found me, I now hug them and say, "I'm Italian!" And I tell people I'm from this big Italian family.

Sometimes the loss of genetic heritage can mean a lack of recognition not only of cultural practices, but on some occasions, unknown opportunities.

Joy~
My [adoptive] mom thought I was East Indian, which could've been Pakistani. I remember

meeting people in my life that were from East India and thinking, "Hey, I want to know you more just because maybe I have a connection to you that I don't know." All the while it was Cherokee American Indian.

Had I known that I would've pursued more information. But we don't get to know any of that.

I remember the details of my first conversation with my birth mother. She got on the phone and said, "Hi, Joy. It's so nice to meet you. We're Cherokee Indians and we're the last of the thinking people."

I was so blown away by that, because why would you lead with all that? I mean it went right to my critical and technical thinking, and the visualization of things I've always had. "Oh my God. I've always known this about me. I'm the last of the thinking people."

Had I known I was an American Indian in any way, I could have legally forced my record open. I have a whole tribe of community I didn't even know I could have had.

Why don't we have the right to know about ourselves? Maybe I would've made different decisions in my life had I known a little bit more.

I am not a creative person. I've never thought of myself as a creative person. I have a creative daughter. I didn't know it, but my biological mom was an artist, and she liked to paint and draw. I feel I missed out on painting and drawing. That might have been part of my life if I would've known that my biological mother was an artist in some way. I may have explored that side of me. Even that is a little bit of a slight.

Darker Revelations

Sometimes more troubling realities surface after reunions. The fictional adoption narrative can be revealed as a cover for the harsher reality.

Brian~
I arrived on my birth mother's doorstep, and we met. She couldn't let go of me. She was holding on so tight it freaked me out. I suddenly became the adult and said, "I'm fine, I'm fine. You're fine. You made a good choice. Everything is okay."

She kept saying, "I didn't want to give you away. I did not want to give you away. I'm so sorry I did this to you."

"What? No! Adoption's a beautiful thing. You did this because you love me. No, look, everything is fine!"

And she said, "No, I didn't want to do it. My parents made me do it. They would've shipped me away if I didn't. I didn't want to leave. I just agreed to give you away if they let me stay at home in Kansas City."

Sharon~
She was sixteen and her parents said, "You can't bring home an illegitimate child." They sent her to one of the Louise Wise homes for unwed mothers to have the baby. They said,

"Place her with us and go home and you can work on your parents." And within twenty-four hours [the agency] sued for custody, citing a minor in need of supervision, which was the law at the time in New York State. It was considered a juvenile offense to be under the age of eighteen and single and pregnant in 1965.

I ended up in foster care for a year because my birth mother refused to sign the consents, and it had to go to court. *She fought for a year.*

The day I completed graduate school, I was pregnant. It was being pregnant and suddenly feeling this connection to my birth mother of how hard that must have been. At the time, I didn't know the story. Only that she was sixteen, because I'd gotten some non-identifying information.

I thought, how hard it must be to relinquish a child and not know if they are okay or not? I suddenly felt this deep desire to connect with her and tell her I was okay. I wanted her to know.

That started my search, and it took a couple of years. I was adopted in New York, and she took her life at twenty-six. Her suicide was a cocktail of overdosed pills and alcohol, very purposely and intentionally. She left a letter.

Her mother, my grandmother, was the first one I connected to on the phone.

She said, "Linda's dead."

"Yes, I know," I said. "I'm so sorry."

"I always kept my phone number listed so you could find me," she told me.

> She was eighty-six years old, and she never told anybody about the reunion, because she was still so ashamed that her daughter had a child out of wedlock. So even though she was so happy to reconnect and teary when she met me and said, "Your voice is hers, and I feel like I have a piece of my daughter," and all that, she still carried the stigma and shame.

These harsher realities can swing both ways, too. Not all birth parents, including mothers, will be all their relinquished children wished or hoped they were. These stories sometimes can leave the adopted adult feeling they may indeed have dodged a bullet by not being raised by them.

> **Jody~**
> She got pregnant, and she made the decision. Her parents wanted to keep me and raise me, and she would not have it. I got this story from my cousin, who came and lived with me for a while.
>
> My cousin said, "Oh yeah, she didn't have to give you up for adoption. She didn't want her parents to raise you because then her parents wouldn't take care of her."
>
> But considering that all four of those daughters [raised by my grandparents] were really fucked up, I question how great that home was.

> **Joy~**
> Some of the questions I asked my mom, when it was right to do so, were such as, "did you

hold me?"

"No, never held you."

"Okay. Did you privately name me?"

"Nope. Never named you."

It was almost like a rejection in every answer, and that was hard. She couldn't have known that I took it as a rejection. I was hurt at first but over time, the more I thought about it, it wasn't wrong for her to do what she did. I was her fifth child. She knew what it probably meant to hold me. So, it wasn't right for her to hold me because then she may have wanted me. Given her circumstances, adoption was the absolute right thing for her to do.

Finding Peace Through Hardship

Many reunions do not look like fairy tales, but they can find a way to work even when there are unexpected challenges.

Rae~

I'm sitting in my living room with my partner nearby and I have a computer in front of me. To my absolute shock, the address on the public record is less than three miles from where I'm sitting.

Then I did a Facebook search, and I found her picture. It was a picture of this really grizzled kind of woman, and she had a very sad look in her eyes. I thought, oh, I don't really know if I want to know that person. That's kind of scary. She seems sad, and she seems like she's living a difficult lifestyle.

Curiosity got the better of me and the

agony of not knowing. I wrote a letter, and I put the address on the public record search on the letter.

Then about a month later, there was an email from somebody named Mark. I don't know this person, but I opened the email to delete it, and it said, "Anne asked me to send this to you." It's my half-brother, and he's writing to me. "She is very excited and very nervous, and she would like to talk to you, but she isn't sure." And so began this correspondence. I sent a couple of emails back and forth to him and therefore to her, by extension.

I hadn't told my adoptive parents at all. Because of my experience growing up, I didn't think this was going to be the sort of thing they wanted to hear. I figured I would wait and see how it went and report back to them after I had some results.

I agreed reluctantly to give her my phone number. We picked a day for the phone call.

In my mind, I'm going to have this really nice conversation and say, "Oh, it's so nice to meet you." We're strangers who are going to get to know each other. I answered the phone. At the exact same moment, she and I both say, "Hello." I cannot tell you what a physiological reaction I experienced because it was something you've never heard of. It was like my entire body experienced an electric jolt because I heard *my* voice say hello back to me through the phone. I had never heard it in another person in the same cadence and the same tone. And my birth mother and I both started crying because we'd never heard the voice of the other.

We're just shocked into this point of, oh my God, it's *you*.

All my plans at that point to form a slow and steady relationship disappeared out the window because of the shock of that biological connection. We agreed to meet the very next day at a dog park.

The next day, I loaded my dog up and I got there forty-five minutes early because I wanted to feel prepared. We were wandering around, and I looked back toward the gate to see a woman standing there. I could tell immediately that it was my mother. I went over to her. She was crying, and I was nervous with all these big emotions. What should I do? She just gave me a big hug. We were able to share a few moments together walking through that park.

It's been a reunion story ever since, but it is also colored by addiction and mental health, which my biological mother suffers from very heavily. Addiction and ADHD really took a toll on her. You can see that in her body. There are things about her that are very familiar, and then there are things about her that are very off-putting. Because you can't quite tell if it's her personality or the addiction and the ADHD that she suffers from?

In that way, it's been hard to form a reunion perhaps in comparison to other adoptees because she's a somewhat disjointed individual. She's well-intentioned, but very intense sometimes. Those have been some difficult challenges in my reunion.

I think there has been a stillness in my soul that came after our reunion despite all the challenges and the pains it has brought to me. It just makes me feel like I know where I came from.

---

1. https://www.psychologytoday.com/us/blog/the-lost-family/202010/why-are-americans-obsessed-genealogy

2. https://www.linkedin.com/pulse/genealogy-products-services-market-analysis-share-size-mitali-pingale-nzwof

3. Hanlon, R., Davi, N., Quade, M., & Lindner, A. (2024). Profiles in adoption: Adult adoptee experiences. National Council For Adoption.

4. Petta, G. A., & Steed, L. G. (2005). The experience of adoptive parents in adoption reunion relationships: A qualitative study. American Journal of Orthopsychiatry, 75(2), 230–241. https://doi.org/10.1037/0002-9432.75.2.230

5. A Preliminary Exploration into Adoption Reunions. Data on when adoptees knew they were adopted. Facebook, 7 2024, 3:19PM, https://www.facebook.com/profile.php?id=61555968231690, Accessed14 Jun 2024.

6. https://www.webmd.com/a-to-z-guides/what-is-my-medical-history

7.https://www.mayoclinic.org/tests-procedures/genetic-testing/about/pac-20384827#:~:text=In%20some%20cases%2C%20a%20genetic,over%20time%20may%20be%20necessary.

Chapter 25
Roadmaps to More Satisfying Reunions

"I want people to be told, this isn't what you think it is, this is like a bomb. There is so much debris inside, dangerous debris that needs to be respected and managed carefully."
~Cathryn Vogeley

The public rarely thinks about adoption, but one of the ways it is brought to their attention is via heartwarming news stories about long-lost siblings or birth parents and their relinquished children finding each other. The coincidences are often remarkable or serendipitous, and everyone appears overjoyed. Videos and pictures fill the screen with hugs, tears, and people in the midst of discoveries everyone believes are happily-ever-afters. Some reunions *do* last forever and become the fairy tale everyone hopes for and envisions. Too many do not last beyond the initial "honeymoon" period.

Ann~
He reassured me he had a good life and didn't want for anything. Probably after that, we would text back and forth every other week. Then, I was going to Arizona, and I was going to call and meet up with him. But something happened, and I ended up not going.

I texted him and said, "Hey, I'm not going to be able to be down there, but you are going to come through Vegas. So, when you come through on your vacation, how about we meet? I would prefer just to meet with you and your wife first, and if you want to bring your kids, that's fine. I have to go in baby steps before I bring my daughter and my parents into this. So, how about we meet?"

I haven't heard back from him since.

I've talked to one person that's adopted. He said, you've put the ball in his court. He needs to understand where you're coming from. If he can't accept that, then maybe you'll just never meet him.

Reunions are full of hopes and expectations from both adoptees and their birth parents. A few small studies have been done on adoption reunions in the US, the UK, and Australia. The number of reunions where the parent(s) and adult adoptees maintain a connection over the long term varies widely.

Some report that after eight years, slightly over 50% of the study participants are still actively in contact.[1] Another cited that 25% of the relationships failed.[2] In one US study, while roughly 70% of these relationships remained in either regular or occasional long-term contact, 17% of them terminated their relationships immediately after the first meeting.[3] The only thing that all of these studies agree on is that the emotions involved are highly charged, and great care is needed to make them successful.

Cathryn~

This is not two people reaching for each other, flesh and blood, hugging after a lifetime and saying, I'm sorry I gave you away. And the other one's saying, it's okay, mom, I love you. It is not that. And that was my notion. But it's not real.

I would like to stress the importance of approaching reunion cautiously. Whether you're an adoptee or a first parent. The romantic notion that you're going to run toward each other and throw your arms around each other and say, "Oh my God, I found you. I love you so much. I'm sorry I gave you up,". The reality is there's been a lot that happened between that pregnancy, the delivery, and the day when you meet each other. A lot of resentment, pain, and complicated feelings have developed. A lot of people are involved. The adoptive parents, the first siblings, the adoptive siblings, and on, and on. Get a specialist and get help.

Cathryn is a writer and author of her memoir "I Need To Tell You" who relinquished her daughter in 1968. Part of her story was shared in Chapter 11. She found her daughter and reunited with her in 2016 when she was working on her book.

Cathryn~
I think it would've helped me a lot had I understood that it's common and natural for an adoptee to feel angry. That an adoptee, even though she's a middle-aged adult, is still a child inside. I am her mother. She's not my sister, and she's not my friend. She learned that I was writing my story. I connected with her during the process of writing my book. She wanted to read what I was writing. She almost begged me to send her what I was writing. She was really supportive of me, as if she was my therapist. She reassured me, and I recognized that, though I thought this

> was not a good idea she pulled it out of me. She would say, she's a grown woman, highly educated, blah, blah, blah. And I fell for that. She said, "There's nothing you can say that I can't handle." I knew better, but I believed her because I wanted to.
>
> She said, maybe if we were on the same coast, [a meeting could] happen. I said, "Okay. How about this? I'll fly into the Atlanta airport, and you can meet me there and we could have lunch or something. Then I'll get back on the plane and go back home. So, nobody has to know, her parents don't have to know, her children don't have to know.
>
> She wrote back and said, "What do you hope to gain from that?"
>
> I said, "I can look into your eyes and tell you I'm sorry. And I could hug you, if you would let me."
>
> She said no. I had to respect her wishes. I do respect her wishes. She had no choice, and that's part of what she said made her angry. She had no choice about what happened to her when she was born, and things were done with her as a baby that she didn't have any control over.

Adoptees can find themselves suddenly angry when faced with the mothers who relinquished them. These same mothers, now women who are much older, are often begging for forgiveness and deeply afraid of their now adult child's emotions.

Adoptees are often as conflicted about their feelings as their newly located birth parents. They may have ignored or suppressed their feelings to fit in or fulfill the desire to belong. Some appeased many people in their lives and needed that mindset. Reunion is bringing all that vulnerability, desire, pain, and loss from the unconscious separation with their first mother and setting it on top for themselves and all to see. It can be overwhelming for everyone involved.

> **Brian~**
> After our initial reunion, I struggled. I didn't even know why. I would just start bawling.
>
> For my birth mother, I'm trying to be the strong one and comforting her. As I got involved with the adoption community, a good thirteen years after my reunion, I understood the birth mother's point of view. When they reunite, they go back to that time of giving birth. Here I am, a twenty-four-year-old man now comforting [what would seem like] my seventeen-year-old mother. Those were her emotions.
>
> In the same way, all my emotions were flooding. I was like a baby again. I was the infant that lost his mother. I didn't have the language to put terms with my feelings. That's why I didn't understand what was going on.
>
> The reunion is such a complicated thing. It's exciting. Everything's new and you're trying to fill in all these gaps and holes, because you're like Swiss cheese growing up. You're looking for connection. But then you have these foreign emotions you don't understand, that just hit you and you're grieving.

Sometimes all these pain points come together in a single story. Adoptees often internalize a plethora of complex feelings. Loyalty conflicts can be internalized completely without adoptive parents' knowledge or fault. It's a feeling for that adoptee by their own creation. Also, the one searching needs to be mindful that, for the "found" person, they may be in their own life situation which may cause them to say, "Not now." *Timing matters.*

Pam~
I'm twenty-eight, and I get a call from the agency that handled my adoption. I was happy with where I was at, who I was with, and my family.

I never had a desire to know more outside of that. I never had that curiosity, yet when I was angry as a teen I would always say, "You're not my mom!" That was just me being rebellious. I just made that connection because I remember never wanting to search for her or know anything else. So that's interesting to me.

The agency told me they would send me documents and all the paperwork. I called my aunt—my mom's sister, who I was so close with. I'm more like my aunt than my mom. I told her what had happened and she was quiet, but she listened and she helped me. I said, "I don't know. I think I need to call my parents and tell them what happened."

We agreed.

I called my mom and dad and let them know. They were on vacation, and, apparently, my mom got quiet and had a really hard time for the rest of her trip after I called. My dad told me that later.

Over a decade goes by, and now Pam is living in Las Vegas and is about to turn forty when she receives her first direct contact from her birth mother.

> I open the envelope and it's a letter from her. Apparently, she had been trying to find me since I was young. She kept placing ads in the paper. So right around when it would be my birthday, she would put in an ad to try to figure out where I was at.
>
> She found me finally because she had a private investigator following me, which pissed me off. But she gave me her name, she gave me all of her information, and she said, "If you would ever want to talk, here I am."
>
> I remember walking into the house, and I said to my husband at the time, "I just got this letter from my natural mother, and I don't know what to do with this."

Pam agreed to meet, and her birth mother came to Las Vegas. After a few mixed communications they do meet up for a few hours one day. Her mother explained how she had become pregnant from her boyfriend, and how Pam's grandmother had convinced the family to have her placed for adoption.

> I didn't feel any connection. I didn't even feel like her daughter. It was like meeting somebody else who's been trying to find you. It was weird. But the memorable part though is not too far after.
>
> I was turning forty, and my then husband threw me a surprise birthday party. A bunch of my friends came, and my parents and my brother. I remember sitting with my mom and dad and I felt like I was cheating on them. My parents have always been amazing. It was just so good to see them and to hug them.
>
> And I felt *so guilty*.

I had this little secret. So, the party was over and within that week, I had received a gift from my natural mother. It was a pillow with a bunch of stuff embroidered on it. I could tell she had it specially made. I remember feeling like she was trying so hard to be in my life, and I was so divided.

I called my brother and my mom's sister, and I told them I had met her. I said I don't think I should tell mom. I thought I could have told my dad—he could handle it. But my dad couldn't keep secrets from her very well. Plus, he had cancer.

So, we all decided, my brother and my aunt and I, the best thing to do right now would be to just not say anything because I think my mom would have been hurt. I remembered back from when I was twenty-eight, and I felt so guilty.

My natural mother kept emailing me and trying to get in touch with me. I felt like she wanted to be my mom.

I made the decision to stop talking to her. I remember, I couldn't do it over the phone. I did it by email. I just said, it's too much for me. I feel too guilty.

I was devastated, because I felt like I was cheating on my parents. That's the best way that I can describe it. But I felt immediate relief when I stopped it. I haven't heard from her since. I think the timing was off, and I can't see myself searching.

I'll be honest with you—I don't remember her name anymore. Somewhere in my paperwork, I've got the letter, I've kept all of that, but I don't think about it. I don't necessarily want it. That said, I think if I were to find out that she passed, I would be sad. It would make me sad.

I think it would change things if my adoptive mom was passed.

Motivations for Searching

Affecting the reunion will be the motivations for the search, and how they differ for both adoptees and birth parents. Another key factor is who has found who. For the "found" person, *they* may not want or have even considered a relationship. One may find the other and be very quickly rebuffed because the party who was not searching is not interested.

Birth parents, and particularly birth mothers' motivations are intensely emotional and are more likely to want a relationship. They *are* mothers and many feel that keenly, which can even cause them to feel entitled to a connection with their now adult child. These mothers wish to know how their child fares and if they have had good lives. They also wish to explain their decisions around relinquishing and tell these adoptees of their love for them. Inner peace and healing are also hoped for.[4] First mothers in particular feel a longing for meaningful connections with their adult child. But how their feelings manifest does not always go well.

Jody~

You go looking for [birth family], you're just like, "Oh my God, these are my people." And there's unrealistic expectations on both sides, again, much like the adoption experience on the other end. You get it on this end too.

Well, I look like her and I have the same mannerisms as her and I talk like her, but I was raised by entirely different people in a different world. I have different boundaries and morals and belief systems.

Then she's very, "Well, I gave up this child and here she is. She's back in my life and I'm her mom." But when I skinned my knee, [my adoptive mom] is the one that wiped my tears. When I had a birthday, she's the one that made me a cake, and she's the one that let me play dress-up in her clothes. She's the one that took me to school and read me to sleep at night. She's my mom. This other lady that I look like and sound like, she's a stranger. You don't get to make that claim on me, and she could not deal with that.

She came into my life, and she wanted to boss me, to make demands. She wanted to use me. I set boundaries and that was not okay with her. I don't *do* abuse—period—end of sentence. I just don't. You want to be abusive with me? There's the door.

Melissa~

My birth mother gave me the book, "The Primal Wound," I think at probably twenty-three, twenty-four years old. I read it and I was, who the hell are you, lady, to give me this book and act like you know who I am and what I'm going through.

I was so mad, and I was so protective of my adoptive parents. I had the best life. None of this is me. I threw it in the garbage, and I didn't pick it up again until a year and a half ago and then reread it. Now I can take what I want and leave what doesn't fit. I can look at it objectively and not react.

I found [my birth mother] in the '90s. She had some medical issues going on. She thought the day I turned eighteen I would try and find her, and I didn't.

I found a bunch of papers from my parents. It was a file with my name on it. What the hell is this? I open it up and there's a letter in there from when I was eighteen, and now I'm twenty. It was addressed to my parents.

I was eighteen and it should have come to me. I'm an adult now. I know nothing about this and could not tell my adoptive parents I had found this information. From what I could gather, my birth mother was having health issues. Her doctors' want to know if I'm having any of these symptoms because they don't know what's wrong with her.

Now I'm like, well, what the frick happened to her? What was it? Because I need to know biological stuff. I was pissed off and hired some ladies called the Snoop sisters. And they found her really quick. They even sent me my original birth certificate.

I'm from California, which is still a closed records state. They wouldn't tell me how they got that stuff, but they sent it to me. So that was weird, seeing my name as a different name on the birth certificate.

So, she was totally ready to meet me. She was, "What took you so long? I thought you were going to try and find me when you were eighteen." I guess she had told the agency that if I did reach out, she was okay connecting with me. But I didn't even know how to go about any of that. I don't even know what agency.

> So that's how I found her. Then, through her I found my dad.

Natural fathers have been studied far less. Adoptees may tend to focus more on their mothers than the male side of their story and can be influenced by the perceived treatment of their mothers by their fathers, especially if his actions appear to have been harsh or neglectful at the time of relinquishment. Even if these stereotypes prove to be inaccurate.[5] These potential issues aside, many adoptees and birth fathers have very successful reunions.

Mel's story as a birth father is briefly featured in Chapter 2. Any of his potential desires were completely set aside by the processes put in place by the parents and (he assumed) the wishes of his then former girlfriend. He lived his life never knowing if he had fathered a boy or a girl. But he never forgot.

Even after his marriage and three subsequent children, he wondered about the one he didn't know. Traveling as a police officer through the northeast, into the town he knew his former girlfriend had been sent to, one night he finally decided he wanted the mystery to end. After gaining the support of his then wife, he contacted the Lund Agency who had handled the adoption.

> **Mel~**
> I made the call that week. The staff person who talked to me was wonderful. I told her who I was, who the birth mother was, and when the likely date was. She said, "Let me check and get back to you." And she did! She didn't take long to look it up in the records.
>
> When she called back, she first said, "I think you'll be glad you called." There was so much messaging going on in those few words that were all positive. She tells me, "You have

a daughter. Her name is Kate, and she lives in Massachusetts." Of course, we were living only twenty miles from Massachusetts! She says, "I can't tell you where she works or what she does. That's all I can tell you."

"She [Kate] has also reached out and sent a letter saying that if my birth parents come forward, you pass my name along." She explained, "Here's how it works. You write her a letter but send it to me." What's funny is that I didn't realize that she would be vetting the language. So, I just wrote this letter, giving too much information. I learned later that you couldn't share your last name, or where you live, as they're editing that information. Because the process is, she looks at it, takes the identification out, and sends it off to Kate.

Kate writes back, and then I get it from them. After about three letters back and forth, our case worker says, "You two were meant for each other."

I finally got to begin my own correspondence with my daughter. It turned out she was near Boston, about two and a half hours away. It didn't take long for us to decide to meet.

We went to a park, and she had her two kids there as well. It was just a wonderful introduction! The kids were wonderful, and they were still young. One sat on my lap while we sat on the grass, just talking away. Kate explained who raised her.

It didn't take long to set up a gathering where we met her adoptive parents, and they were both wonderful. Initially, her adoptive

> mother didn't take lightly this idea of me coming into the scene. Kate admitted "Mom is not happy about this."
>
> But she relented. Once we had that meeting, it was fine. [My wife] and she were both travelers and activists back in the day, and they bonded. I got the story from their perspective, a little bit of what it was like for them.
>
> But you couldn't have asked for better parents, adoptive or birth, because they were just loving and did the right things.

The Stages of Reunion

There is a somewhat predictable "course" of events or more accurately, emotional transitions that occur in reunions once first contact is made. These stages vary by individual but tend to follow similar trends. Both parties will move fluidly in and out of these stages as the relationship progresses.

One online resource shares these following stages, which seem particularly sound and are similar to others found in researching the topic:

> **Excitement**—this can also be known as the fantasy or honeymoon stage at the beginning of the reunion. Emotions are giddy and feel almost surreal, whether this has been dreamt of for decades or more recent.
>
> **Obsession**—infatuation can begin to feel like an obsession. Family members may caution the parties to not "lose their heads" or get "too carried away." Both parties may think of little else during this

phase, but if their needs are not meshing with each other, one pulling back can be sensed by the other.

Confusion— it starts to get complicated. As real life and real relationships need to be dealt with, the reunion enters a new phase. How do they wish to interact with other family members? How much and what kind of contact? What do we call each other? Pulling back while both assess their feelings and intuit their way may be needed to help them establish physical and emotional boundaries.

Figuring it Out—eventually both adoptees and their parents start to normalize their relationships and sort through some of these challenges. It is during these times that a reunion can either solidify and become stronger, or potentially break down. Mastering communications and managing expectations honestly and compassionately help smooth the way.

Acceptance—this can be the most difficult aspect of reunion to achieve. If there were unrealistic expectations from the beginning and are not overcome, they may remain in the relationship but feel forever disappointed. Both parties want to make up for lost time, but that is not possible in a true sense. There will never be a full reparation of the damage from separation. If a sense of personal peace can be found, finding acceptance that this is enough can be rewarding.[6]

There is no "guidebook" or "Seven Habits to Highly Effective Adoption Reunions." Both the adult adoptee and their birth parent(s) need to show up for themselves and each other as honestly, openly, and authentically as they can. The sheer vulnerability required to participate in such a process is daunting. If either one of these parties does not want such an emotional undertaking and requests to not meet or connect, that must be respected. The process of "coming out of the fog" and facing each other can be too much.

For some birth parents or adoptees, the request to leave the past alone is a permanent one and may never change. Others find it can shift, and maybe all that's needed is a gentle push to see if the door remains closed, or possibly reopens.

Dirk is a transracial, domestic adoptee who has already established a successful reunion with his birth father, whom he favors physically. Many of his half-siblings are also regularly in touch, and he was generally welcomed into the family. His mother is white, and his father is black. When he was born back in 1960, these mixed relationships were viewed negatively. He never had success forging a reunion with his mother whom he found years ago. At the time, she wanted "the past to stay in the past."

> **Dirk~**
> I was in one of the men's adoptee support groups, and I said, "You know what? I know where she lives. Before one of us dies, I'm thinking about going." I asked the group, "What do you guys think?"
>
> One guy said, "When I found my birth dad, it was at a cemetery."
>
> I booked a flight and rented a car that week.
>
> I knew she was in an assisted living home.

I made this whole plan on how I was going to get in to see her. It's a secure building. I got my story all ready to get me in there and then what I'm going to say to her. I had all these scenarios in my head.

The one thing I didn't plan on was her having a roommate. I walk up and see her room and the name plates there. Her nameplate is there but there is also another one. Now I'm freaking out because I'm about ready to meet my birth mom after all these years. I'm sixty-one at the time.

The door was open, so I just popped my head in. I saw her right away. I knew it was her. She was sleeping, and the other bed wasn't made up.

I walked in. I'm staring at my birth mom. I thought, "If she wakes up, she's going to boot me out of here so fast." I reached in my pocket to grab my phone and take a picture of her. As soon as I put my hand on the phone, her eyes opened. She looked at me and said, "Who are you?" And she really ironed me down.

I shook my head and said, "Do you know who I am?"

"You're Darren Scott, aren't you?" That was my original name [from my birth certificate]. It was Darren Scott Cooper.

I said, "Yes, I'm Darren Scott."

"I thought this was going to happen someday, and it's okay you're here."

I apologized and said, "I just wanted to come and see you once."

"No, no, it's okay."

We just started to talk. I had my iPad and started showing her a bunch of pictures. I flew on Allegiant, and if you know them, you fly in on certain days, you fly out on certain days. So, I was going to be there for three days whether I liked it or not.

I told her the first day, "I'm going to be here for a few days, is it okay if I come back tomorrow?" She agreed. So, I spent three days with her. About an hour and a half each time because she would get tired.

We just talked. It was amazing. I asked, "Should I be upset with my birth dad?"

She said, "No. I want you to know that he and I really loved each other, but back then was back then. It just wasn't going to happen. It wasn't realistic."

But it was interesting having that talk with her. Realizing I had a life before I was three weeks old and got picked up by my mom and dad. So that was amazing. At the end of our visit, I knew the answer, but I had to ask, "Is it okay, just every now and then, I send you a text or something with a picture?" She didn't say anything, but I could just see it on her face. I said, "No, no, don't worry about it."

I gave her a kiss on the cheek, and we prayed together. And we each said, "I love you." Then, I walked out.

That was my three days with Rose.

Complications are Everywhere

The emotions in reunions are both conscious and unconscious. There are the surface level concerns, such as traveling to see one another and how they choose to communicate. Navigating these issues alone can cause people to misinterpret each other's feelings. Someone not responding quickly to a text or an email sends regular, everyday family, friends, or romantic interests into a tailspin.

Beneath the surface there is even more turmoil. Adoptees, even those who want a reunion and may have been the ones that initiated contact, might find themselves in deep waters and not know how to traverse them. This is why therapeutic intervention and finding those who have helped others with this process can be so invaluable.

> **Brian~**
> I love my adoptive family, but I have always had that urge in me to know my biological family, to be connected. I knew something was missing. I'm not saying it was good or bad, I'm just saying something was missing and that's what I was looking for.
>
> Once we reunited, I was a little overwhelmed. I think subconsciously, I said and did things that [my birth mom] felt were pushing her away. So, she just kind of stopped everything and put the ball in my court.
>
> She told me, "I felt like you were pushing me away, like you didn't want me as prevalent in your life. You said things like, 'I have my family,'" which I'm sure I said, but I didn't mean it that way.
>
> She put the ball in my court, which was kind of okay for a little bit. But after a while it got exhausting, because she would never call, never reach out again. So, it just went 180 degrees. And thanks to support groups, I finally gathered the courage to have a conversation.
>
> "I want you to be a part of my life. I want my kids to be a part of your life. They know you as Grandma Beth." I mean, let me be clear.

> If I did call, we were fine. It was a normal conversation. When I went to Kansas City, and we visited her, it was great. We caught everybody up on each other. Her husband was always there, who's an amazing human being. I'm actually talking to her more now. I've said, "Call me, and I wouldn't mind if you called me on my birthday." But no, she still won't.

Can Reunion Work?

Yes. For all the cautionary tales contained in this chapter there are good stories to share. What they have in common are openness and honesty, along with very careful handling and respect for each other's feelings in the process. It is also about meeting each other where they are, and acceptance of who each other has already become prior to meeting. This story is a great example from birth mom Jean, of all these principles.

> **Jean~**
> To get to know her, to be in her energy, to hear her voice, just to see who she became and is becoming. You have this person that you love so deeply, but you don't know them. It was the weirdest feeling to be in that space.
>
> I remember thinking her voice was deeper than I thought it would be. The way she parents her daughter. Just witnessing who she is and getting to see her, how she's moving through the world, was fascinating to me. It made me wonder, would she be different if I had raised her versus the upbringing she was in?
>
> I explained to her, I loved you so freaking much I refused to bring you into this hell I was living in. I just couldn't fathom another

> innocent little soul being tormented like this.
>
> She connected with her father on Facebook. They had one conversation, and she called me afterwards and said, "Thank you for not letting that man be my father."
>
> Being an alcoholic and addict, he was in and out of prison for years. He was recently released when Katie had a conversation with him. After that, she finally gained a deeper understanding of what life with him would have been like.

There are therapists who have made it part of their professional work to help escort these mothers and their children through their often volatile and chaotic emotions. One such Psychotherapist is Jeanette Yoffe, MA, MFT, and founder of the Celia Center in Los Angeles, a non-profit community center supporting those in foster care and all members of the adoption constellation. She talks about beginning with a few key stipulations that need to be agreed to up front:

- Everyone has been victimized
- Everyone has experienced loss
- Each person's loss is incomparable
- Everyone will make mistakes
- Practice forgiveness over and over and over again[7]

From her work at the Celia Center, Jeanette has created the following guidelines she calls "A Framework for a Successful Adoption Reunion." Within it, she shares eight pacts that both the adoptee and their birth parent should commit to:

Have Empathy – hear each other, which may take some time. Try to understand each other's experiences by "walking in their shoes." Respect what they share and do not assume the other's story.

Ask Permission – ask each other for permission when sharing important or personal information. This includes photos, letters, or birth documents. This is needed to help build trust. Also, do not invite other people into the relationship without first gaining each other's permission.

Create a level of contact – neither party has the right to control contact. Negotiate this together about what feels safe or natural. Text? Phone? Email? Talk about holidays and gift giving expectations.

Share your stories – provide space for each other to share their full story. Remember, revisiting this can be re-traumatizing to that person. Reframe from blaming, and also remember that no one's pain is worse than the others.

Be responsible for your own healing – they are not responsible for each other's wounds, and they cannot fill the void for each other. Both parties will likely regress to the age of the relinquishment. All are encouraged to get therapy individually or together and attend support groups. They cannot "rescue" each other.

Respect the relationship – committing to this process and the relationship is a critical step. Do not abandon or "ghost" each other as this is yet another form of betrayal. Stay in communication, even if one or both need a break from each other.

Sharing with others—secrets hurt. Plan together on when and how to tell other members of each other's respective families. Ask permission on when it's okay to let other friends and important people into your reunion journey.

Recognition of your trust tree—respect the loved ones closest to you and the other relationships that are essential to your lives.[8]

Through all these tenuous threads of pain and love, failure and triumph, a new kind of healing and acceptance is at least possible. When that comes together, these newly forged relationships create their own strength and beauty.

Rae~

It's been very healing, I think, for everyone involved, for my biological mother, for myself, for my relationship with my adoptive parents, which had been very tenuous before reunion. But I think a lot of the pressure was off when I finally met my biological mother. And for my partner too. He said the transformation was visible after I connected with my biological mother.

He says, "You did change after reunion. You became much surer of yourself. It's like for the first time in your life, you weren't just grasping at straws. You were sure of where your feet were on the ground. You knew what path you were following."

I can agree with that.

1. Howe, D., & Feast, J. (2000). Adoption, Search and Reunion.

2. Clapton, G. (2018). Close relations? the long-term outcomes of adoption reunions. Genealogy, 2(4), 41. https://doi.org/10.3390/genealogy2040041

3. SACHDEV, P. (1992). Adoption Reunion and After: A Study of the Search Process and Experience of Adoptees. Child Welfare, 71(1), 53–68. http://www.jstor.org/stable/45398877

4. https://www.adoptionbirthmothers.com/ongoing-adoption-reunions/

5. Nola L. Passmore & Judith A. Feeney (2009) Reunions of Adoptees Who Have Met Both Birth Parents: Post-Reunion Relationships and Factors that Facilitate and Hinder the Reunion Process, Adoption Quarterly, 12:2, 100-119, DOI: 10.1080/10926750902978865

6. https://catholiccharitiesks.org/adoption-reunification/

7. https://www.jeanetteyoffe.com/post/roadmap-to-reunion-a-framework-for-a-successful-adoption-reunion

8. https://www.jeanetteyoffe.com/post/roadmap-to-reunion-a-framework-for-a-successful-adoption-reunion

Chapter 26
The Curse of Adoptee Birth Certificates and Politics

"Never doubt that a small group of thoughtful, committed citizens can change the world; indeed, it's the only thing that ever has."
~Margaret Mead

Adoptee advocates and allies have been pushing for decades to improve access to their original birth certificates. It is an issue many adopted adults see as a matter of their personal rights and dignity as human beings.

To quickly review, a child is born, and a birth certificate is issued. In an adoption, once the birth parent(s) have signed over their rights, the adoption process begins. When completed, a new, amended birth certificate is issued listing the adoptive parents as though they are the natural ones. The original certificate, technically, has no legal standing. It has been replaced. Then, in every state other than Alaska and Kansas, the procedure has been to seal these documents away from view. In some states, only a court order can reopen or allow them to be seen, even by the adoptee or the birth parent.

The average citizen never faces this scenario. Their birth certificate is always available to them or easily requested if lost. Many in the general, non-adoptive public are unaware of the situation or its long-term impacts. When they learn the circumstances endured by adopted adults, they are often stunned at the lack of access adoptees have.

Minnesota's law in 1917 was the first one to seal away adoption records. As adoption laws spread across the US, states tended to "borrow" statutes from each other and use them as templates. Minnesota's law was one of the most notable ones used as such. But ironically, this trend does not appear to apply in the reverse as activists work to re-open these sealed records. They must each plead their cases tirelessly with mixed results, and these legislative bodies are slow to amend their practices based upon other states' experiences.

Current Access of Records

The easiest way to show the current levels of access is with a map.

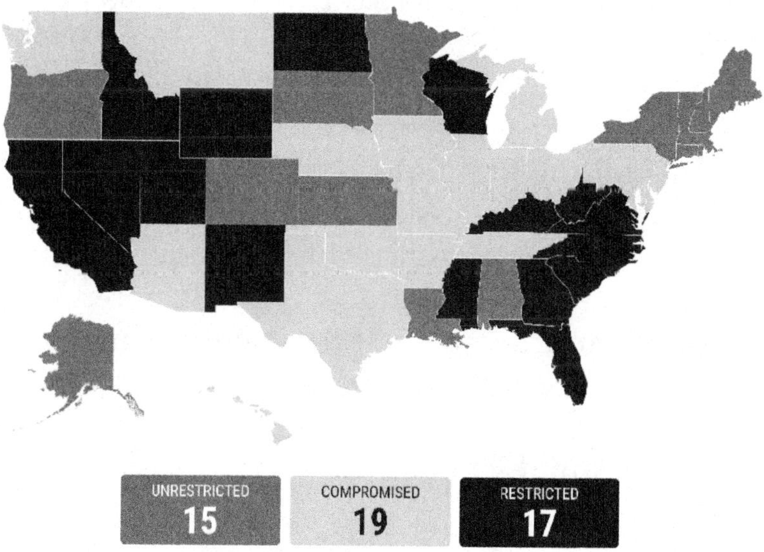

From the Adoptee Rights Law Center, accurate as of Jan. 2025[1]

As of July 1, 2024, Minnesota became the fifteenth state in the US to provide unrestricted access for adoptees to their birth records. The Adoptee Rights Law Center breaks these different state statutes into three different categories, as follows:

- **Unrestricted Access**—an adopted person can receive their original birth certificate without interference.
- **Compromised Access**—there are uneven practices in state statutes preventing some adopted adults from getting their records.
- **Restricted Access**—the adopted adult can only receive information or their records via a court order, and the potential additional requirement of having their birth parent's written consent or be able to prove their birth parent(s) have perished.[2]

The patchwork quilt of legal access is impacted by many factors and often depends on how recently adoption laws in each state were last revised by their legislatures. When states revisit their laws it is often to make adoptions easier or faster to complete, and does little or nothing to help adopted adults or their first parents. In 2018, Georgia revamped its statutes for the first time in thirty years. The bill eased regulations for both in-state and out of state adoptions and removed a six-month residency requirement. It also dropped the revocation window for birth parents from ten days down to four, even while the state remains completely closed as far as adoptee access to records.[3]

Personal Impacts of Closed Records

One example of the absurd situations created by sealed records was shared by birth mother Katie. Her daughter was adopted by a couple outside of the US. Her now twenty-year-old daughter has moved back to Georgia where she was originally born and where Katie still lives.

Her daughter wishes to verify her citizenship, gain a social security number, and thus be able to work, live, and go to school. Note—*she was born in the US*, but once she was relinquished and her original birth certificate replaced and sealed, it is no longer the legal record of her birth. She *is* a citizen, but according to the official record, she had to fight to prove that.

> **Katie~**
> She moved here when she was twenty, but she had to get a driver's license. She needed to set herself up legally. So, we're going to the Social Security Administration.
>
> Finally, after six months, we had another meeting with Social Security, and this guy had worked with us through this whole time. He was very empathetic and very sweet through all of this.
>
> He had his monitor in front of him and we were on the other side of his desk. He says, "I'm looking at it. You exist. I'm looking at your birth certificate. I wish I could turn my monitor."
>
> We weren't even allowed to see it.
>
> We were both sitting there. This was our information. I'm on the record as her mother. This was her existence. The social security guy could look at it, but she couldn't look at her own birth record.
>
> We hug each other and have a little cry. She was able to get her driver's license and everything from that point forward. But that's why I'm on the committee here in Georgia to open original birth certificates.

Sharon was relinquished and then adopted in Minnesota in 1960. Through much personal effort and digging she was able to locate her birth mother in 1982.

> **Sharon~**
> In 2008, I attempted for the first time to legally receive my full file, and they refused to give it to me. What I wanted most was to see a picture of my birth. What did I look like when I was first born? Then, in 2023, I contacted a big adoption lawyer to finally get my full unredacted adoption file. By this point I'd had a relationship with both my birth mother and father. The lawyer got the file for me.
>
> If you have any wondering about what some adoption professionals think about adoptees, let me tell you, I now have the emails. They say things like, "Well, we think this woman must have manipulated her parents into signing releases."
>
> The internal emails are, "How would these parents have agreed to let her see this file unless she manipulated them? She must have done something." And there's dialogue in which an attorney writes, "If she takes us to court, I can't defend that all four of these people signed releases to say that they want her to have the unredacted file." The adoption professional people are saying, "Well, we don't know what the context was. Maybe she pushed them into it."

It is infantilizing to adoptees to be patted on the head and told they should just be grateful for being alive and provided for. The juxtaposition of adoption practices being all about "the welfare of the adopted child" falls apart.

The lack of understanding makes adopted adults feel frustrated, disrespected, and irate. However, these feelings are not effective in improving access. Tangible facts, not emotions, are what create change. And lawmakers think differently than ordinary citizens, because that is their role.

Activism in Action

"Where did I come from? Why am I here, and where am I going? If you don't have number one, it's really hard to get to numbers two and three." These words from Richard Uhrlaub are some he has used many times over the years when testifying before state legislative committees. He says these statements resonate with legislators. Rich is well known in the national adoption community as a long-time activist and adoptee. He is on the board of the Adoption Search Resource Connection (https://www.asrconline.org) and is part of the team that saw birth and certain adoption records for adoptees open for Colorado and has been part of other states efforts to do the same.

Rich joined the cause of protecting and advocating for adoptee rights when in the mid-1990s there was a movement started by the National Conference of State Legislators to *seal adoption records for 99 years.* A public hearing was held and he and other Coloradans testified successfully against it.

That was the beginning for him, and Rich found a home in the movement of fighting for direct access to records for adult adoptees. But one of the things he emphasizes to no end, is that these advocates need to play a smart and savvy game. This is not for the faint of heart, and emotions are best left outside the door.

Winning and Losing Points

Rich~
Sometimes our angst and anger and outrage works against us. We spent years here in Colorado, going down to the Capitol to testify, weeping and hoping the legislators would get how it feels to be us. And most of them just can't. They're dealing with 600 to 1000 bills a year with other people who have problems too. So, we shifted our focus to create the best practices rooted around truth and transparency in adoption.

That's one thing we learned; stop pounding the table about adoptee rights. As soon as you say that to somebody you're off to the races. Some legislators are going to say, what about birth parent rights? What about adoptive parent rights? It creates an adversarial perception that all the parties are at odds with each other and lawmakers need to step in and protect somebody from the marauding adoptee who's out to ruin their family and tell all their secrets.

Once you've done that, you've set yourself up for compromised legislation where nobody gets everything they want.

But something that resonates a lot better is we *oppose shame and secrecy* in all these areas, and we *support truth and transparency.* Because that really is the broader picture, and it means we are all on the same side: adoptive parents, birth parents, adoptees, ethical social workers, ethical agencies. Who's going to say, "No, I promote shame and secrecy!"

When we talk about restoring access to adoptee records, there's the stated reasons for opposing it, and *the real reasons* for opposing it.

The most common argument is that agencies made promises of privacy to birth mothers. However, privacy from the general public and anonymity from one's own offspring are two separate issues.

If you investigate legislative history, the primary reason the records were sealed was to keep birth parents from coming back to the adoptive family and trying to get their child back. When our records were sealed, they said there were three intentions, and this is true across most states.

One, they wanted to protect birth mothers from any hasty or coerced relinquishment decisions.

Two, they wanted to protect adoptive parents from being at risk of losing their child. Some adoptions were kind of a "loosey-goosey" thing for decades. There are some sensational situations where the child was never legally relinquished. The third reason is to protect parents from adopting children whom they knew nothing about. So, they started gathering information about the child [from the birth mother].

So that was the history behind sealed records in the US. But that evolved into, "We made this promise."

In virtually every state, with one exception that I know of, had a provision where the adoptee could get the records, or the adoptive parents were handed some of the records that had identifying information on it. Or state laws included a provision where an adoptee could demonstrate good cause to get those records, though in many cases it was not an easy process. So, the notion that there was this absolute, ironclad promise of anonymity from your own offspring simply wasn't true and never existed.

Case law from Tennessee and in Oregon following retroactive legislative changes, affirm that the birth mother does not have an absolute right to anonymity from their own child. So the distinction between confidentiality from the public and anonymity from your offspring is significant.

There are several things lawmakers don't understand, and they need to. First, there is no absolute promise of anonymity that could ever be enforced.

We also really try to emphasize that our pursuit of records access only applies to adult adoptees from an infant adoption. These bills are not designed to, "throw open the records" to people who have had their parental rights terminated as some legislators have claimed. It's important to clarify the terms of what we're talking about.

One legislator can get up and make an inaccurate allegation about a bill and kill it on the spot.

> I believe in the adoptees' unqualified right to have access, and to know where they come from. At the same time, we have to be sensitive and tactful, and thoughtful enough to understand this isn't just a big bad system trying to keep us from our truth. There are some legitimately touchy situations out there we have to be sensitive to. They're rare, a tiny fraction of a percentage in some cases, but they're real.

DNA Testing and Impacts on Confidentiality

DNA testing companies building out their databases are tempting for many people to participate in, "just for fun." However, if adopted adults are seeking their birth parents, and they cannot get personal access to an original birth certificate, they will turn to this resource if they have decided to search.

Advocates point out to lawmakers and those arguing against personal access that *DNA testing shreds anonymity.* Consider the following—as shown from the birth parent chapters, mothers in particular, may still harbor shame and may have kept the relinquishment a secret from her entire family. Fathers may not know anything about their child's existence. Then, the adopted individual does a DNA test, with the specific hope of learning their parentage.

Any members of that family who have also been tested, now find this stranger among them. A typical scenario then unfolds. The online family tree shows the DNA connections. The adoptee is writing carefully worded messages to those relatives attempting to locate their parent(s). Which gets the family talking—who gave up a baby, and when? Now, this birth mother's secret is exposed.

Sometimes this goes smoothly, but other times it can be catastrophic for that mother's secret being revealed in this way. Advocates point out the difference between anonymity and privacy. The legal information shared above clearly shows that no government can forever shield someone from remaining unknown by their offspring. But denying adoptees access to the names of their birth parents by not allowing them to have their records, along with the availability of DNA testing, contributes to this scenario. People *will* do these tests within families, and when things pop up, they will be discovered.

What it comes down to is truly respecting someone's privacy in adoption if they have relinquished a child. When adoptees have a name, they can search and then respectfully, *directly*, reach out to that person and ask them if they wish to connect. Is this not the most considerate way to manage this delicate situation? When lawmakers deny adoptees their original birth certificate, this is one of the expected outcomes from lack of access.

The debate is one of many instances in this society where the available technology has moved beyond the current scope of the law. Legislators have meaningful obligations around privacy. The promises lawmakers believe they made and need to protect are now impossible for them to guarantee because of the breadth and commonality of these consumer accessible DNA databases.

When talking to activists, lawmakers will still object to open access to records. Their reasoning is that while they recognize the impacts DNA testing has on the above scenarios, they wish to still attempt to hold back the impacts from these tests as long as possible. It is an argument unlikely to be settled any time soon.

Wisdom from the Battleground States

When one connects with activists for personal access to records, one of the surprising data points is how many years these people have worked on their projects. In Colorado, for example, adoptees had been actively lobbying for change since the 1980s, but it took them until 2014 for it to pass. Advocates in New Jersey worked for over thirty years to get that legislation done. Texas has been at it for thirty-five years. It's exhausting, and these advocates sometimes need to take breaks or pace themselves in their efforts.

Ohio

Another activist who is widely admired throughout the US is adoptee Betsie Norris, founder of Adoption Network Cleveland. She is also responsible for spearheading major legislation which passed in 2013 in Ohio. Many note, the bill has compromises contained within, but it is still considered landmark legislation.

She became active in the cause for adoptee access to records in 1988 when she was 28 because she believed it was a social justice issue. At the time she herself had personal access to her records but most adoptees in her state didn't. She watched a bill to open records be proposed and later fail.

She joined the Ohio Coalition of Adoption Reform on that first bill, then put together several bills through Adoption Network Cleveland over the following decades, all of which also failed to pass.

> **Betsie~**
> One of the things I've learned over the years is that legislators and hearings are important,

but equally, or more so, are all the other interested parties. Everything else that swirls around has an impact – in the state house and the individual conversations, even if they're in the hallway.

When I was a lone activist, often the minute I walked out of a lawmaker's office, some lobbyists from some other organization with an interest would walk in. The state legislator will say "Oh, Betsie was just in here about this. What do you think about that?"

If I hadn't anticipated that first and brought them over to our side before I left the room, I hadn't done my job. In addition, public perception is important. During one of our bills in the '90s, I went into this lawmaker's office to tell them what I'm there to talk about. She literally says, "Oh, you don't have to tell me anything. I watch Oprah. I know all about this." She was serious.

The opposition to our bills came primarily from The National Council for Adoption, and a state-level pro-life organization. They had fears about what would happen if adult adoptees were allowed to access their original birth certificates.

We looked at Kansas and Alaska, which at the time were the only two states that had access to records because they'd never closed them. There wasn't more abortion, there wasn't less adoption. All the things they thought would happen weren't happening, at least in those two states. And we strongly believed they wouldn't happen in other states if our changes passed.

We watched very closely as Tennessee passed a complicated law that improved access to records. Then, Oregon passed a voter initiative that allowed adoptees to have their records. Both laws ended up in court challenged by the religious right but were upheld. We watched very closely and tried to document as best we could what was happening with abortion rates, adoption rates. Did "the sky fall" in those states? No it didn't. We led more legislated attempts over the years, but I had some good data by the time we came back in 2013.

Our last group of sponsors that got it through in the end were amazing. We had the main sponsor, whose siblings are adopted. He had watched what they'd gone through. We had a sister of a birth mother. We had an adoptive parent in an open adoption, and then an adoptee whose records were closed because of the current law. We started only attending meetings in triads to be sure someone could speak to whatever issues were raised.

The bill sailed through for eleven of the twelve months. At the last minute, one state senator who had been supportive, woke up one day and said, "Oh, a birth parent should be able to take their name off the birth certificate." He was powerful enough to block the bill from coming to a vote. Our bottom line was the birth certificate is the adoptee's birth certificate. It belongs to the adoptee. So, nobody should be able to keep that record closed from them.

There's a big difference between a birth parent saying the adult child can't get their record, or they can get that record with everything else intact, but my name is off. We didn't want that either, but it was more palatable. It still maintained the adoptee's name, the address for the birth parent was there, the hospital, all the other stuff was intact.

We could have pulled the plug and said we're withdrawing our support. However, our sponsor made it clear he was deep enough in this bill it was going to pass—with us, or without us. So, we had a choice. Do we make it the least harm done? Or do we pull the plug? We took that choice point very seriously, and it was heartbreaking.

But we were able to negotiate. There was already a one-year waiting period before it was going to be fully implemented so that vital statistics could prepare for the release of records. We proposed that during that one year only the birth parent would have the right to redact their name, and then that sunsets. They saw the logic and agreed. We also asked for them to require the birth parent to file a full medical history if they were redacting their name. We made the language ironclad.

We projected forward what this would look like. This powerful senator would probably be in power in that role and could deep six our bill one way or the other. We estimated it would be for another ten years. We statistically figured out how many birth parents and how many adoptees would likely die in these next ten years without access. I don't remember the numbers, but there would have been many, many, people who statistically would have died without their information. It was a bitter pill to swallow.

Of the 400,000 records on file, only 229 birth parents redacted their name off the birth certificate. It was absolutely not what we wanted, but it was still a major success. I do in my heart believe "leave no one behind." But in effect, we would have left 400,000 people behind if we didn't do it.

Texas

Lobbyists have been active in Texas since the 1990s. Bills have been consistently introduced since 2013 and pass the state House with ease but are always stopped in the Senate.

In 2023, House Bill 2006 passed easily through the state House before stalling out as others before it. The only time a proposed bill made it to the floor of the Senate for a public hearing was in 2017, when over forty activists spoke in favor of passage. There is one powerful Senator who is blocking these bills, and she is adoptive parent and State Senator, Donna Campbell.[4]

She has four adoptive children, three of whose mothers are deceased, and one from a closed adoption. "She said that her seventeen-year-old daughter has not expressed an interest in finding her birth parents—and that she would not encourage her to look because she promised the birth mother that she would keep her identity a secret."[5]

Many view her opposition as a personal interest that is

now swaying legislation affecting 600,000 adult adoptees in Texas. The crux of this issue brings to the forefront the friction between adoptee rights advocates, and the pro-life, anti-abortion movements. There is widespread belief that if closed adoptions were taken away as an option, there would potentially be more abortions. However, many studies have shown that data doesn't play out. Another study recently released in 2023 shows that women weighing their options when facing an unplanned pregnancy, do not see adoption as an alternative to abortion.[6]

The debate over the difference between secrecy and privacy in adoption continues. None of the current adoptees lobbying for change agreed to be interviewed for the book, because they did not want to make themselves public figures amid this ongoing effort. These volunteer advocates are smart and tenacious and will continue their battle.

Idaho

A recent effort in Idaho is worth reviewing. HB544 was introduced in early 2024 and quickly sailed through the House. Within it, not only was it modifying an already complex reunion registry process for birth parents or adoptees, it also proposed significantly altering the age of access. The bill stated that for an adopted adult to gain access to their records, they had to be *forty years old*. This would be a significant increase from what most states require, which is between the ages of eighteen and twenty-one, the outlier being Rhode Island who says the adoptee must be twenty-five.

A recording of Representative Julianne Young was made describing HB544 on February 21, 2024. In it she states, "I began asking members of the Senate, okay, if we were uncomfortable just opening those records up, at what age do we believe an existing adoptee has sufficient maturity and life experience to be able to make these decisions. And forty was the random number that we picked."[7]

Conversely, a citizen and young adult at the age of eighteen can vote, own property, get a loan or a credit card, own a business, or join the military and be sent to war. The founders and authors of the Constitution believed that someone was of sufficient "maturity and life experience" to become President of the United States at age thirty-five.[8]

Had it passed, this would have become the most restricted state in the nation for adoptee records. Fortunately, this died in the Senate committee process.

Michigan

This state is an example of what incremental changes in the law create if significant forethought is not put into decisions around adoption policies and practices. Volunteer advocate Erica Curry VanEe has been lobbying their state lawmakers to modernize and streamline the states adoption policies for the past decade.

In the 2023-24 legislative session, an adoptee rights bill package was introduced that would have granted unrestricted access to original birth certificates for adult adoptees and their lineal descendants. When the bipartisan bills went before their state legislature, the measure passed the House with a landslide majority but never made it out of the Civil Rights, Judiciary, and Public Safety committee in the Senate.

Erica explained, "Michigan's adult adoptees face various challenges depending on what year their adoption was finalized. The most restrictive timeframe is referred to as the 'donut hole' and impacts those who's adoptions were finalized between May 28, 1945- September 12, 1980.

While all adult adoptees in Michigan face discriminatory practices not experienced by the non-adoptees, those in the donut hole face the harshest inequities that make it virtually impossible for an adult to access their original birth record."

According to Curry-VanEe, the sticking point for the adoptee rights bills proposed in the 2023-24 legislative session was the form DHS-1919, titled "Parent's Consent/ Denial to Release Information to Adult Adoptee." This document is utilized by the Michigan Department of Health and Human Services (MDHHS) Central Adoption Registry and allows birth parents to consent to or deny the release of their identifying information to their adopted child once they reach 18 years of age. "Some interest groups that opposed the adoptee rights bills based their position on a perceived right to privacy. They wanted a redaction clause included for biological parents which would have allowed their name to be removed from the original birth certificate, or worse, a signed affidavit from adult adoptees promising not to contact our first parents. There was a fundamental misinterpretation of form DHS-1919. While it facilitates the process for birth parents to express their preferences regarding the release of identifying information, the form itself is not a law or a guarantee of lifetime anonymity or privacy."

This process began before the widespread usage of computer databases, so Michigan has no idea how many parents have submitted a Form DHS-1919, or if they do, they are not releasing it, despite multiple FOIA requests. It could be dozens or thousands. "Unfortunately, we know for sure that hundreds of thousands of adult adoptees continue to face the discriminatory practices born from archaic policies," claimed Curry Van Ee. Despite the concessions offered by advocates to replace Form DHS-

1919 with a contact preference form, the number of opposing organizations grew as they demanded an opt-out clause, and the bill never made it out of committee. In the end, some lawmakers believed a privacy right had been granted and did not want to take that away.

> "We went in with a clean bill that would have created equitable access to original birth certificates and replace Form 1919 with an updated contact preference form. We wanted holistic reform and when it was clear that would not be possible, our coalition pulled support for the bills".

When talking to Erica, one can feel her frustration and determination. For now, Michigan remains a compromised state, but the work will continue. The question that haunts her now is worrying how many adult adoptees will die not having this vital information of their origins, and what will it take to change? "I recognize that MI legislators are trying to balance the needs of what they see as two vulnerable population groups, adult adoptees and biological parents, but after a 25 years of advocacy to secure the right to my original birth certificate from my birth state of Ohio, along with a decade of advocacy in my home state of Michigan, I am tired of fighting for what I believe should be a birthright. I really thought 2024 was the year we would get it right and make it equal, and now, I am not sure if this will ever happen in my lifetime. I have decided it's time for me to release, step aside and let others who will be directly impacted by this legislation lead the way forward."

1. https://adopteerightslaw.com/maps/

2. https://adopteerightslaw.com/maps/

3. https://newschannel9.com/news/local/new-georgia-adoption-law-takes-effect-saturday

4.https://www.texasstandard.org/stories/texas-adoptee-original-birth-certificates-donna-campbell/

5.https://www.texasstandard.org/stories/texas-adoptee-original-birth-certificates-donna-campbell/

6. Liza Fuentes, Megan L. Kavanaugh, Lori F. Frohwirth, Jenna Jerman, Nakeisha Blades, "Adoption is just not for me": How abortion patients in Michigan and New Mexico factor adoption into their pregnancy outcome decisions, Contraception: X, Volume 5, 2023, 100090,ISSN 2590-1516

7. https://adopteerightslaw.com/hb544/

8. Point credited to the Adoptee Rights Law Center: https://adopteesunited.org/legislation/state/2024-sessions/#id

Chapter 27
Child Centered Solutions

Do the best you can until you know better.
Then when you know better, do better.
~ Maya Angelou

What does it mean to be truly child centered when considering adoption? It begins with listening, sincerely and without dismissal, to the adoptees involved. Most importantly, being child centered in adoption means that the interests of the adults are set aside, and the needs of the child are prioritized over all others.

If adoption is to be child centered, it must first be *family* centered. If families are more stable, there are fewer relinquishments and less need for foster care.

Administrative Change

What if one of the first improvements in the practice was to change the way an adoption is handled and administered with its most basic element—sealing original birth certificates.

Let Kansas and Alaska become the template for that structure, opening them up in each state. It is the simplest solution and the most respectful one if adoptions remain a common part of this culture.

The lack of awareness and understanding created by the current system smacks of willful dismissal of the rights of adopted individuals. Replacing someone's heritage in the name of their welfare or personal safety is the opposite of prioritizing and caring for their needs. It declares their allegiance to their new family be so absolute they must leave everything else behind, losing all contact with their first relatives. In the case of foster care, why should the price of a child's safety mean they lose *everyone* in their family?

Chester Jackson is a gentleman who is himself a late discovery adoptee and adoptive parent from foster care and has spent most of the last thirty years working with both youngsters and teenagers as a foster care advocate in New York and Pennsylvania.

> **Chester~**
> I really couldn't understand why people couldn't understand that nobody wants to be in somebody else's family. This is not something these kids should feel good about. Kids shouldn't have to prove that they're worthy of somebody caring for them.
>
> How can destroying families be in the best interest of any child? We know better than that.
>
> But because we're protecting children, then that gives us license to destroy their families. Now, of course, there are going to be children that are going to have to be removed from their immediate family for whatever reason. That doesn't mean they have to stop being a Smith or a Johnson.

One doubts if the above administrative suggestion will gain much traction with lawmakers, but it is worthy of consideration, as are other ideas floated by other advocates for change in the adoption community.

Family Preservation

Family preservation is a hot topic among child welfare providers and policy makers. The child welfare industry knows it has problems with bias and the impacts of high housing costs, poverty, and the rates at which people of color struggle financially.

Current estimates claim nearly half of the US adult population has less than $500 in personal savings.[1] According to a report by Chapin Hall, a policy and research center based at the University of Chicago, almost 50% of US families are at risk of poverty before their child enters kindergarten. Before they turn 65, more than 50% of all Americans will spend one year living below that threshold, and 84% of Black Americans will do so. However, nearly half of all families who fall into poverty will come out of that a year later.[2]

If a family is already struggling to meet everyday needs and then experiences a financial shock, such as a lost job or layoff, loss of transportation, an accident or illness, that can plunge them into crisis. In 2023 the poverty threshold nationally is $30,000 for a family of four.[3]

If the family experiences a negative income shock the risk of a CPS investigation increases by 18%. However, if they receive some public benefits this buffers that family, and the risk of child welfare involvement drops dramatically for reports of neglect or abuse.[4]

The Harshest Truths

There is a need for an unbiased and principled study on the full impact of adoption. It deserves to happen because lives are at stake, and this country remains entrenched in the practice.

When talking to birth parents, there is little to no information given to them about separation trauma and that relinquishment could potentially harm their child. Nothing like this is ever disclosed to them within the industry in general. There are thousands of agencies and workers who interact with these couples, and it is impossible to know or track what may or may not be explained.

When these birth parents find out much later in life how these decisions impacted the well-being of their relinquished children, they are often furious. Good parents will sacrifice or endure *anything* to spare their children pain. Birth parents were promised, "their child will have a better life." Having their maternal instincts used against them is an overwhelming betrayal.

There are a great many good families and good parents who have adopted children. For adoptees who say, "I don't feel traumatized," the answer should be, "Great! Happy for you!" But saying these issues don't relate *to an individual* fails to grasp the larger picture.

If the mental health community, counselors, policy makers, and educational institutions are unwilling to move past the bias that everyone wins in adoption, then this society will continue to create dysregulated individuals with nervous systems negatively impacted by their earliest days of existence. Worse, they won't understand what is wrong or where to seek answers. When families don't have the correct information things will be missed in their young person. Then they reach an age where they may start acting out some of that trauma, but no one will have a name for what is happening.

An adoption competent and trained therapist will spot this behavior and identify it. The collective denial of adoption's inherent trauma, even by adoptees themselves, perpetuates these problems, and harms everyone in the long run.

The Case for Guardianship

An idea that has gained a lot of ground in the adoptee community is the idea to replace adoption with guardianship. The idea also has traction in the foster care community. It is worthy of examination as well and may be a solution for some families and situations, but not others.

Many adoptees have flocked to these ideas in part because of their frustrations with the closed adoption systems and the treatment of their original birth certificates. Guardianship in the US is practiced when a family takes in a youngster and is responsible for the care of that person until they reach eighteen, but no formal lifetime attachment is created. Surnames for example are not changed, and children are not renamed. There is also no assumption of an inheritance, which adoption guarantees.

There are many shifts the states are talking about in the foster care system regarding a new emphasis on family preservation. Chester shares more of his insight.

> **Chester~**
> What's changed? Honestly, in the years since 2020, since George Floyd was murdered, we're having conversations that I would have bet money we would never be having in child

welfare. Talking about abolishing the system, racism, all kinds of things you just did not talk about before. So, that's been a real change, and people are talking about abolishing the system.

Serious people, not the lunatic fringe. People saying that termination of parental rights is something that should be off the table. The reason parental rights get terminated is because any tool you have on your belt, especially the most potent one, is going to be used.

You don't want to follow the program? We will just terminate your rights. If we took that off the table then agencies would have to do something else, and that something else is to be more realistic about what it is we really need. Is it housing they need? Is it rehab?

The problem is that the heart of the matter hasn't changed. Foster care is still a terrible, terrible system. You lose your rights in a way most people can't really fathom when you become a foster child. You are nobody's responsibility, and that's not only a psychologically terrible place to be, it's also a dangerous place to be with children.

That calls into question the whole adoption industry and its transactional nature. Where are the kids coming from? Is it taking advantage of people in their most desperate times? These are all social problems, and at some point we're going to have to come to grips with them. We'll never do right by it until we're willing to actually look at the causes where people are thinking about giving up their children. Or the causes that led to having them taken.

It's not rocket science, and it's not witchcraft. We don't have to have algorithms and all that stuff. We have to do what mothers, in particular, have done for generations. We have to care for children the best we can, and it's not always going to look the same.

The word adoption is not the problem. Guardianship, foster, kinship, whatever you want to call it, as long as you're going to do the job, and the job is to be the parent, I don't care what you call it. But adoption is not the problem, the word is not the problem.

That's really a reaction to the market. It's really a reaction to this idea that adoption is something magical or something that should be celebrated. Adoption is awful. Adoption is a tragedy. That means that some children live away from their parents, their mother in particular, for whatever reason. That's a tragedy. Always.

Now, that doesn't mean it didn't need to happen. Adoptive parents need to understand the fact that parenting in this way is buying into the tragedy. Be willing to do whatever you have to do to help your child bear this burden. You can't fix it or take it away. It's one of those things that will affect every aspect of their life forever, just like anything else they might have been born with.

Extending and Preserving Families

Family preservation requires a different kind of will and commitment to helping families stay together. It requires creativity and an understanding that hasn't always been encouraged, especially by the child welfare system. Susan Tucker, an adoptee interviewed for the book, is also an Assistant Regional Administrator of the Department of Children and Family Services of Los Angeles County. During her interview she talked about her own life growing up in a dysfunctional household and her reunion story with her birth mother's extended family, who welcomed her warmly. It influenced her, not just personally, but also in the way she and her staff now interact with adoptive families and the first families of the children they place.

Susan~
I teach my staff, and they teach their workers that we need to be gracious and look at the whole situation and who can be a support as you have this child, whether it's for a short placement or a permanent one. And how can we do that? How can we do that and establish what's good for this kid? And so, we've been able to bring a lot more into that. Unless it's so toxic one side's just not going to be able to hold up their end of it.

I've been able to bring in the birth family who were always thought of as little more than perpetrators. Now I'm saying, nope, they're parents. They've got family members who had nothing to do with this and deserve to be part of this child's life, and this child deserves to know them.

> To humanize it in a way beyond the system that really, if you're not careful, can exclude people. We've had a lot of conversations with our staff about how the media portrays parents who have had abuse and neglect reported. I've encouraged the staff to look a little deeper. What was it that happened when [those parents] were growing up? What is it that happened to *them* because they too may have been victims, and they just have never been able to get the skills or the opportunity to make this right. So we don't create a second generation of kids in our system.
>
> Let's figure out how to get support. Let's figure out how to make the best family for this kid. It's not just one-sided. So, now we bring those conversations in very early on instead of at the last second before an adoption is finalized.

These more holistic views encompass a few common threads. They revolve around, first, the commitments to do the right thing by a family, regardless of what has created the intervention or interaction of adoption or child welfare workers. They also incorporate the respect for biological and familial ties that deserve to be maintained, and back up the idea that whenever possible it is better for every child, no matter how they ended up being raised by others. Lastly, what it comes down to is the commitment and respect of the raising or adoptive parents to show up for the long haul of their child's life with a full awareness of what they will live through and never give up on their youngster.

Chester~
Adoption is not magic. It's an adult making a commitment to a child. The answer is love. It's love, and I feel weird saying that because I've been in so many meetings lately where people have said it. What it comes down to is if I truly cared about you, on just a human-to-human basis, there are things that I would not do. And I'm talking adult to adult, I'm not even talking adult to a child. You have an obligation to parent them from someplace that's helping them.

Most of these kids [in foster care] want what everybody else has. They want to belong. They want to have a space. They want to have people that care about them. That's a home. All it requires from you, as an adult, is to make the commitment. Then just treat them like you would somebody you actually cared about, and it becomes easy.

Solutions to these problems are hard to come by. Adoption competent therapists, adoptee allies and child welfare advocates often feel like they are shouting into a hurricane to get others to understand the inherent loss and trauma that is always part of any adoption. If a child needs to be raised by someone other than their parents, all avenues should be exhausted to find relatives or kin the youngster identifies with first. But if an adoption occurs it must be oriented about what is best for the child in terms of their physical and mental wellbeing for the long run. This will help build a safer and saner world for kids to call home.

1. mike_wintrs. (2024, January 24). How much money Americans have in their savings accounts-nearly half have less than $500. CNBC. https://www.cnbc.com/2024/01/24/how-much-money-americans-

have-in-savings.html

2. Anderson, C.,Grwal-Kok, Y., Cusick, G., Weiner, D., & Thomas,K. (2023). Family and child well-being system: Economic and concrete supports as a core component. [Power Point slides.] Chapin Hill at the University of Chicago.

3. Prior HHS Poverty Guidelines and Federal Register references. ASPE. (n.d.). https://aspe.hhs.gov/topics/poverty-economic-mobility/poverty-guidelines/prior-hhs-poverty-guidelines-federal-register-references

4. Anderson, C.,Grwal-Kok, Y., Cusick, G., Weiner, D., & Thomas,K. (2023). Family and child well-being system: Economic and concrete supports as a core component. [Power Point slides.] Chapin Hill at the University of Chicago.

Chapter 28
My New View:
A Journey Through the Fire

This is not the book I intended to write. Initially, my vision was to gather stories from all sides of the constellation and explore adoption's emotional complexities. At the time it seemed a worthy endeavor as there wasn't another published book quite like it.

What came of that intention is this work. As I listened to stories from adoptees and first mothers and learned their struggles the landscape shifted. Adoptive parents also surprised me with their input. In 2022, I hired two wonderful UNLV students to help me with the research. As we dug through mountains of study and moved through these topics, time and again we found data that was painful and disturbing. I did not have an agenda when I began. This book wrote itself and took the turns it did because this is where the research and the interviews led me.

I am grateful to have met many amazing people, and it has been my greatest honor to record these personal stories. Thank you. At times the weight of hearing your testimonies and putting them into this work was overwhelming. I hope you feel I was a good steward with your words.

These intimate and personal stories create a vibrant fabric bursting with color and texture, beauty and pain. I carry a piece of each of you in my heart and am touched beyond measure by your bravery and trust.

I have been and continue to be transformed by the evolution of my own personal adoption story. Much remains unfinished and unknown about my birth family. I have found my first mother, but so far, she has rejected personal contact.

My natural mother may have made mistakes. I don't romanticize her but see her for who and what she was. Her full story is unknown to me, but from the non-identifying information in my file, she was an eighteen-year-old young woman with an abusive stepfather, and a boyfriend who couldn't support her and wouldn't marry her.

But she is more than just a sad story and deserved the opportunity to prove that. Assuming she was automatically incapable of parenting me is a myth, and she likely would have made a good mother. My adoptive parents also made mistakes and, in spite of that, were good parents whom I love, respect, and cared for through the end of their days. They all dwell within me.

When people with power exert coercive pressures or treat my mother with a lack of care, harsh judgements, or disrespect, you are treating me the same, whether you understand this or not. Biases about her create the belief about my "need" to be "rescued." If her options were limited, and you think they deserved to be because she got herself into that predicament, then please recall a certain parable about people throwing stones in glass houses.

She had sex and may not have been as responsible as she could have been about using birth control. Likely, none was available. Now, the baby forming in her womb was unplanned, but that does not mean she didn't want to parent. When you judge her, you are judging my existence. And because she was "a bad girl" I therefore need to be better provided for by others. Maybe some view her as no longer having the same value as before. These biases were applied to my mother back in 1965 and are still present today.

I am angry at the way many birth parents have been treated in the past and continue to be. During the baby scoop, some mothers were left to labor in hospital hallways because delivery rooms were only for proper married ladies. In 2010, when Shayanne (who readers met in Chapters 15 and 16) was in labor, she was left to lie for four hours in her amniotic fluid after her water broke. The dignity extended to these women has not improved as much as one might hope.

The outcome of an adoption means that barely out of the womb, I'm separated from the one person I need and know more than any other. This was done supposedly for my welfare, and people will say she did a good thing by being so noble and brave. Society then declares me lucky, and insists I agree.

Everyone needs to understand the bond between a natural mother and her infant is not a casual one, and that breaking us apart has consequences. When we use adoption as part of our social safety net, we fail everyone involved.

I've been an entrepreneur and business owner for decades. Since 1999, the only money my husband and I have earned was generated through our own labor, drive, and intellect. In general, I'm a capitalist and thrive with an entrepreneurial spirit. It's far from perfect. Of the economic systems we've created so far, capitalism seems to have great potential, but it must be practiced ethically.

A capitalist society is good at identifying needs and solving problems. We needed better ways to carry goods and people. In response, we built trains and railways and, eventually, cars and airplanes. We wanted to send information to each other faster and more efficiently. We went from creating overnight delivery, to fax machines, to the internet, and now stream content and share information at lightning speed.

Capitalism created all of that, and it improves lives daily. It's great at enticing creative problem-solving and rewarding someone financially when they're successful.

We are now the only nation on earth with this adoption marketplace. My hope is someday it can be reimagined.

Private, for-profit markets and entities are good at many things. But they should not have infiltrated the child welfare system as is happening in foster care, nor should they be part of adoption.

I believe international adoptions to non-kin should stop or should be dramatically overhauled. We cannot guarantee that any such child has not been trafficked, and there are far too many instances of international corruption already discovered and more seem to surface regularly. If we want to improve the plight of children overseas, then leverage the vast array of nonprofits capable of assisting in those countries.

"Nonprofits" who exist solely to provide services related to adoption who are not also providing services for family preservation ought to be identified for what they are—for-profit adoption businesses. An evaluation of some agencies' classification is long overdue.

Burning this industry to the ground and starting over is unlikely. However, it is past time we acknowledge that many states who "do things this way because that's the way we've always done them," is thoughtless governance. It's failing to serve modern families and the needs of children.

Incremental change is more likely. What we need are strong voices, *and hordes of them*. One responsibility I lay firmly at the feet of adoptive parents is the gauntlet for change on closed adoptions and sealed records. Support for closed adoptions and closed records must end. The need for the safety of a closed adoption should be respected when necessary but understood for how rare it is. Truth and transparency must win in adoption *every day*.

I have great empathy for adoptive parents and their understandable desires, personal egos, and pains, and have no wish to rip apart or belittle their good intentions and yearnings to parent.

I also implore, insistently, that they join birth parents and adoptees. Together we can educate the public and lawmakers that change is warranted. *Nothing will happen without adoptive parents and the public helping us.* My adoptive parents, if they were alive today, would join us.

We need to trust the servants in the cause of child welfare. I won't dare speak for others, but after the interviews I have conducted it's clear to me there are allies everywhere, and legislation isn't necessarily the answer. It's about people coming together who are clear about what it looks like to commit to the wellbeing of a child, for their entire lifespan, and showing up for that.

A source for ideas is reviewing how other countries handle their internal adoption and child welfare processes. They have different mechanisms we can learn from. There also needs to be a reckoning of how we view parenting and privilege, and who should be the "chosen ones" to build families among us.

There are so many good adoptive parents out there, my own included. They loved me unconditionally, celebrated my unique personality and differences, and never allowed me to be belittled by anyone. They were always honest and, overall, got more things right in adoption than wrong.

My father, as a school psychologist of his time, quoted

the "blank slate theory" and believed it, as it was the dominant view then. Were he alive and still mentally active today he would be reading the work of Gabor Maté, Bessel van der Kolk, and others, and learning how wrong these older notions were.

It would crush him to know that his ignorance at the time may have harmed me or the formation of my little self as I grew up. I wish he'd known. If his essence carries on watching over us, I know he's listening closely and is proud of me. The same is true of my mother. I love my raising parents and cannot regret being their daughter.

To the adoptive parents I know and those interviewed for the book I don't criticize them for their choices, their adoptions, or growing their families in this way. My problems with the structure of the system do not mean I personally condemn them. I honor their journey because their adoptees need and love them.

I run into problems when adoptive parents don't seem to fully commit to their children. I did not meet or interview any like this but have been around others who appear to parent for self-centered and ego driven reasons. The results of this can be seen when adopted children are rehomed or sent back into the foster care system.

Younger adoptees I'm surrounded by in support groups and on social media relate jaw dropping stories of selfishness displayed by their raising parents. We must own these shortcomings and work to solve them. Good adoptive parents exist everywhere, but they need help and the right resources to guide them.

I cannot profess to know the answers, but I know they begin by setting aside the false assumptions that have been built by our culture's simplified rhetoric that adoption is a beautiful way to build a family. As a fellow adoptee and good friend recently said, "We've all been bamboozled!"

The paradox arises from the idea that when adoption is necessary, it can be or at least should be beautiful. *It should be.* If you have a child who is unsafe in their home or truly cannot be raised by its natural mother, then being raised by a new family and given the ability to belong and be healed *can* be beautiful.

Healing is possible and necessary and, for many, is a lifelong journey. For me it comes down to finding grace and understanding for everyone involved. My first mother and father could not figure out how to make it work, and the world they lived in was uninclined to assist. My adoptive parents loved me dearly, and I them, but collectively we didn't know what we didn't know.

I've worked hard on myself for years to heal from the more visible and clearly understood problems created through my adoptive mother's alcoholism and my father's denial of it. I'm grateful for the Adult Children of Alcoholics groups and mentors who helped me. Those wounds are still present, but the new information learned in writing this book has created a personal revolution. In spelunking through the internal caverns of my implicit memories, I now understand my adoption's impacts. I've always believed I was fine, and that adoption never affected me. Ironically, I've found peace in understanding how it did.

New revelations surface where suddenly things fit. I have a chronic inability to understand when I need help from others, and I don't ask for help, ever. That tendency likely formed because when I was born and separated from my mother, my little baby brain thought she abandoned me. I received loving care, but no one understood I needed *her* and had no words to tell anyone. My implicit memory formed under the emotion of loss, and my cries never brought me the help I needed. Which made it very likely I was less able to bond to my already psychologically insecure adoptive mother. We were all harmed by the lack of knowing.

I had another epiphany about my innate hyper-vigilism which many adoptees share. My nervous system is geared for subliminal stress. If life doesn't create stressors for me, I will manufacture them because that is my normal. Even if things are calm, I feel an unease, waiting for the proverbial shoe to drop.

Putting these patterns of behavior into proper perspective has been profound, because no other therapy has been able to touch these struggles. Now I know. It's hard to compose an explanation for what might have been different.

Seeing all of this with a clear lens gives me the power and freedom to heal. Being around other adoptees and first mothers has been cathartic. In them I have a community and safety I never expected. Other powerful allies are the adoptive parents who are aware of these complexities. Healing in community is powerful, and I invite everyone in the constellation to join.

To those who are struggling, I beg them to not give up hope and seek help from the right therapists. We can all heal and find answers. Please let any person or family in need make use of the resources provided on my website.

Everyone in an adoption must take responsibility and be accountable for their roles. As the adopted child, we have no agency until we are grown. Awakening to new complexities can create a great deal of anger in some adoptees and feelings of betrayal at being used. These feelings are valid and should not be dismissed.

This is why money's influences in adoption processes and the commodification of children is so dangerous. In the early days of adoption in the US there was profiteering, but not on the scale happening today. It warps the thing every child most deserves, which is a safe and loving family, and manipulates it. How *should* someone expect me or any other adoptee to feel about that?

However, staying stuck in anger or even rage is unhealthy. Feeling anger at what happened is common. It flames bright and is liberating for a while. But claiming an identity consumed or fueled by it won't ultimately serve someone long-term. There is no way around it, it must be felt. But we can move *through* it. The journey toward healing is worth it, even with all its scary and uncomfortable parts.

Appreciating something that is flawed, holding this duality of thinking and emotional intelligence is *hard*. My love for both my first and second set of parents is unending. It swirls around and feeds back on itself escorted by an eternal flame. One first lit inside of me by my natural mother, then tended by my adoptive parents, and now lives under my care. It glows bright and steady and is mine alone, which is as it should be.

Adoption contains love and loss and forces the human spirit to entertain new ways to experience both of those emotions at the same time. This duality is always present.

Adoption is a paradox.

Acknowledgments

There are so many people to thank for their help in creating this work, I'm certain I'll miss some but will try my best. Firstly, to my publisher Jo A. Wilkins, C.E.O. at Mystic Publishers. You plucked this new author out of a critique group, and I'm indebted to your unwavering support for the topic. To my editor, Janelle Evans, thank you for taking my writing and turning it into something special I'm proud of.

A shout out is needed for the Henderson Writers Group – with Audrey at the helm along with the critiques of Wolf, Tonya, Bryn, Donald (RIP), Ray, Pat, Raymond, Elliot, John and countless others. You pushed me to keep improving and reminding me I can always write a better sentence.

Thank you to Dr. Cynthia Anderson for your immediate support and belief in the necessity of this book. My friends and beta readers are too many to name, but a few are: Peter, Hannah, Alan, Anne, Peggy, Katherine, Laura, Tracey, Shannon, Mikayla, Dayrn and so many others who shared your impressions and guidance.

I must also mention all the current thought leaders in the adoption space, pushing us all into greater consciousness. These authors, teachers, counselors, podcasters, playwrights, film makers and influencers deserve credit for laying the groundwork to support adoptee voices. I hope this work contributes to the cause.

Friends who don't find your names ultimately in the book, I was devastated each time a name or storyline had to be condensed or cut. Your input is not forgotten and with your permission they will become part of other future work. All our words deserve the clear light of day upon them.

To my cheerleaders and friends, near and far, I'm grateful. Thanks for bearing with me on the journey. I'd like to say we can stop talking so much about adoption now, but I fear that's a lie. Hanging out at our local watering hole and elsewhere, you've literally watched me transform before your eyes. Thank you for your continued acceptance and support.

For my adoptive parents who raised me, somewhere on another plane of existence if this journey becomes part of your consciousness, know I am and always will be grateful and proud to be your daughter. Auntie Ann, thanks for not flinching at the hard stuff.

My bonus mom, Dora, you know all you do for us and your love has always been healing. To my husband Kyle, best friend and love of my life, you stabilize me and continue to ask me to believe in and love myself as much as you do. Someday I'll get there.

Barb, you *are* a good person, and did nothing wrong. You've done your best. Please own your journey and allow yourself to be fully seen for your whole story. My door remains open.

Appendix

Resources for adoptive families are growing and changing now constantly. This is a great trend but makes creating a single printed resource challenging. Because of that, I've amassed an online section of my website, that I will endeavor to keep updated regularly at:

https://adoptionparadox.com/information-resources/

Jean is a domestic adoptee born in 1965 and raised in Washington State. After having a mostly positive adoption experience growing up, she now shares her story, as it continues to evolve navigating adoption's complexities. Jean is a marketing consultant and joint venture affiliate marketing expert and along with her husband has built and sold two e-commerce companies. She is the owner of a local news and information blog in her small town, which expanded her love of storytelling and writing. Jean is also a member of a local Rotary Club and volunteers with the Adoption Knowledge Affiliates organization. She currently lives in Southern Nevada with her husband and two dogs.

Printed in Dunstable, United Kingdom

79379017R30271